Microsoft® Official Academic Course

HTML5 Application Development Fundamentals, Exam 98-375

WILEY

VP & PUBLISHER	Don Fowley
EDITOR	Bryan Gambrel
DIRECTOR OF SALES	Mitchell Beaton
EXECUTIVE MARKETING MANAGER	Chris Ruel
MICROSOFT PRODUCT MANAGER	Rob Linsky of Microsoft Learning
EDITORIAL PROGRAM ASSISTANT	Jennifer Lartz
ASSISTANT MARKETING MANAGER	Debbie Martin
SENIOR PRODUCTION MANAGER	Janis Soo
ASSOCIATE PRODUCTION MANAGER	Joel Balbin
CREATIVE DIRECTOR	Harry Nolan
COVER DESIGNER	Georgina Smith
TECHNOLOGY AND MEDIA	Tom Kulesa/Wendy Ashenberg

This book was set in Garamond by Aptara, Inc. and printed and bound by Bind-Rite Robbinsville.
The cover was printed by Bind-Rite Robbinsville.

Microsoft, ActiveX, Excel, InfoPath, Microsoft Press, MSDN, OneNote, Outlook, PivotChart, PivotTable, PowerPoint, SharePoint, SQL Server, Visio, Visual Basic, Visual C#, Visual Studio, Windows, Windows 7, Windows Mobile, Windows Server, and Windows Vista are either registered trademarks or trademarks of Microsoft Corporation in the United States and/or other countries. Other product and company names mentioned herein may be the trademarks of their respective owners.

The example companies, organizations, products, domain names, e-mail addresses, logos, people, places, and events depicted herein are fictitious. No association with any real company, organization, product, domain name, e-mail address, logo, person, place, or event is intended or should be inferred.

The book expresses the author's views and opinions. The information contained in this book is provided without any express, statutory, or implied warranties. Neither the authors, John Wiley & Sons, Inc., Microsoft Corporation, nor their resellers or distributors will be held liable for any damages caused or alleged to be caused either directly or indirectly by this book.

ISBN 978-1-118-35993-8

Printed in the United States of America

10 9 8 7 6 5 4 3 2 1

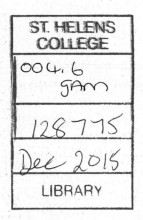

Foreword from the Publisher

Wiley's publishing vision for the Microsoft Official Academic Course series is to provide students and instructors with the skills and knowledge they need to use Microsoft technology effectively in all aspects of their personal and professional lives. Quality instruction is required to help both educators and students get the most from Microsoft's software tools and to become more productive. Thus our mission is to make our instructional programs trusted educational companions for life.

To accomplish this mission, Wiley and Microsoft have partnered to develop the highest quality educational programs for Information Workers, IT Professionals, and Developers. Materials created by this partnership carry the brand name "Microsoft Official Academic Course," assuring instructors and students alike that the content of these textbooks is fully endorsed by Microsoft, and that they provide the highest quality information and instruction on Microsoft products. The Microsoft Official Academic Course textbooks are "Official" in still one more way—they are the officially sanctioned courseware for Microsoft IT Academy members.

The Microsoft Official Academic Course series focuses on *workforce development*. These programs are aimed at those students seeking to enter the workforce, change jobs, or embark on new careers as information workers, IT professionals, and developers. Microsoft Official Academic Course programs address their needs by emphasizing authentic workplace scenarios with an abundance of projects, exercises, cases, and assessments.

The Microsoft Official Academic Courses are mapped to Microsoft's extensive research and job-task analysis, the same research and analysis used to create the Microsoft Technology Associate (MTA) and Microsoft Certified Solutions Developer (MCSD) exams. The textbooks focus on real skills for real jobs. As students work through the projects and exercises in the textbooks they enhance their level of knowledge and their ability to apply the latest Microsoft technology to everyday tasks. These students also gain resume-building credentials that can assist them in finding a job, keeping their current job, or in furthering their education.

The concept of life-long learning is today an utmost necessity. Job roles, and even whole job categories, are changing so quickly that none of us can stay competitive and productive without continuously updating our skills and capabilities. The Microsoft Official Academic Course offerings, and their focus on Microsoft certification exam preparation, provide a means for people to acquire and effectively update their skills and knowledge. Wiley supports students in this endeavor through the development and distribution of these courses as Microsoft's official academic publisher.

Today educational publishing requires attention to providing quality print and robust electronic content. By integrating Microsoft Official Academic Course products, *WileyPLUS*, and Microsoft certifications, we are better able to deliver efficient learning solutions for students and teachers alike.

Joseph Heider

General Manager and Senior Vice President

Preface

Welcome to the Microsoft Official Academic Course (MOAC) program for HTML5 Application Development Fundamentals. MOAC represents the collaboration between Microsoft Learning and John Wiley & Sons, Inc. publishing company. Microsoft and Wiley teamed up to produce a series of textbooks that deliver compelling and innovative teaching solutions to instructors and superior learning experiences for students. Infused and informed by in-depth knowledge from the creators of Microsoft products, and crafted by a publisher known worldwide for the pedagogical quality of its products, these textbooks maximize skills transfer in minimum time. Students are challenged to reach their potential by using their new technical skills as highly productive members of the workforce.

Because this knowledge base comes directly from Microsoft, creator of the Microsoft Certified Solutions Developer (MCSD) and Microsoft Technology Associate (MTA) exams (www.microsoft.com/learning/certification), you are sure to receive the topical coverage that is most relevant to students' personal and professional success. Microsoft's direct participation not only assures you that MOAC textbook content is accurate and current; it also means that students will receive the best instruction possible to enable their success on certification exams and in the workplace.

■ The Microsoft Official Academic Course Program

The *Microsoft Official Academic Course* series is a complete program for instructors and institutions to prepare and deliver great courses on Microsoft software technologies. With MOAC, we recognize that, because of the rapid pace of change in the technology and curriculum developed by Microsoft, there is an ongoing set of needs beyond classroom instruction tools for an instructor to be ready to teach the course. The MOAC program endeavors to provide solutions for all these needs in a systematic manner in order to ensure a successful and rewarding course experience for both instructor and student—technical and curriculum training for instructor readiness with new software releases; the software itself for student use at home for building hands-on skills, assessment, and validation of skill development; and a great set of tools for delivering instruction in the classroom and lab. All are important to the smooth delivery of an interesting course on Microsoft software, and all are provided with the MOAC program. We think about the model below as a gauge for ensuring that we completely support you in your goal of teaching a great course. As you evaluate your instructional materials options, you may wish to use the model for comparison purposes with available products.

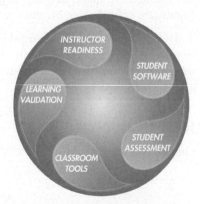

Illustrated Book Tour

▪ Pedagogical Features

The MOAC textbook for HTML5 Application Development Fundamentals is designed to cover all the learning objectives for that MTA exam 98-375, which is referred to as its "objective domain." The Microsoft Technology Associate (MTA) exam objectives are highlighted throughout the textbook. Many pedagogical features have been developed specifically for *Microsoft Official Academic Course* programs.

Presenting the extensive procedural information and technical concepts woven throughout the textbook raises challenges for the student and instructor alike. The Illustrated Book Tour that follows provides a guide to the rich features contributing to *Microsoft Official Academic Course* program's pedagogical plan. Following is a list of key features in each lesson designed to prepare students for success as they continue in their IT education, on the certification exams, and in the workplace:

- Each lesson begins with an **Exam Objective Matrix**. More than a standard list of learning objectives, the Exam Objective Matrix correlates each software skill covered in the lesson to the specific exam objective domain.

- Concise and frequent **Step-by-Step** instructions teach students new features and provide an opportunity for hands-on practice. Numbered steps give detailed, step-by-step instructions to help students learn software skills.

- **Illustrations:** Screen images provide visual feedback as students work through the exercises. The images reinforce key concepts, provide visual clues about the steps, and allow students to check their progress.

- **Key Terms:** Important technical vocabulary is listed with definitions at the beginning of the lesson. When these terms are used later in the lesson, they appear in bold italic type and are defined. The Glossary contains all of the key terms and their definitions.

- Engaging point-of-use **Reader Aids**, located throughout the lessons, tell students why this topic is relevant (*The Bottom Line*) and provide students with helpful hints (*Take Note*). Reader Aids also provide additional relevant or background information that adds value to the lesson.

- **Certification Ready** features throughout the text signal to students where a specific certification objective is covered. They provide students with a chance to check their understanding of that particular MTA objective and, if necessary, review the section of the lesson where it is covered. MOAC offers complete preparation for MTA certification.

- **End-of-Lesson Questions:** The Knowledge Assessment section provides a variety of multiple-choice, true-false, matching, and fill-in-the-blank questions.

- **End-of-Lesson Exercises:** Competency Assessment case scenarios and Proficiency Assessment case scenarios are projects that test students' ability to apply what they've learned in the lesson.

■ Lesson Features

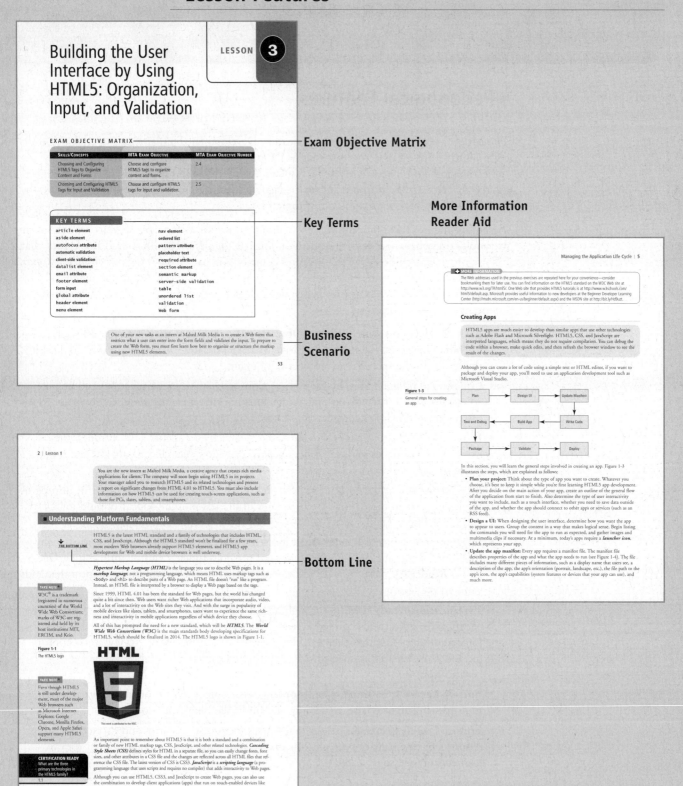

Exam Objective Matrix

Key Terms

More Information
Reader Aid

Business
Scenario

Bottom Line

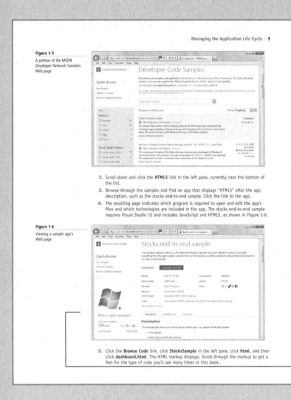

Figure 1-5
A portion of the MSDN Developer Network Samples Web page

2. Scroll down and click the **HTML5** link in the left pane, currently near the bottom of the list.
3. Browse through the samples and find an app that displays "HTML5" after the app description, such as the stocks end-to-end sample. Click the link to the app.
4. The resulting page indicates which program is required to open and edit the app's files and which technologies are included in the app. The stocks end-to-end sample requires Visual Studio 12 and includes JavaScript and HTML5, as shown in Figure 1-6.

Figure 1-6
Viewing a sample app's Web page

5. Click the **Browse Code** link, click **StocksSample** in the left pane, click **html**, and then click **dashboard.html**. The HTML markup displays. Scroll through the markup to get a feel for the type of code you'll see many times in this book.

Screen Images

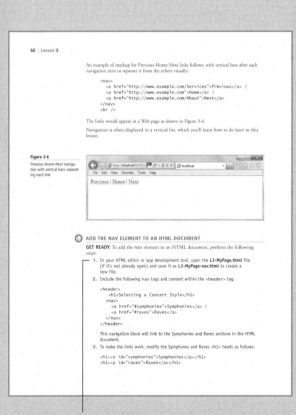

60 | Lesson 3

An example of markup for Previous-Home-Next links follows, with vertical bars after each navigation item to separate it from the others visually:

```
<nav>
    <a href="http://www.example.com/Services">Previous</a> |
    <a href="http://www.example.com">Home</a> |
    <a href="http://www.example.com/About">Next</a>
</nav>
<br />
```

The links would appear in a Web page as shown in Figure 3-6.

Navigation is often displayed in a vertical list, which you'll learn how to do later in this lesson.

Figure 3-6
Previous-Home-Next navigation with vertical bars separating each link

Previous | Home | Next

ADD THE NAV ELEMENT TO AN HTML DOCUMENT

GET READY. To add the nav element to an HTML document, perform the following steps:

1. In your HTML editor or app development tool, open the **L3-MyPage.html** file (if it's not already open) and save it as **L3-MyPage-nav.html** to create a new file.
2. Include the following nav tags and content within the <header> tag:

```
<header>
    <h1>Selecting a Concert Style</h1>
    <nav>
        <a href="#symphonies">Symphonies</a> |
        <a href="#raves">Raves</a>
    </nav>
</header>
```

This navigation block will link to the Symphonies and Raves sections in the HTML document.

3. To make the links work, modify the Symphonies and Raves <h1> heads as follows:

```
<h1><a id="symphonies">Symphonies</a></h1>
<h1><a id="raves">Raves</a></h1>
```

Step-by-Step Exercises

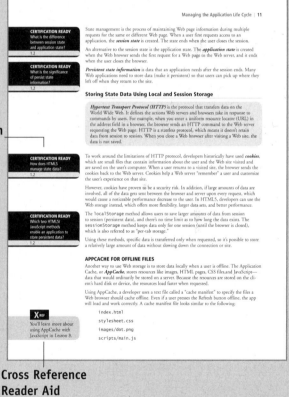

> **CERTIFICATION READY**
> What is the difference between session state and application state?
> 1.2

State management is the process of maintaining Web page information during multiple requests for the same or different Web page. When a user first requests access to an application, the *session state* is created. The state ends when the user closes the session.

An alternative to the session state is the application state. The *application state* is created when the Web browser sends the first request for a Web page to the Web server, and it ends when the user closes the browser.

> **CERTIFICATION READY**
> What is the significance of persist state information?
> 1.2

Persistent state information is data that an application needs after the session ends. Many Web applications need to store data (make it persistent) so that users can pick up where they left off when they return to the site.

Storing State Data Using Local and Session Storage

Hypertext Transport Protocol (HTTP) is the protocol that transfers data on the World Wide Web. It defines the actions Web servers and browsers take in response to commands by users. For example, when you enter a uniform resource locator (URL) in the address field in a browser, the browser sends an HTTP command to the Web server requesting the Web page. HTTP is a stateless protocol, which means it doesn't retain data from session to session. When you close a Web browser after visiting a Web site, the data is not saved.

Certification Ready Alert

> **CERTIFICATION READY**
> How does HTML5 manage state data?
> 1.2

To work around the limitations of HTTP protocol, developers historically have used *cookies*, which are small files that contain information about the user and the Web site visited and are saved on the user's computer. When a user returns to a visited site, the browser sends the cookies back to the Web server. Cookies help a Web server "remember" a user and customize the user's experience on that site.

However, cookies have proven to be a security risk. In addition, if large amounts of data are involved, all of the data gets sent between the browser and server upon every request, which would create a noticeable performance decrease to the user. In HTML5, developers can use the Web storage instead, which offers more flexibility, larger data sets, and better performance.

> **CERTIFICATION READY**
> Which two HTML5 JavaScript methods enable an application to store persistent data?
> 1.2

The localStorage method allows users to save larger amounts of data from session to session (persistent data), and there's no time limit as to how long the data exists. The sessionStorage method keeps data only for one session (until the browser is closed), which is also referred to as "per-tab storage."

Using these methods, specific data is transferred only when requested, so it's possible to store a relatively large amount of data without slowing down the connection or site.

APPCACHE FOR OFFLINE FILES

Another way to use Web storage is to store data locally when a user is offline. The Application Cache, or *AppCache*, stores resources like images, HTML pages, CSS files, and JavaScript—data that would ordinarily be stored on a server. Because the resources are stored on the client's hard disk or device, the resources load faster when requested.

Using AppCache, a developer uses a text file called a "cache manifest" to specify the files a Web browser should cache offline. Even if a user presses the Refresh button offline, the app will load and work correctly. A cache manifest file looks similar to the following:

> **XREF**
> You'll learn more about using AppCache with JavaScript in Lesson 8.

```
index.html
stylesheet.css
images/dot.png
scripts/main.js
```

Cross Reference Reader Aid

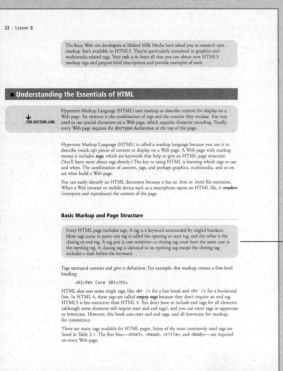

Take Note
Reader Aid

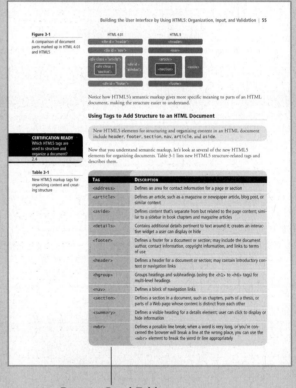

Easy-to-Read Tables

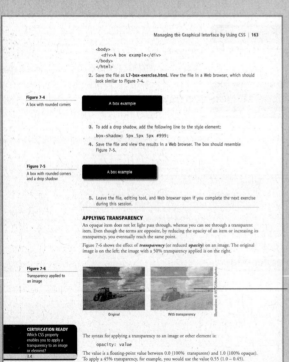

Photos

Skill Summary Matrix

Understanding CSS Essentials: Layouts | 133

Although this example used the auto keyword, you can use any of the values for grid-rows and grid-colums as listed in Table 5-2.

The specification for grid template layouts is very much in draft format and isn't supported by any Web browsers at the time of this writing. However, you might come across grid templates on the MTA 98-375 exam. Therefore, you should check the latest W3C CSS Grid Template Layout Module specification when preparing to take the exam.

SKILL SUMMARY

IN THIS LESSON YOU LEARNED:

- User interfaces can be clean and simple or more complex with several sections, buttons, and controls.
- Designing an interface that renders well on large PC screens and small mobile devices used to require a lot of markup and code. Today, the CSS Flexbox Box and Grid Layout models reduce the amount of code required for cross-device compatibility. Because the CSS specifications are not yet final, you'll need to use vendor prefixes before CSS property names to make everything work.
- Flexboxes are designed for toolbars, menus, forms, and similar elements in Web pages and applications. Grids are better suited to more complex designs.
- Both a flexbox and its contents can be configured to change size, horizontally and vertically, when the screen on which they're displayed changes size. You can also reverse the direction and order of flexboxes with one line of code.
- A flexbox can include child boxes that are flexible by height and width. You use the flex property to work with child boxes. The flex-flow property sets the flex-direction and flex-wrap properties of a flexbox (the parent box) at the same time.
- Grid layouts are similar to spreadsheets in that they use columns, rows, and cells, but you can create many different types of layouts that, in the end, don't look like a spreadsheet at all.
- You use the CSS properties display:grid (or display:inline-grid), grid-columns, and grid-rows to create grid structures. The size of columns and rows can be fixed or flexible.
- Flexboxes and grids are designed to scale proportionally.
- The flex-order property enables you to change the order of child items in a flexbox, rearranging them in any order you like without having to change them in the HTML markup.
- A grid template uses alphabetical characters to represent the position of items in a grid. You use the alpha characters with the grid-template, grid-rows, and grid-columns properties to create a grid into which data flows.

■ Knowledge Assessment

Fill in the Blank

Complete the following sentences by writing the correct word or words in the blanks provided.

1. A _____ is the portion of a Web site or application with which a user interacts.

2. In the original W3C CSS box model, the _____ is the space between border and the content of the box.

Knowledge Assessment Questions

Understanding CSS Essentials: Layouts | 133

Although this example used the auto keyword, you can use any of the values for grid-rows and grid-colums as listed in Table 5-2.

The specification for grid template layouts is very much in draft format and isn't supported by any Web browsers at the time of this writing. However, you might come across grid templates on the MTA 98-375 exam. Therefore, you should check the latest W3C CSS Grid Template Layout Module specification when preparing to take the exam.

SKILL SUMMARY

IN THIS LESSON YOU LEARNED:

- User interfaces can be clean and simple or more complex with several sections, buttons, and controls.
- Designing an interface that renders well on large PC screens and small mobile devices used to require a lot of markup and code. Today, the CSS Flexbox Box and Grid Layout models reduce the amount of code required for cross-device compatibility. Because the CSS specifications are not yet final, you'll need to use vendor prefixes before CSS property names to make everything work.
- Flexboxes are designed for toolbars, menus, forms, and similar elements in Web pages and applications. Grids are better suited to more complex designs.
- Both a flexbox and its contents can be configured to change size, horizontally and vertically, when the screen on which they're displayed changes size. You can also reverse the direction and order of flexboxes with one line of code.
- A flexbox can include child boxes that are flexible by height and width. You use the flex property to work with child boxes. The flex-flow property sets the flex-direction and flex-wrap properties of a flexbox (the parent box) at the same time.
- Grid layouts are similar to spreadsheets in that they use columns, rows, and cells, but you can create many different types of layouts that, in the end, don't look like a spreadsheet at all.
- You use the CSS properties display:grid (or display:inline-grid), grid-columns, and grid-rows to create grid structures. The size of columns and rows can be fixed or flexible.
- Flexboxes and grids are designed to scale proportionally.
- The flex-order property enables you to change the order of child items in a flexbox, rearranging them in any order you like without having to change them in the HTML markup.
- A grid template uses alphabetical characters to represent the position of items in a grid. You use the alpha characters with the grid-template, grid-rows, and grid-columns properties to create a grid into which data flows.

■ Knowledge Assessment

Fill in the Blank

Complete the following sentences by writing the correct word or words in the blanks provided.

1. A _____ is the portion of a Web site or application with which a user interacts.

2. In the original W3C CSS box model, the _____ is the space between border and the content of the box.

86 | Lesson 3

10. What is the format for the HTML5 tag that validates an email address?
   a. <input label="email" name="URL",
   b. <form id="email">
   c. <label for="email">Email</label>
   d. <input type = "email" name = "email">

True / False

Circle T if the statement is true or F if the statement is false.

T F 1. In a table, the tfoot element must appear before the tbody element.

T F 2. You can use numbers or letters for each item in an ordered list.

T F 3. You can specify the height of an input element using the size attribute.

T F 4. The label element displays the caption, or title, for a table.

T F 5. The nav element defines a block of navigation links.

Competency Assessment

■ Competency Assessment

Scenario 3-1: Markup for a Newsletter Article

Sally Rowe, the document controller at Malted Milk Media, wants to publish a series of articles on the company intranet regarding document security and versioning. She needs to create a skeleton of the HTML5 markup for an article that will appear in the monthly online newsletter created by one of the Web developers. Each article will have a title and subtitle, several paragraphs of text, and her name and the article date in the footer. What should her article markup look like?

Scenario 3-2: Displaying Long Tables in HTML

Vince generates accounting reports for the VP of Finance at Momentum Strategies, a PR firm geared toward political campaigns. Vince regularly prints tables that are two- or three-pages long and delivers hard copies to senior management staff. He wants to publish them to a secure area of the company intranet, but the rows of data separate from the column headings and totals line at the end. He wants to know how to present the tables properly in HTML5. What do you tell him?

Proficiency Assessment

■ Proficiency Assessment

Scenario 3-3: Creating a Glossary of Terms

Waylon is a student working on a term paper. His instructor requires each student to format the paper for display on the Web. Waylon wants to include a glossary of terms at the end of the paper but can't produce the right "look" using an unordered list. Which markup would be better suited for Waylon's glossary?

Scenario 3-4: Using Proper Input Types in a Web Form

Margie is creating and testing a Web form that includes an email field, a Web address field, and a zip code field, among others. When she has a few co-workers test the form, she finds they often enter the email address in the Web address field by mistake, and sometimes enter too many or too few numbers in the zip code field. She doesn't want to use a pattern expression because she says it's too complicated. What other input types can Margie use?

www.wiley.com/college/microsoft *or*
call the MOAC Toll-Free Number: 1+(888) 764-7001 (U.S. & Canada only)

Conventions and Features Used in This Book

This book uses particular fonts, symbols, and heading conventions to highlight important information or to call your attention to special steps. For more information about the features in each lesson, refer to the Illustrated Book Tour section.

CONVENTION	MEANING
↓ **THE BOTTOM LINE**	This feature provides a brief summary of the material to be covered in the section that follows.
CLOSE	Words in all capital letters indicate instructions for opening, saving, or closing files or programs. They also point out items you should check or actions you should take.
CERTIFICATION READY	This feature signals the point in the text where a specific certification objective is covered. It provides you with a chance to check your understanding of that particular MTA objective and, if necessary, review the section of the lesson where it is covered.
TAKE NOTE*	Reader aids appear in shaded boxes found in your text. *Take Note* provides helpful hints related to particular tasks or topics.
X REF	These notes provide pointers to information discussed elsewhere in the textbook or describe interesting features of HTML5 that are not directly addressed in the current topic or exercise.
Alt + Alt	A plus sign (+) between two key names means that you must press both keys at the same time. Keys that you are instructed to press in an exercise will appear in the font shown here.
Example	Key terms appear in bold italic.

Instructor Support Program

The *Microsoft Official Academic Course* programs are accompanied by a rich array of resources that incorporate the extensive textbook visuals to form a pedagogically cohesive package. These resources provide all the materials instructors need to deploy and deliver their courses. Resources available online for download include:

- **DreamSpark Premium** is designed to provide the easiest and most inexpensive developer tools, products, and technologies available to faculty and students in labs, classrooms, and on student PCs. A free 3-year membership is available to qualified MOAC adopters.

  Note: Microsoft Visual Studio and Micrsoft Expression can be downloaded from DreamSpark Premium for use by students in this course.

- The **Instructor Guides** contains Solutions to all the textbook exercises and Syllabi for various term lengths. The Instructor Guides also includes chapter summaries and lecture notes. The Instructor's Guide is available from the Book Companion site (http://www.wiley.com/college/microsoft).

- The **Test Bank** contains hundreds of questions in multiple-choice, true-false, short answer, and essay formats, and is available to download from the Instructor's Book Companion site (www.wiley.com/college/microsoft). A complete answer key is provided.

- A complete set of **PowerPoint presentations and images** are available on the Instructor's Book Companion site (http://www.wiley.com/college/microsoft) to enhance classroom presentations. Approximately 50 PowerPoint slides are provided for each lesson. Tailored to the text's topical coverage and Skills Matrix, these presentations are designed to convey key concepts addressed in the text. All images from the text are on the Instructor's Book Companion site (http://www.wiley.com/college/microsoft). You can incorporate them into your PowerPoint presentations, or create your own overhead transparencies and handouts. By using these visuals in class discussions, you can help focus students' attention on key elements of technologies covered and help them understand how to use it effectively in the workplace.

Wiley Faculty Network

- When it comes to improving the classroom experience, there is no better source of ideas and inspiration than your fellow colleagues. The **Wiley Faculty Network** connects teachers with technology, facilitates the exchange of best practices, and helps to enhance instructional efficiency and effectiveness. Faculty Network activities include technology training and tutorials, virtual seminars, peer-to-peer exchanges of experiences and ideas, personal consulting, and sharing of resources. For details visit www.WhereFacultyConnect.com.

DREAMSPARK PREMIUM—FREE 3-YEAR MEMBERSHIP AVAILABLE TO QUALIFIED ADOPTERS!

DreamSpark Premium is designed to provide the easiest and most inexpensive way for universities to make the latest Microsoft developer tools, products, and technologies available in labs, classrooms, and on student PCs. DreamSpark Premium is an annual membership program for departments teaching Science, Technology, Engineering, and Mathematics (STEM) courses. The membership provides a complete solution to keep academic labs, faculty, and students on the leading edge of technology.

Software available in the DreamSpark Premium program is provided at no charge to adopting departments through the Wiley and Microsoft publishing partnership.

And tools that professors can use to engage and inspire today's technology students.

Contact your Wiley rep for details.

For more information about the DreamSpark Premium program, go to:

https://www.dreamspark.com/

Note: Microsoft Visual Studio and Microsoft Expression can be downloaded from DreamSpark Premium for use by students in this course.

■ Important Web Addresses and Phone Numbers

To locate the Wiley Higher Education Rep in your area, go to http://www.wiley.com/college and click on the "*Who's My Rep?*" link at the top of the page, or call the MOAC Toll Free Number: 1 + (888) 764-7001 (U.S. & Canada only).

To learn more about becoming certified and exam availability, visit www.microsoft.com/learning/mcp/mcp.

▪ Additional Resources

Book Companion Web Site (www.wiley.com/college/microsoft)

The students' book companion site for the MOAC series includes any resources, exercise files, and Web links that will be used in conjunction with this course.

Wiley Desktop Editions

Wiley MOAC Desktop Editions are innovative, electronic versions of printed textbooks. Students buy the desktop version for up to 40% off the U.S. price of the printed text, and get the added value of permanence and portability. Wiley Desktop Editions provide students with numerous additional benefits that are not available with other e-text solutions.

Wiley Desktop Editions are NOT subscriptions; students download the Wiley Desktop Edition to their computer desktops. Students own the content they buy to keep for as long as they want. Once a Wiley Desktop Edition is downloaded to the computer desktop, students have instant access to all of the content without being online. Students can also print out the sections they prefer to read in hard copy. Students also have access to fully integrated resources within their Wiley Desktop Edition. From highlighting their e-text to taking and sharing notes, students can easily personalize their Wiley Desktop Edition as they are reading or following along in class.

▪ About the Microsoft Technology Associate (MTA) Certification

Preparing Tomorrow's Technology Workforce

Technology plays a role in virtually every business around the world. Possessing the fundamental knowledge of how technology works and understanding its impact on today's academic and workplace environment is increasingly important—particularly for students interested in exploring professions involving technology. That's why Microsoft created the Microsoft Technology Associate (MTA) certification—a new entry-level credential that validates fundamental technology knowledge among students seeking to build a career in technology.

The Microsoft Technology Associate (MTA) certification is the ideal and preferred path to Microsoft's world-renowned technology certification programs, such as Microsoft Certified Solutions Developer (MCSD). MTA is positioned to become the premier credential for individuals seeking to explore and pursue a career in technology, or augment related pursuits such as business or any other field where technology is pervasive.

MTA Candidate Profile

The MTA certification program is designed specifically for secondary and post-secondary students interested in exploring academic and career options in a technology field. It offers students a certification in basic IT and development. As the new recommended entry point for Microsoft technology certifications, MTA is designed especially for students new to IT and software development. It is available exclusively in educational settings and easily integrates into the curricula of existing computer classes.

MTA Empowers Educators and Motivates Students

MTA provides a new standard for measuring and validating fundamental technology knowledge right in the classroom while keeping your budget and teaching resources intact. MTA helps institutions stand out as innovative providers of high-demand industry credentials and is easily deployed with a simple, convenient, and affordable suite of entry-level technology certification exams. MTA enables students to explore career paths in technology without requiring a big investment of time and resources, while providing a career foundation and the confidence to succeed in advanced studies and future vocational endeavors.

In addition to giving students an entry-level Microsoft certification, MTA is designed to be a stepping stone to other, more advanced Microsoft technology certifications, like the Microsoft Certified Solutions Developer (MCSD) certification.

Delivering MTA Exams: The MTA Campus License

Implementing a new certification program in your classroom has never been so easy with the MTA Campus License. Through the purchase of an annual MTA Campus License, there's no more need for ad hoc budget requests and recurrent purchases of exam vouchers. Now you can budget for one low cost for the entire year, and then administer MTA exams to your students and other faculty across your entire campus where and when you want.

The MTA Campus License provides a convenient and affordable suite of entry-level technology certifications designed to empower educators and motivate students as they build a foundation for their careers.

The MTA Campus License is administered by Certiport, Microsoft's exclusive MTA exam provider.

To learn more about becoming a Microsoft Technology Associate and exam availability, visit www.microsoft.com/learning/mta.

■ Activate Your FREE MTA Practice Test!

Your purchase of this book entitles you to a free MTA practice test from GMetrix (a $30 value). Please go to www.gmetrix.com/mtatests and use the following validation code to redeem your free test: **MTA98-375-3324376A6A85.**

The **GMetrix Skills Management System** provides everything you need to practice for the Microsoft Technology Associate (MTA) Certification.

Overview of Test features:

- Practice tests map to the Microsoft Technology Associate (MTA) exam objectives
- GMetrix MTA practice tests simulate the actual MTA testing environment
- 50+ questions per test covering all objectives
- Progress at own pace, save test to resume later, return to skipped questions
- Detailed, printable score report highlighting areas requiring further review

To get the most from your MTA preparation, take advantage of your free GMetrix MTA Practice Test today!

For technical support issues on installation or code activation, please email support@gmetrix.com.

Acknowledgments

▪ MOAC MTA Technology Fundamentals Reviewers

We'd like to thank the many reviewers who pored over the manuscript and provided invaluable feedback in the service of quality instructional materials:

Yuke Wang, University of Texas at Dallas
Palaniappan Vairavan, Bellevue College
Harold "Buz" Lamson, ITT Technical Institute
Colin Archibald, Valencia Community College
Catherine Bradfield, DeVry University Online
Robert Nelson, Blinn College
Kalpana Viswanathan, Bellevue College
Bob Becker, Vatterott College
Carol Torkko, Bellevue College
Bharat Kandel, Missouri Tech
Linda Cohen, Forsyth Technical Community College
Candice Lambert, Metro Technology Centers
Susan Mahon, Collin College
Mark Aruda, Hillsborough Community College
Claude Russo, Brevard Community College
Heith Hennel, Valencia College
Adrian Genesir, Western Governors University
Zeshan Sattar, Zenos

Douglas Tabbutt, Blackhawk Technical College
David Koppy, Baker College
Sharon Moran, Hillsborough Community College
Keith Hoell, Briarcliffe College and Queens College—CUNY
Mark Hufnagel, Lee County School District
Rachelle Hall, Glendale Community College
Scott Elliott, Christie Digital Systems, Inc.
Gralan Gilliam, Kaplan
Steve Strom, Butler Community College
John Crowley, Bucks County Community College
Margaret Leary, Northern Virginia Community College
Sue Miner, Lehigh Carbon Community College
Gary Rollinson, Cabrillo College
Al Kelly, University of Advancing Technology
Katherine James, Seneca College
David Kidd, Western Governors University

www.wiley.com/college/microsoft *or*
call the MOAC Toll-Free Number: 1+(888) 764-7001 (U.S. & Canada only)

Brief Contents

Lesson 1: Managing the Application Life Cycle 1

Lesson 2: Building the User Interface by Using HTML5: Text, Graphics, and Media 21

Lesson 3: Building the User Interface by Using HTML5: Organization, Input, and Validation 53

Lesson 4: Understanding CSS Essentials: Content Flow, Positioning, and Styling 87

Lesson 5: Understanding CSS Essentials: Layouts 110

Lesson 6: Managing Text Flow by Using CSS 137

Lesson 7: Managing the Graphical Interface by Using CSS 159

Lesson 8: Understanding JavaScript and Coding Essentials 189

Lesson 9: Creating Animations, Working with Graphics, and Accessing Data 215

Lesson 10: JavaScript Coding for the Touch Interface, Device and Operating System Resources, and More 243

Appendix 268

Index 269

Contents

Lesson 1: Managing the Application Life Cycle 1

Exam Objective Matrix 1

Key Terms 1

Understanding Platform Fundamentals 2
What's New in HTML5? 3
Creating Apps 5
Exploring Packaging and the Runtime Environment 7
Understanding the Host Process 7
Understanding the App Package and App Container 8
Understanding Credentials and Permission Sets 10

Understanding and Managing Application States 10
Storing State Data Using Local and Session Storage 11
AppCache for Offline Files 11

Understanding Touch Interfaces and Gestures 12
Leveraging Existing HTML5 Skills and Content for Slate/Tablet Applications 13

Debugging and Testing HTML5 Apps 13
Validating HTML5 Code 14
Validating a Package 14

Publishing an Application to a Store 16

Skill Summary 17

Knowledge Assessment 18

Competency Assessment 20

Proficiency Assessment 20

Lesson 2: Building the User Interface by Using HTML5: Text, Graphics, and Media 21

Exam Objective Matrix 21

Key Terms 21

Understanding the Essentials of HTML 22
Basic Markup and Page Structure 22
Using Attributes 23
Nesting Elements 24
Understanding Entities 24
Understanding the Doctype 25
Exploring the Markup of a Simple Web Page 26

Choosing and Configuring HTML5 Tags to Display Text Content 29
Text Elements from HTML 4 with New Meaning or Functionality 29
New Text Elements in HTML5 31
Text Elements Not Used in HTML5 32

Choosing and Configuring HTML5 Tags to Display Graphics 34
Using the figure and figcaption Elements 35
Creating Graphics with Canvas 38
Canvas Basics 39
Creating an Outline of a Shape 40
Providing an Alternate Image or Text for Older Browsers 41
Creating Graphics with SVG 42
When to Use Canvas Instead of SVG 44

Choosing and Configuring HTML5 Tags to Play Media 45
Understanding and Using Video Tags 45
Understanding and Using Audio Tags 47

Skill Summary 49

Knowledge Assessment 49

Competency Assessment 51

Proficiency Assessment 52

Lesson 3: Building the User Interface by Using HTML5: Organization, Input, and Validation 53

Exam Objective Matrix 53

Key Terms 53

Choosing and Configuring HTML5 Tags to Organize Content and Forms 54
Understanding Semantic HTML 54
Using Tags to Add Structure to an HTML Document 55
The header and footer Elements 56
The section Element 57
The nav Element 59
The article Element 61
The aside Element 61
Using Tags to Create Tables and Lists 64
Creating Tables 64
Creating Lists 69

Choosing and Configuring HTML5 Tags for Input and Validation 72
Understanding Input and Forms 73
Exploring Form Creation, Input Attributes, and Values 77
Understanding Validation 81
Skill Summary 83
Knowledge Assessment 84
Competency Assessment 86
Proficiency Assessment 86

Lesson 4: Understanding CSS Essentials: Content Flow, Positioning, and Styling 87

Objective Domain Matrix 87
Key Terms 87
Understanding CSS Essentials 87
Using the Appropriate Tools 88
Exploring the Link between HTML and CSS 89
Separating Content from Style 91
Understanding Selectors and Declarations 92
Understanding Fonts and Font Families 94
Managing Content Flow 96
Positioning Individual Elements 99
Applying Float Positioning 99
Applying Absolute Positioning 100
Managing Content Overflow 102
Understanding Scrolling Overflow 102
Understanding Visible Overflow and Hidden Overflow 104
Skill Summary 105
Knowledge Assessment 106
Competency Assessment 108
Proficiency Assessment 109

Lesson 5: Understanding CSS Essentials: Layouts 110

Exam Objective Matrix 110
Key Terms 110
Arranging User Interface (UI) Content by Using CSS 111
Using Flexbox for Simple Layouts and Using Grid for Complex Layouts 112
Using a Flexible Box to Establish Content Alignment, Direction, and Orientation 114
Work with Flexboxes and Flexbox Items 116

Applying Proportional Scaling within a Flexbox 116
Changing the Direction of Child Items in a Flexbox 122
Ordering and Arranging Content 126
Using Grid Layouts to Establish Content Alignment, Direction, and Orientation 128
Creating a Grid Using CSS Properties for Rows and Columns 130
Understanding Grid Templates 132
Skill Summary 133
Knowledge Assessment 133
Competency Assessment 135
Proficiency Assessment 136

Lesson 6: Managing Text Flow by Using CSS 137

Exam Objective Matrix 137
Key Terms 137
Managing the Flow of Text Content by Using CSS 137
Understanding and Using Regions to Flow Text Content between Multiple Sections 139
Flowing Content through Containers Dynamically 140
Overflowing Text 142
Microsoft's Implementation of CSS Regions 142
Using Columns and Hyphenation to Optimize the Readability of Text 145
Creating Columns 146
Using Hyphenation 150
Using CSS Exclusions to Create Text Flow around a Floating Object 152
Skill Summary 155
Knowledge Assessment 155
Competency Assessment 157
Proficiency Assessment 158

Lesson 7: Managing the Graphical Interface by Using CSS 159

Exam Objective Matrix 159
Key Terms 159
Managing the Graphical Interface with CSS 159
Creating Graphics Effects 160
Creating Rounded Corners 160
Creating Shadows 161
Applying Transparency 163
Applying Background Gradients 164

Understanding Typography and the Web
    Open Font Format   166
Applying 2D and 3D Transformations   167
    2D Translation   168
    2D Scaling   169
    2D and 3D Rotation   171
    2D and 3D Skewing   172
    Understanding 3D Perspective, Transitions, and Animations   173
    Applying SVG Filter Effects   179
    Using Canvas to Enhance the GUI   182
Skill Summary   185
Knowledge Assessment   186
Competency Assessment   188
Proficiency Assessment   188

Lesson 8: Understanding JavaScript and Coding Essentials   189

Objective Domain Matrix   189
Key Terms   189
Managing and Maintaining JavaScript   189
    Creating and Using Functions   193
    Using jQuery and Other Third-Party Libraries   197
Updating the UI by Using JavaScript   199
    Locating and Accessing Elements   201
    Listening and Responding to Events   203
    Showing and Hiding Elements   206
    Updating the Content of Elements   208
    Adding Elements   209
Skill Summary   211
Knowledge Assessment   212
Competency Assessment   214
Proficiency Assessment   214

Lesson 9: Creating Animations, Working with Graphics, and Accessing Data   215

Objective Domain Matrix   215
Key Terms   215
Coding Animations by Using JavaScript   216
    Creating Animations   216
Working with Images, Shapes, and Other Graphics   219

Manipulating the Canvas with JavaScript   220
Sending and Receiving Data   224
    Transmitting Complex Objects and Parsing   227
Loading and Saving Files   229
    Using the Application Cache (AppCache)   231
    Understanding and Using Data Types   233
Using JavaScript to Validate User Form Input   233
Understanding and Using Cookies   235
Understanding and Using Local Storage   237
Skill Summary   239
Knowledge Assessment   240
Competency Assessment   242
Proficiency Assessment   242

Lesson 10: JavaScript Coding for the Touch Interface, Device and Operating System Resources, and More   243

Exam Objective Matrix   243
Key Terms   243
Responding to the Touch Interface   244
    Capturing and Responding to Gestures   246
Coding Additional HTML5 APIs   249
    Coding to Capture GeoLocation   249
    Understanding Web Workers   252
    Understanding WebSockets   255
    Using File API for File Uploads   258
Accessing Device and Operating System Resources   260
    Accessing In-Memory Resources   260
    Accessing Hardware Capabilities   262
        Understanding Global Positioning System (GPS)   263
        Understanding Accelerometer   263
        Accessing a Camera   263
Skill Summary   264
Knowledge Assessment   265
Competency Assessment   267
Proficiency Assessment   267

Appendix   268
Index   269

Managing the Application Life Cycle

EXAM OBJECTIVE MATRIX

SKILLS/CONCEPTS	MTA EXAM OBJECTIVE	MTA EXAM OBJECTIVE NUMBER
Understanding Platform Fundamentals	Understand the platform fundamentals.	1.1
Understanding and Managing Application States	Manage the state of an application.	1.2
Understanding Touch Interfaces and Gestures	Understand the platform fundamentals.	1.1
	Debug and test an HTML5-based touch-enabled application.	1.3
Debugging and Testing HTML5 Apps	Debug and test an HTML5-based touch-enabled application.	1.3
Publishing an Application to a Store	Publish an application to a store.	1.4

KEY TERMS

app container

app package

AppCache

application programming interface (API)

application state

Cascading Style Sheets (CSS)

cookies

debugging

gesture

Hypertext Markup Language (HTML)

Hypertext Transport Protocol (HTTP)

HTML5

identity permissions

JavaScript

launcher icon

localStorage

markup language

media queries

Metro-style user interface (UI)

namespace

permission sets

persistent state information

platform-independent

scripting language

session state

sessionStorage

touch event

touch-screen simulator or emulator

validator

Windows Runtime (WinRT)

Windows Store

World Wide Web Consortium (W3C)

You are the new intern at Malted Milk Media, a creative agency that creates rich media applications for clients. The company will soon begin using HTML5 in its projects. Your manager asked you to research HTML5 and its related technologies and present a report on significant changes from HTML 4.01 to HTML5. You must also include information on how HTML5 can be used for creating touch-screen applications, such as those for PCs, slates, tablets, and smartphones.

■ Understanding Platform Fundamentals

THE BOTTOM LINE

HTML5 is the latest HTML standard and a family of technologies that includes HTML, CSS, and JavaScript. Although the HTML5 standard won't be finalized for a few years, most modern Web browsers already support HTML5 elements, and HTML5 app development for Web and mobile device browsers is well underway.

Hypertext Markup Language (HTML) is the language you use to describe Web pages. It is a *markup language*, not a programming language, which means HTML uses markup tags such as <body> and <h1> to describe parts of a Web page. An HTML file doesn't "run" like a program. Instead, an HTML file is interpreted by a browser to display a Web page based on the tags.

Since 1999, HTML 4.01 has been the standard for Web pages, but the world has changed quite a bit since then. Web users want richer Web applications that incorporate audio, video, and a lot of interactivity on the Web sites they visit. And with the surge in popularity of mobile devices like slates, tablets, and smartphones, users want to experience the same richness and interactivity in mobile applications regardless of which device they choose.

All of this has prompted the need for a new standard, which will be **HTML5**. The **World Wide Web Consortium (W3C)** is the main standards body developing specifications for HTML5, which should be finalized in 2014. The HTML5 logo is shown in Figure 1-1.

TAKE NOTE*

W3C® is a trademark (registered in numerous countries) of the World Wide Web Consortium; marks of W3C are registered and held by its host institutions MIT, ERCIM, and Keio.

Figure 1-1

The HTML5 logo

This work is attributed to the W3C.

TAKE NOTE*

Even though HTML5 is still under development, most of the major Web browsers such as Microsoft Internet Explorer, Google Chrome, Mozilla Firefox, Opera, and Apple Safari support many HTML5 elements.

An important point to remember about HTML5 is that it is both a standard and a combination or family of new HTML markup tags, CSS, JavaScript, and other related technologies. *Cascading Style Sheets (CSS)* defines styles for HTML in a separate file, so you can easily change fonts, font sizes, and other attributes in a CSS file and the changes are reflected across all HTML files that reference the CSS file. The latest version of CSS is CSS3. *JavaScript* is a *scripting language* (a programming language that uses scripts and requires no compiler) that adds interactivity to Web pages.

Although you can use HTML5, CSS3, and JavaScript to create Web pages, you can also use the combination to develop client applications (apps) that run on touch-enabled devices like

CERTIFICATION READY
What are the three primary technologies in the HTML5 family?
1.1

PCs, slates, tablets, and smartphones. Essentially, the same technologies developers use to build Web pages are now beginning to be used to build applications that run on different devices.

HTML5 is also ***platform-independent***. That means you can create apps using the HTML5 family of technologies that can run on different desktop and mobile device operating systems, such as Microsoft Windows, Internet Explorer, and Windows Phone. You can also run them in Mac OS X, Android, iOS, and Blackberry OS. Because HTML5 is built on an open standard, users of HTML5 apps do not have to download a plug-in or use devices that have plug-in support. Instead, you can use any Web browser, whether on your PC or mobile device, and get the same rich Web experience.

Finally, an important part of app development in the Windows environment is the ***Metro style user interface (UI)***, which is the UI used by the latest Microsoft Windows version: Windows 8. The Metro style UI includes features like a clean, uncluttered look and feel, use of the full screen, large hubs (graphical buttons), and a focus on lateral scrolling, to name a few. See Figure 1-2 as an example.

Figure 1-2

The Windows 8 Start screen is a Metro style UI

Because this book helps prepare you for the Microsoft Technology Associate (MTA) 98-375 certification exam, HTML5 Application Development Fundamentals, examples in the lessons use Microsoft tools as much as possible. However, the exam does not focus on a specific set of tools. You can work with the HTML5 family using many different tools from many different companies. Even a simple text editor like Notepad or Notepad++ does the trick when working with HTML markup, CSS, and JavaScript. You need the more comprehensive tools, like Visual Studio, when debugging a lot of code, packaging apps for distribution, and similar tasks. Free development tools for creating Metro style apps are available at http://bit.ly/K8nkk1.

What's New in HTML5?

The HTML5 family includes many new markup tags and technologies like media queries, geolocation, Modernizr, and much more. These technologies add a lot of functionality to HTML-based apps and help make the finished product more stylish.

The following is a short list of these new features and brief descriptions:

- **Audio and video tags:** Embeds audio and video multimedia using the HTML5 markup tags `<audio>` and `<video>`.
- **Canvas:** An HTML5 element that creates a container for graphics, and uses JavaScript to draw the graphics as needed.
- *Media queries:* A CSS3 feature that detects the user's type of screen and sizes the output accordingly.
- **New application programming interfaces (APIs):** Give apps access to a plethora of resources, such as files, webcams, and hardware-accelerated animations.
- **Geolocation:** Uses JavaScript to detect the location (geographic positioning) of a client device, whether it's a Windows Phone, Android phone, or a PC.
- **Modernizr:** A JavaScript library that helps you deliver the new capabilities of HTML5 and CSS3 in older browsers.

This is a small sampling of the available features and technologies. You'll learn how to use many of these in lessons throughout the course.

 EXPLORE THE HTML5 STANDARD

GET READY. To learn about the HTML5 standard, perform the following steps:

1. Go to the W3C Web site at http://www.w3.org/TR/html5/.
2. Read the content on the first few pages, until you reach the Table of Contents and then address the following questions:
   - What is the latest published version of the standard?
   - Which working group is responsible for the specification?
   - What is the name of the Web page that tracks bugs, and what are three bugs that have not yet been addressed?
   - What is the name of the Web page that tracks outstanding issues, and what are three issues that have not yet been addressed?
3. On the main HTML5 Web page, spend about 15 minutes browsing the remainder of the page to become familiar with the topics.

 EXPLORE APP DEVELOPER RESOURCES

GET READY. To learn about app develop resources provided by Microsoft, perform the following steps:

1. Go to the Beginner Developer Learning Center Web site at http://msdn.microsoft.com/en-us/beginner/default.aspx.
2. Click the **Getting started with Windows Metro style apps development** link. On the resulting page, browse the information. Which technologies or development tools can you use to create Metro style apps?
3. Go to the HTML/CSS for Metro style apps Web page at http://bit.ly/N48F0L.
4. Click the **HTML and DOM reference** link and then answer the following question:
   - What is the Document Object Model (DOM) and what is its significance to Metro Style apps?
5. Return to the **HTML/CSS for Metro style apps** page at http://bit.ly/N48F0L. Click the **Cascading style sheets reference** link and then address the following:
   - Name three elements of Web pages that are controlled using CSS.
6. Go to the MSDN site at http://bit.ly/Hd9uzt. Browse the information to become familiar with the site.

+ MORE INFORMATION

The Web addresses used in the previous exercises are repeated here for your convenience—consider bookmarking them for later use. You can find information on the HTML5 standard on the W3C Web site at http://www.w3.org/TR/html5/. One Web site that provides HTML5 tutorials is at http://www.w3schools.com/html5/default.asp. Microsoft provides useful information to new developers at the Beginner Developer Learning Center (http://msdn.microsoft.com/en-us/beginner/default.aspx) and the MSDN site at http://bit.ly/Hd9uzt.

Creating Apps

HTML5 apps are much easier to develop than similar apps that use other technologies such as Adobe Flash and Microsoft Silverlight. HTML5, CSS, and JavaScript are interpreted languages, which means they do not require compilation. You can debug the code within a browser, make quick edits, and then refresh the browser window to see the result of the changes.

Although you can create a lot of code using a simple text or HTML editor, if you want to package and deploy your app, you'll need to use an application development tool such as Microsoft Visual Studio.

Figure 1-3

General steps for creating an app

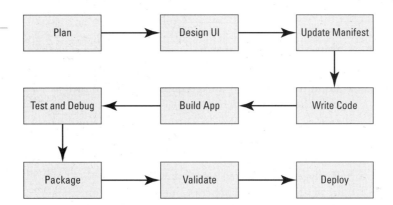

In this section, you will learn the general steps involved in creating an app. Figure 1-3 illustrates the steps, which are explained as follows:

- **Plan your project:** Think about the type of app you want to create. Whatever you choose, it's best to keep it simple while you're first learning HTML5 app development. After you decide on the main action of your app, create an outline of the general flow of the application from start to finish. Also determine the type of user interactivity you want to include, such as a touch interface, whether you need to save data outside of the app, and whether the app should connect to other apps or services (such as an RSS feed).

- **Design a UI:** When designing the user interface, determine how you want the app to appear to users. Group the content in a way that makes logical sense. Begin listing the commands you will need for the app to run as expected, and gather images and multimedia clips if necessary. At a minimum, today's apps require a *launcher icon*, which represents your app.

- **Update the app manifest:** Every app requires a manifest file. The manifest file describes properties of the app and what the app needs to run (see Figure 1-4). The file includes many different pieces of information, such as a display name that users see, a description of the app, the app's orientation (portrait, landscape, etc.), the file path to the app's icon, the app's capabilities (system features or devices that your app can use), and much more.

Figure 1-4

An example of a manifest file

```xml
<?xml version="1.0" encoding="utf-8"?>
<Package xmlns="http://schemas.microsoft.com/appx/2010/manifest">
   <Identity Name="CompanyX.Samples.App1"
             Version="1.0.0.0"
             Publisher="CN=Company X, O=Company X, L=Coolsville, S=TX, C=USA" />
   <Properties>
     <DisplayName>Samples App1</DisplayName>
     <PublisherDisplayName>Company X</PublisherDisplayName>
     <Logo>images\CompanyX-logo.png</Logo>
   </Properties>
   <Prerequisites>
     <OSMinVersion>6.2</OSMinVersion>
     <OSMaxVersionTested>6.2</OSMaxVersionTested>
   </Prerequisites>
   <Resources>
     <Resource Language="en-us" />
   </Resources>
   <Applications>
     <Application Id="App1" StartPage="default.html">
       <VisualElements DisplayName="App1" Description="A handy little app."
           Logo="images\icon.png" SmallLogo="images\icon-sml.png"
           ForegroundText="dark" BackgroundColor="#FFFFFF">
         <SplashScreen Image="images\splash.png" />
       </VisualElements>
     </Application>
   </Applications>
</Package>
```

- **Write code:** During this phase, you compose the code for your application, which might include a combination of HTML, CSS, and JavaScript.
- **Build the app:** Using an app development tool such as Visual Studio, convert your code and other resources into an actual application.
- **Debug and test:** You must test your app thoroughly and fix any problems that appear. If the app uses a touch interface, it's highly important to test the app on a touch device or use a touch emulator.
- **Package:** Packaging an app creates a container that holds all of the various files required by the app, such JavaScript, images, and so on.
- **Validate:** Validating your app means running it through a validation program to ensure nothing is missing,
- **Deploy:** Upload your app to a marketplace such as the Windows Store.

Apps that you plan to deploy to many people, especially through a marketplace such as an app store, must be reliable and secure. Many apps are also designed to run on multiple operating systems. Be sure you have tested your app thoroughly and validated it with the proper tools. You should also consider providing technical support for more complex apps.

 PREPARE FOR APPLICATION DEVELOPMENT

GET READY. To prepare to work with HTML5 and develop apps, perform the following steps:

1. Look for sources of free, non-copyrighted images on the Web. Even if you're capable of creating many of your own graphics, having resources to draw from will come in handy.

2. To work with HTML5, CSS, and JavaScript files, download and install a text or HTML editor, such as Notepad++. (Just search for Notepad++ using a Web browser.) A more full-featured tool is Visual Studio Express for Web, available from the Visual Studio Web site at http://bit.ly/eBUygk. Express for Web lets you open your files into a Web browser with one click and provides lots of templates to help you create files quickly.

3. Ensure you have the latest versions of your browser installed.

4. To create apps for the Windows Store, download Microsoft Visual Studio 2012 Express for Windows 8 from http://bit.ly/K8nkk1 and install it. The program requires Windows 8 to be installed.

Exploring Packaging and the Runtime Environment

The Windows Runtime environment is the foundation of the Windows 8 operating system and provides functionality to Metro-style apps.

When an application is launched, it's considered to be in a runtime environment (RTE). This is the environment in which developers test their applications, and where users run the apps. Windows has its own runtime environment, called *Windows Runtime (WinRT)*.

The WinRT is the foundation of the Windows 8 operating system, and is made up of layers that provide functionality to Metro-style apps and the Windows shell. WinRT supports apps written in different languages that use the Metro UI.

The Windows Core layer is at the base. This layer includes the Windows kernel, services, and user mode. Moving up, the Windows Runtime Core includes additional services like memory management and globalization. Above the Windows Runtime Core are layers related to devices, along with media, networking, local and remote storage, and more. The UI layer supports HTML5 apps, along with others.

The WinRT works with C#, C++, Visual Basic, and JavaScript. You can build Metro style apps with the WinRT and Windows Library for JavaScript APIs. An *application programming interface (API)* is simply a list of instructions letting a program communicate with another program. In a Web app, an API enables a Web browser or a Web server to communicate with other programs. There are hundreds of APIs available for many different uses.

TAKE NOTE*

The Document Object Model (DOM) is an important API to keep in mind. The DOM is designed for HTML and Extensible Markup Language (XML), and allows programs and scripts to update content, structure, and styles on the fly—essentially anything in an HTML or XML file can be modified. The DOM is neither HTML nor JavaScript, but it ties them together.

CERTIFICATION READY
Which environment gives developers access to a user's device?
1.1

The Windows Library for JavaScript includes JavaScript and CSS files which developers can use to create Metro style apps more easily and quickly. You use the library along with HTML, CSS, and the WinRT to create apps.

The runtime environment is responsible for access to devices, media, networking, local and remote storage, and other items. A developer can use APIs and the runtime environment to request access to user devices within an app. In a Windows 8 app, for example, the device could be a keyboard, mouse, touchpad, printer, webcam, or microphone.

➕ MORE INFORMATION

For more information about Windows Runtime, visit the "HTML, CSS, and JavaScript features and differences" Web page at http://bit.ly/xrofoB.

UNDERSTANDING THE HOST PROCESS

Whether an app is a Web app or whether it's created for Windows, an app requires a runtime host to start it. For example, when you start Internet Explorer, a host process in the operating system controls the overall execution of the browser. (A "process" is simply a program that's being executed.) In this case, each browser tab gets its own process, so if you have three tabs open, the system has three processes running for each of those tabs.

When you run a Metro style app that was created with JavaScript, Internet Explorer renders the HTML much like when you browse to a Web page, but the browser is hosted by a different process, called WWAHost.exe. This process runs the app inside of an app container. (You'll learn about app containers in the next section.) WWAHost passes the HTML, CSS, and JavaScript into the default.html page that is the start of your app.

To keep things orderly, the code running in a Metro style app container is restricted to certain actions, by default. If you want your app to access a device, another app, the Internet, or anything outside of itself, you must declare (specify) the interaction in the app manifest. These declarations are located in the Capabilities section of the manifest. When the end user installs the app, the user must give permission for the requested access.

Metro style apps use contracts, which are essentially agreements, and something called extensions when creating interactions between apps. WinRT APIs handle the communication between the apps.

UNDERSTANDING THE APP PACKAGE AND APP CONTAINER

The purpose of an app package is for ease of distribution and deployment. Application packaging bundles an app's files and folders into a distributable package. An app container ensures the application runs in its own memory space and doesn't corrupt the operating system.

Application packaging is the process of bundling an application and its various files into a distributable file, making it easy to deploy the app. The *app package* is the result of the packaging process. Packaging is similar to archiving a folder that contains files and subfolders. It would be difficult to send all of the files and subfolders to someone as is, but the job is much easier when you compress everything into a single archive file. App development packages like Visual Studio provide the functionality to create app packages. A user acquires an app package, usually from an online app store, and installs it on a PC or device. The application executes in a runtime *app container*, which means a separate memory space. An app container prevents corruption of the operating system if the application fails for some reason and enables a user to cleanly uninstall the app.

Some things you should know about packages are as follows:

- A package may contain Web pages, code, database tables, and procedures. When a package has a user interface, it's referred to as an application.
- A package can contain other packages.
- You can move one or more elements in or out of a package. Because a package is in its own container, if you move a package, then everything in the package moves as a unit.
- A user can install, upgrade, or remove a package.

A single package can have a lot of functionality. To keep all of the components separated so they don't conflict, a package defines a *namespace*. Think of a namespace as a work area for related objects (pages, code, etc.).

EXPLORE APP SAMPLES

GET READY. To explore the kinds of sample apps that are available for download, perform the following steps:

1. Go to the MSDN Developer Network Samples Web page (see Figure 1-5) at http://bit.ly/H57ZVh. Microsoft provides a wide range of sample apps and code samples, which you can download and open in an app development tool like Visual Studio. You can also view the code for many sample apps online.

Figure 1-5

A portion of the MSDN Developer Network Samples Web page

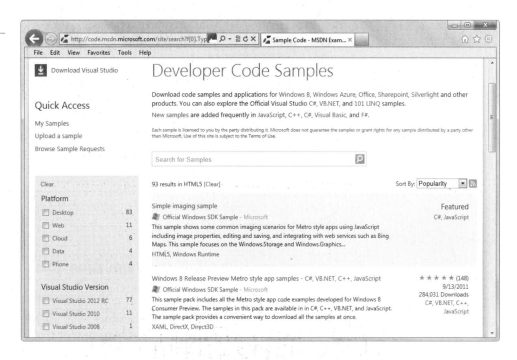

2. Scroll down and click the **HTML5** link in the left pane, currently near the bottom of the list.

3. Browse through the samples and find an app that displays "HTML5" after the app description, such as the stocks end-to-end sample. Click the link to the app.

4. The resulting page indicates which program is required to open and edit the app's files and which technologies are included in the app. The stocks end-to-end sample requires Visual Studio 12 and includes JavaScript and HTML5, as shown in Figure 1-6.

Figure 1-6

Viewing a sample app's Web page

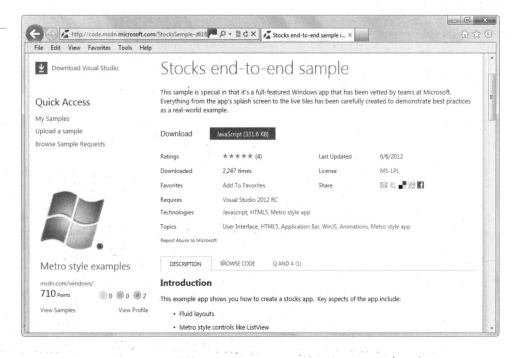

5. Click the **Browse Code** link, click **StocksSample** in the left pane, click **html**, and then click **dashboard.html**. The HTML markup displays. Scroll through the markup to get a feel for the type of code you'll see many times in this book.

6. Click **css** in the left pane and then click **dashboard.css**. The CSS code displays.

7. Click **js** in the left pane and then click **default.js**. The JavaScript code displays.

8. If you have an app development tool (like Visual Studio) already installed, feel free to download and open the sample app to browse all of the files in the package.

9. You can also go to the HTML5Rocks.com Web site, click the **Posts & Tutorials** menu at the top of the screen, check the **Samples** check box, and then browse how each sample works along with its code.

10. Close any open windows.

+ MORE INFORMATION

For more information about the app package, visit the "App packages and deployment" Web page at http://bit.ly/H9rsFz.

Understanding Credentials and Permission Sets

The .NET Framework provides a secure environment in which HTML5/JavaScript apps can run. The framework uses security transparency to separate different kinds of code while running, and uses permission sets and identity permissions to control the environment.

Code security is a priority with app developers. The monetary loss from viruses, Trojans, cross-site scripting attacks, and other malware distributed across the Internet increases each year. Creating a safe and secure environment for apps to run in is vitally important to most individuals and organizations today.

The good news is that the .NET Framework 4.0 supports building and running Metro style apps, among other technologies. The .NET Framework is a Windows component that runs in the background, providing the code-execution environment for scripted or interpreted code (like JavaScript), helping them run with relatively few problems. It also provides an object-oriented programming environment for object code.

The .NET Framework now relies more heavily on security "transparency" than in past versions. Transparency prevents application code from running with infrastructure code. The .NET Framework uses permission sets and identity permission. *Permission sets* are groups of permissions. Transparent code executes commands that don't exceed the limitations of a permission set, and transparent code is even more limited when it comes to critical code.

The .NET Framework defines several levels of permission sets, which range from Nothing (no permissions exist and code cannot run) to Full Trust (code can access all resources fully).

Identity permissions protect assemblies (compiled code libraries) based on evidence, which is information about the assembly. Each identity permission represents a particular kind of evidence, or credentials, that an assembly must have in order to run.

■ Understanding and Managing Application States

↓ **THE BOTTOM LINE**

A session state is created when a user first requests access to an application, and it ends when the session closes, such as when a user logs off. An application state exists from the time a Web browser requests a Web page until the browser closes. Persistent state information is data that exists after a session ends. In HTML5, developers can use the **localStorage** and **sessionStorage** JavaScript methods to deal efficiently with state data. In addition, AppCache enables a user to load data ordinarily stored on a server even when the user is offline.

CERTIFICATION READY
What is the difference between session state and application state?
1.2

CERTIFICATION READY
What is the significance of persist state information?
1.2

State management is the process of maintaining Web page information during multiple requests for the same or different Web page. When a user first requests access to an application, the *session state* is created. The state ends when the user closes the session.

An alternative to the session state is the application state. The *application state* is created when the Web browser sends the first request for a Web page to the Web server, and it ends when the user closes the browser.

Persistent state information is data that an application needs after the session ends. Many Web applications need to store data (make it persistent) so that users can pick up where they left off when they return to the site.

Storing State Data Using Local and Session Storage

Hypertext Transport Protocol (HTTP) is the protocol that transfers data on the World Wide Web. It defines the actions Web servers and browsers take in response to commands by users. For example, when you enter a uniform resource locator (URL) in the address field in a browser, the browser sends an HTTP command to the Web server requesting the Web page. HTTP is a stateless protocol, which means it doesn't retain data from session to session. When you close a Web browser after visiting a Web site, the data is not saved.

CERTIFICATION READY
How does HTML5 manage state data?
1.2

To work around the limitations of HTTP protocol, developers historically have used *cookies*, which are small files that contain information about the user and the Web site visited and are saved on the user's computer. When a user returns to a visited site, the browser sends the cookies back to the Web server. Cookies help a Web server "remember" a user and customize the user's experience on that site.

However, cookies have proven to be a security risk. In addition, if large amounts of data are involved, all of the data gets sent between the browser and server upon every request, which would cause a noticeable performance decrease to the user. In HTML5, developers can use the Web storage instead, which offers more flexibility, larger data sets, and better performance.

CERTIFICATION READY
Which two HTML5/JavaScript methods enable an application to store persistent data?
1.2

The `localStorage` method allows users to save larger amounts of data from session to session (persistent data), and there's no time limit as to how long the data exists. The `sessionStorage` method keeps data only for one session (until the browser is closed), which is also referred to as "per-tab storage."

Using these methods, specific data is transferred only when requested, so it's possible to store a relatively large amount of data without slowing down the connection or site.

APPCACHE FOR OFFLINE FILES

Another way to use Web storage is to store data locally when a user is offline. The Application Cache, or *AppCache*, stores resources like images, HTML pages, CSS files,and JavaScript—data that would ordinarily be stored on a server. Because the resources are stored on the client's hard disk or device, the resources load faster when requested.

Using AppCache, a developer uses a text file called a "cache manifest" to specify the files a Web browser should cache offline. Even if a user presses the Refresh button offline, the app will load and work correctly. A cache manifest file looks similar to the following:

X REF
You'll learn more about using AppCache with JavaScript in Lesson 8.

```
index.html

stylesheet.css

images/dot.png

scripts/main.js
```

> ✚ **MORE INFORMATION**
>
> For more information about state management, and local and session storage, see the "Storing and retrieving state efficiently" Web page at http://bit.ly/H9wH3u.

■ Understanding Touch Interfaces and Gestures

THE BOTTOM LINE

On a touch-screen device, a finger move is called a gesture, and the response by the app to that gesture is called an event. Developing touch-enabled apps requires thorough knowledge of how fingers interact with the screen and planning for different sizes of fingers. You can use JavaScript to create touch-enabled apps, primarily using the `touchstart`, `touchend`, and `touchmove` events.

CERTIFICATION READY
What is a gesture, and what is its significance with touch devices?
1.3

Today's mobile devices and many PC monitors incorporate touch-screen technology, which makes it easier for many users to interact with the devices and their programs. A simple finger tap selects an object or presses a button, a finger swipe scrolls a list of photos on the screen, and a pinch zooms out on an image.

Any finger move is referred to as a **gesture**, which can involve a single finger (one-touch, such as press, tap, press and hold, slide to pan, and so on) or a finger and a thumb (two-touch, such as a pinch and stretch or a turn to rotate). The action the application takes in response to a gesture is called a **touch event**. You can use JavaScript to create touch events in touch-enabled apps. In JavaScript, the three primary touch events are `touchstart`, `touchend`, and `touchmove`.

X REF

You'll learn how to create JavaScript code for touch interfaces in Lesson 9.

When designing apps for a touch-screen environment, gesture responsiveness is key. Slow performance will frustrate most users. Incorporate physics effects such as acceleration and inertia to create a more fluid interaction between the user and screen.

Visual feedback for successful interactions and other notifications is highly important. This allows the user to understand whether he or she is using the touch landscape appropriately. Snap points help users stop at a location within the interface where intended, even if a gesture is a little off the mark.

You should also keep in mind that users have different size fingers, and it's a best practice to design for wider rather than narrower digits. And of course, users will be either right- or left-handed, so a well-designed app uses vertically symmetric navigation and provides for flipping the screen 90 degrees to go from portrait to landscape or vice versa.

CERTIFICATION READY
What are some touch-enabled best practices you should test for?
1.3

Multi-touch occurs when a user must press multiple buttons or locations at once. This is common with games on a touch-screen device, where the user often uses several fingers and both thumbs simultaneously or in very rapid succession. In this situation, swipes and gestures don't work well, resulting in unintended zooming and scrolling instead. The fix is to disable zooming and scrolling in JavaScript.

Another item to test for in a multi-touch app is the reaction to touch events. There will be many events occurring at the same time, which requires proper tracking of fingers and rendering in a loop to get the best performance.

When developing any touch-enabled app, be sure to test for the following:
- Overall responsiveness and fluidity
- Tapping, pinching, rotating, and other common gestures
- Controlled scrolling
- Controlled panning

- Ability to disabled scrolling and panning
- Accuracy of snap points
- Unintended zooming or scrolling, especially in a multi-touch environment
- Proper touch event reaction, especially in a multi-touch environment

Designing and developing well-formed touch-enabled apps takes practice, and a lot of testing. If you don't have a touch-screen device, you can use MouseTouch events and a touch-screen emulator or simulator. Try Microsoft Surface SDK and Runtime for Windows 7, or the Windows Simulator tool in Visual Studio 11. A *touch-screen simulator* or *emulator* imitates a system that only has touch capabilities. Several free emulators are available online.

 LEARN ABOUT GESTURES AND TOUCH-ENABLED APPS

GET READY. To learn about different kinds of gestures, perform the following steps:

1. Go to the Touch interaction design Web page at http://bit.ly/GAJjDL.
2. Read the content on the Web page.
3. Bookmark the page for future reference or locate and click the link that downloads a PDF version of the Web page to your computer.
4. Close the browser window.

➕ **MORE INFORMATION**

You can find the WC3 touch specifications at http://bit.ly/gBZUjo. For more information about touch and gestures, visit the "Responding to user interaction" Web page at http://bit.ly/H7uO5Q.

Leveraging Existing HTML5 Skills and Content for Slate/Tablet Applications

> An advantage for seasoned developers who want to create Metro style apps is that their existing HTML5 skills and code lend themselves well to Metro app development.

CERTIFICATION READY
Does a Web developer need to gain new skills to be able to create Metro style apps for touch devices?
1.1

A highly flexible aspect of developing touch-enabled Metro style apps is that it doesn't require a big learning curve for developers who are already using HTML5 and other methods of app development. They can apply their existing skills and code to creating Metro style apps almost immediately. A Web developer's experience with HTML, CSS, JavaScript, and JavaScript libraries is an advantage when transitioning to touch-enabled Metro app development.

In addition, Microsoft.NET Framework and Silverlight developers can apply their XAML, C#, and Visual Basic experience to Metro projects. Game programmers who are well versed with Microsoft DirectX 11 can also apply their skills creating Metro apps.

■ Debugging and Testing HTML5 Apps

 THE BOTTOM LINE All apps must be thoroughly tested and debugged to ensure they run reliably and as error-free as possible before distribution and deployment.

Debugging an application involves detecting, finding, and correcting logical or syntactical errors. A syntax error is a typo in the code or a similar error, which is usually revealed during runtime for interpreted apps. A logic error results in the app behaving differently than expected.

CERTIFICATION READY
What can a developer do to help ensure that a new app is reliable and as error-free as possible?
1.3

Testing and debugging code is a standard part of app development, and the majority of tools like Visual Studio have debugging features built in to the software. Some errors are easy to detect and fix, whereas others can require hours or even days to resolve, depending on the complexity of the application.

Either way, the testing and debugging phase is highly important for several reasons:

- Your goal is to provide a reliable, secure, and useful app to customers. Debugging and testing help to ensure all three are met.
- High-quality apps garner high ratings, which can boost your profits and drive sales of future apps.
- If you plan to publish your app through the Windows Store or another reputable online app marketplace, the store will require validation or certification that your app has been tested.

Validating HTML5 Code

One of the first steps in the debugging and testing phase is to validate your HTML5 code. Validation means verifying the validity of your code. A *validator* looks for anything that could cause the code to be interpreted incorrectly, such as missing or unclosed tags, an improper DOCTYPE declaration, a trailing slash, deprecated code, and so on. (Don't worry about those details right now. You'll learn about them in Lesson 2.)

The W3C provides a code validation service for all active versions of HTML on its Markup Validation Service Web page at http://validator.w3.org/. The service is free for anyone to use. You simply click a link to upload your file to the service, or copy and paste the content of your file into a text box on the Web site. After that, click the Check button. The validation service checks your code and reports any errors or problems you need to fix.

A validator is not the same as an emulator or a simulator. A validator actually tests the code and reports inaccuracies, giving you an opportunity to make changes. Emulators and simulators simply provide an environment in which to run code.

TAKE NOTE * The W3C also provides a link checker at http://validator.w3.org/checklink. This service checks that all links in your HTML file are valid. The CSS Validation Service at http://jigsaw.w3.org/css-validator/ checks your CSS files.

Validating a Package

Microsoft provides a free tool called the Windows App Certification Kit for testing local apps. The kit is a type of validator that tests your app on your computer before you attempt to package and publish it to the Windows Store.

The Windows App Certification Kit is included in the Windows Software Development Kit (SDK) for Metro style apps, available on the Microsoft Web site. To use the kit, you must first package and install the app locally using an app development tool. Then open the kit, select the application you want to validate, and run the validator. A report displays noting any problems with the app. The Windows App Certification Kit might also be available as a menu choice within your app development tool.

Correct the problems in an app development tool and then test the application again. You'll repeat this process until your app validates.

USE THE W3C MARKUP VALIDATION SERVICE

GET READY. To become familiar with the W3C Markup Validation Service, perform the following steps:

1. Go to the W3C Markup Validation Service Web page at http://validator.w3.org/.
2. Click the **Validate by File Upload** tab.
3. Click **Browse**.
4. Navigate to and select an HTML file from one of your sample apps. Click **Open**, and then click **Check**.
5. Scroll down the page and read the errors and warnings, if any. Figure 1-7 shows an example.

Figure 1-7

Errors and warnings as a result of attempting to validate an HTML Web page

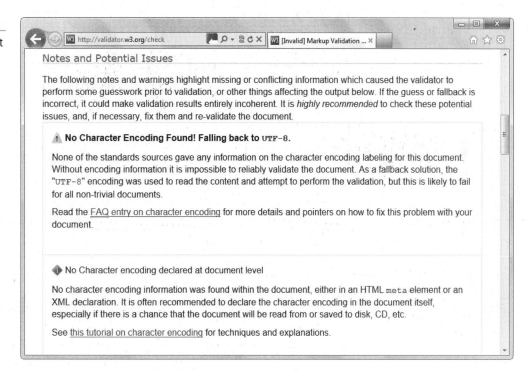

6. If the validator provides links to more information about errors or warnings, click through to at least two of them and read the information.
7. When you're finished, leave the Web browser open.

 USE THE W3C CSS VALIDATION SERVICE

GET READY. To become familiar with the W3C CSS Validation Service, perform the following steps:

1. Go to the W3C CSS Validation Service Web page at http://jigsaw.w3.org/css-validator/ (see Figure 1-8).
2. Click the **By file upload** tab.
3. Click **Browse**.
4. Navigate to and select a CSS file from one of your sample apps. Click **Open**, and then click **Check**.

Figure 1-8

The W3C CSS Validation Service
Web page

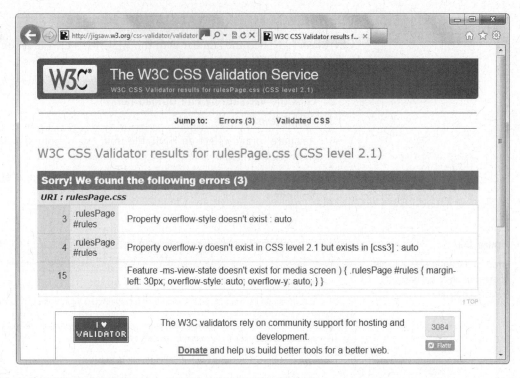

5. Scroll down the page and read the errors and warnings, if any.

6. If the validator provides links to more information about errors or warnings, click through to at least two of them and read the information.

7. When you're finished, leave the Web browser open.

■ Publishing an Application to a Store

↓ THE BOTTOM LINE

Once your app has been tested, debugged, and the code validated or certified, you need to take a few more steps to prepare it for upload to a marketplace such as the Windows Store. You can use Visual Studio 12 or Visual Studio 12 Express to complete the project.

Publishing your app to a public marketplace like the Windows Store is the pinnacle of all of your planning, designing, coding, and testing. The *Windows Store* is an online global marketplace for Metro style apps. Publishing your app for distribution through the store can possibly turn a good idea into a lucrative venture.

Another bonus to selling through the Windows Store is that you get access to several handy tools, such as Microsoft Visual Studio Express and Microsoft Expression Blend. You can also download personalized app telemetry data, which can greatly speed up app creation and deployment.

Before publishing your app to the Windows Store, you must do the following:

- Sign up and pay for a Windows Store developer account, and reserve a name for your app. You'll also need to edit your app's manifest file.
- Go through the app submission checklist at http://bit.ly/HAPmbk. The checklist includes tasks such as naming your app, choosing selling details such as selecting appropriate pricing and a release date, assigning an age rating, describing your app, and more.

CERTIFICATION READY
How do you publish an app to the Windows Store?
1.4

- Use the Windows App Certification Kit to test your app, if you haven't done so already.
- Capture some screen shots of significant or unique features of your app to showcase in the store. You can use the Snipping Tool, which is built into Windows 7 and Windows 8, to capture screen shots or you can use another tool of your choice.
- Have other testers or developers test your app on as many different devices and platforms as possible, especially if you tested it only in a simulator or emulator.
- Include a privacy statement if your app gathers personal information or uses copyrighted software to run.

TAKE NOTE *

You must sign up and pay for a Windows Store developer account to add your app to the store menu.

When you're ready, use your app development tool (such as Visual Studio 12 or Visual Studio 12 Express for Windows 8) to create a final app package and then upload it to the Windows Store.

It's customary to wait for approval from the store. If approved, your app will be certified and listed. However, even after all of your preparatory work, your app could be rejected, which means you must fix any problems noted by app store personnel if you want to retest and republish the app.

 BECOME FAMILIAR WITH THE WINDOWS STORE MARKETPLACE

GET READY. To learn more about Windows Store requirements, perform the following steps:

1. Open Internet Explorer, then go to www.bing.com.
2. Search for Windows Store Marketplace and go to the site.
3. Browse the categories of apps. Note the three highest rated apps, and another three apps that interest you.
4. Read the description of each app and make notes that could help you write an appealing description for your app.
5. Note the number and quality of screen shots provided for those apps.
6. Note the quality of the launcher icon and any other graphical details.
7. Note the price and age rating of each app.
8. Note any other details that might help you sell your app when it's ready.
9. When you're done, close all open windows.

SKILL SUMMARY

IN THIS LESSON YOU LEARNED:

- HTML5 is the latest HTML standard and a family of technologies that includes HTML, CSS, and JavaScript. Although the HTML5 standard won't be finalized for a few years, most modern Web browsers already support HTML5 elements, and HTML5 app development for Web and mobile device browsers is well underway.
- The HTML5 family includes many new markup tags and technologies like media queries, geolocation, Modernizr, and much more.
- The general steps for creating an app are: plan the project, design a UI, update the app manifest, write code, build the app, debug and test the app, package the app, and deploy the app.
- The Windows Runtime (WinRT) environment is the foundation of the Windows 8 operating system and provides functionality to Metro style apps.
- Metro style apps created with JavaScript and that are opened in Internet Explorer are run by the WWAHost.exe process. This is a different process than the host process that ordinarily runs Internet Explorer.
- The purpose of an app package is for ease of distribution and deployment. Application packaging bundles an app's files and folders into an app package.

- The .NET Framework provides a secure environment in which HTML5/JavaScript apps can run. The framework uses security transparency to separate different kinds of code while running, and uses permission sets and identity permissions to control the environment.
- A session state is created when a user first requests access to an application, and it ends when the session closes.
- An application state exists from the time a Web browser requests a Web page until the browser closes.
- Persist state information is data that exists after a session ends.
- In HTML5, developers can use the `localStorage` and `sessionStorage` JavaScript methods to deal efficiently with state data.
- AppCache is a type of Web storage that enables a user to load data that's ordinarily stored on a server even when the user is offline.
- On a touch-screen device, a finger move is called a gesture, and the response by the app to that gesture is called an event.
- Developing touch-enabled apps requires thorough knowledge of how fingers interact with the screen and planning for different sizes of fingers.
- You can use JavaScript to create touch-enabled apps, primarily using the `touchstart`, `touchend`, and `touchmove` events.
- An advantage for seasoned developers who want to create Metro style apps is that their existing HTML5 skills and code lend themselves well to Metro app development.
- All apps must be thoroughly tested and debugged to ensure they run reliably and as error-free as possible before distribution and deployment.
- Once your app has been tested, debugged, and the code validated or certified, you need to take a few more steps to prepare it for upload to a marketplace such as the Windows Store. You can use Visual Studio 11 or Visual Studio 11 Express to complete the project.

■ Knowledge Assessment

Fill in the Blank

Complete the following sentences by writing the correct word or words in the blanks provided.

1. HTML is a _____ language, not a programming language, which means HTML uses markup tags such as <body> and <h1> to describe parts of a Web page.

2. _____ defines styles for HTML in a separate file, so you can easily change fonts, font sizes, and other attributes.

3. Windows 8 users the _____ user interface (UI).

4. The _____ is the foundation of the Windows 8 operating system, and is made up of layers that provide functionality to Metro style apps and the Windows shell.

5. _____ is the process of bundling an application and its various files into an app container, making it easy to distribute and deploy the app. The app package is the result of this process.

6. The _____ state is created when the Web browser sends the first request for a Web page to the Web server and it ends when the user closes the browser.

7. The _____ method keeps data only for one session (until the browser is closed), which is also referred to as "per-tab storage."

8. Any finger move is referred to as a _____, which can involve a single finger (one-touch) or a finger and a thumb (two-touch).

9. A _____ looks for anything that could cause code to be interpreted incorrectly, such as missing or unclosed tags, an improper DOCTYPE declaration, a trailing slash, deprecated code, and so on.

10. The _____ is an online global marketplace for Metro style apps.

Multiple Choice

Circle the letter that corresponds to the best answer.

1. Which three components are the primary elements of the HTML5 family?
   a. XML
   b. HTML
   c. CSS
   d. JavaScript

2. JavaScript is a type of:
   a. Program compiler
   b. Markup language
   c. Scripting language
   d. Validator

3. All of the following are true of HTML5 except:
   a. It requires Windows 8
   b. It can be used to create Web apps and PC and device apps
   c. It is platform-independent
   d. It is built on an open standard

4. Which operating system environment allows a developer to access a camera or webcam?
   a. `localStorage`
   b. WinRT
   c. the session state
   d. Metro

5. You are developing a Metro style app and want the app to access another app. Where do you declare the interaction?
   a. App manifest
   b. CSS
   c. At the top of the HTML file
   d. Nowhere; you do not have to declare the interaction

6. Which of the following is used to create an app package?
   a. JavaScript
   b. CSS
   c. DOM
   d. An app development tool

7. Which API allows programs and scripts to update content, structure, and styles on the fly?
   a. JavaScript
   b. WinRT
   c. The DOM
   d. RTE

8. `AppCache`, `localStorage`, and `sessionStorage` are forms of:
   a. Web storage
   b. HTML commands
   c. Standards
   d. Namespaces

9. Which of the following does not usually work well with multi-touch environments and should be disabled? (Choose two.)
   a. Tracking
   b. Zooming
   c. Scrolling
   d. Gesturing

10. Which tool is a type of validator that tests your app on your computer before you attempt to package and publish it to the Windows Store?
    a. WinRT
    b. Windows 8
    c. W3C Markup Validation Service
    d. Windows App Certification Kit

True / False

Circle T if the statement is true or F if the statement is false.

T F **1.** An application programming interface (API) is a list of instructions letting a program communicate with another program.

T F **2.** A best practice is to publish your app without validation to perform live online testing.

T F **3.** An emulator searches HTML and CSS documents, looking for errors.

T F **4.** It's a best practice to design touch-enabled apps for wider rather than narrower digits.

T F **5.** A platform-independent app can run on different desktop and mobile device operating systems.

■ Competency Assessment

Scenario 1-1: Understanding New Features in the HTML5 Family

Your manager, Marylyne, wants to learn about the HTML5 family to decide if the company should begin using it on new projects. She asks you to provide her a list of five or six new features. What items do you include in the list?

Scenario 1-2: Creating an App

Marylyne approaches you again, this time wanting to know what is involved in creating an HTML5 app. She asks you to provide an outline. What steps do you include in the outline?

■ Proficiency Assessment

Scenario 1-3: Sharing Touch-Enabled App Development Tips

Antoine is working on a touch-enabled app and asks you for development tips and items he should be sure to test on his tablet. What do you tell him?

Scenario 1-4: Publishing an App to the Windows Store

Sammy created his first app and wants to publish it to the Windows Store. What are three preparatory steps he should take?

Building the User Interface by Using HTML5: Text, Graphics, and Media

EXAM OBJECTIVE MATRIX

SKILLS/CONCEPTS	MTA EXAM OBJECTIVE	MTA EXAM OBJECTIVE NUMBER
Understanding the Essentials of HTML		
Choosing and Configuring HTML5 Tags to Display Text Content	Choose and configure HTML5 tags to display text content.	2.1
Choosing and Configuring HTML5 Tags to Display Graphics	Choose and configure HTML5 tags to display graphics.	2.2
Choosing and Configuring HTML5 Tags to Play Media	Choose and configure HTML5 tags to play media.	2.3

KEY TERMS

attribute

audio element

canvas element

codec

compression

deprecation

doctype

element

empty tag

entity

figcaption element

figure element

global attribute

nesting

raster image

render

Scalable Vector Graphics (SVG)

tags

valid

vector image

video compression

video element

The busy Web site developers at Malted Milk Media have asked you to research new markup that's available in HTML5. They're particularly interested in graphics and multimedia-related tags. Your task is to learn all that you can about new HTML5 markup tags and prepare brief descriptions and provide examples of each.

■ Understanding the Essentials of HTML

THE BOTTOM LINE

Hypertext Markup Language (HTML) uses markup to describe content for display on a Web page. An element is the combination of tags and the content they enclose. You may need to use special characters on a Web page, which requires character encoding. Finally, every Web page requires the doctype declaration at the top of the page.

Hypertext Markup Language (HTML) is called a markup language because you use it to describe (mark up) pieces of content to display on a Web page. A Web page with markup means it includes *tags*, which are keywords that help to give an HTML page structure. (You'll learn more about tags shortly.) The key to using HTML is learning which tags to use and when. The combination of content, tags, and perhaps graphics, multimedia, and so on are what build a Web page.

You can easily identify an HTML document because it has an .htm or .html file extension. When a Web browser or mobile device such as a smartphone opens an HTML file, it *renders* (interprets and reproduces) the content of the page.

Basic Markup and Page Structure

Every HTML page includes tags. A tag is a keyword surrounded by angled brackets. Most tags come in pairs; one tag is called the opening or start tag, and the other is the closing or end tag. A tag pair is case sensitive—a closing tag must have the same case as the opening tag. A closing tag is identical to an opening tag except the closing tag includes a slash before the keyword.

Tags surround content and give it definition. For example, this markup creates a first-level heading:

```
<h1>Pet Care 101</h1>
```

HTML also uses some single tags, like <br /> for a line break and <hr /> for a horizontal line. In HTML 4, these tags are called *empty tags* because they don't require an end tag. HTML5 is less restrictive than HTML 4. You don't have to include end tags for all elements (although some elements still require start and end tags), and you can enter tags in uppercase or lowercase. However, this book uses start and end tags, and all lowercase for markup, for consistency.

There are many tags available for HTML pages. Some of the most commonly used tags are listed in Table 2-1. The first four—<html>, <head>, <title>, and <body>—are required on every Web page.

Table 2-1

Common HTML tags

TAG	DESCRIPTION
`<html>`	Identifies the page as an HTML document. The `<html>` tag encompasses everything on the page other than the doctype declaration at the top.
`<head>`	Contains markup and code used by the browser, such as scripts that add interactivity, and keywords to help search engines find the page. Content in the `<head>` tag can also include formatting styles for the page.
`<title>`	Displays the title of the Web page, which appears at the top of the Web browser, usually on the page's tab in a tabbed browser.
`<body>`	Surrounds content that's visible on the Web page when viewed in a Web browser.
`<a href=URL>`	Generally used to anchor a URL to text or an image; can also create a named anchor within a document to allow for linking to sections of the document.
`<b>`	Applies boldface to text.
`<hx>`	Creates a heading, which can be first level (h1) through sixth level (h6).
`<img>`	Inserts an image from a file or another Web site.
`<p>`	Defines text as a paragraph.

A tag pair or an empty tag is also called an **element**. An element can describe content, insert graphics, and create hyperlinks.

USING ATTRIBUTES

Not all tags describe data on their own or at least not in enough detail for rendering, so some elements must include **attributes**, which are modifiers of HTML elements that provide additional information.

Attributes are easy to use and are just extensions of elements. You add attributes to elements according to this basic syntax:

```
<tag attribute="value">
```

Notice that the attribute and its value are both inside a tag. You must include an attribute within a tag so that the Web browser knows how to handle the attribute. A good example of an attribute is when creating a hyperlink, as follows:

```
<a href="http://www.example.com">This is a link.</a>
```

The Web browser uses the combination of the anchor element and the href attribute to display a hyperlink. Figure 2-1 shows how a Web browser interprets this bit of markup.

TAKE NOTE*

A good Web page editor or app development tool should show you which attributes you can use with an element, which is a time saver. The tool should also help you debug the markup if you used an attribute incorrectly.

Figure 2-1

A hyperlink is the result of the anchor element using the `href` attribute

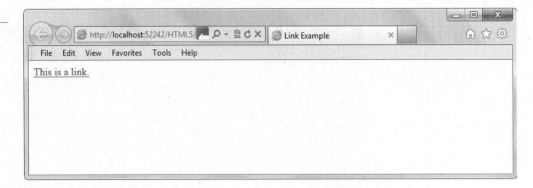

Two of the most common uses of attributes are to create hyperlinks and to insert simple graphics. You'll learn how to work with graphics later in this lesson. HTML5 includes several *global attributes*, which you can use with any HTML5 element. Examples of global attributes include `id`, `lang`, and `class`, among many others.

NESTING ELEMENTS

How a Web browser displays your HTML depends on the way you combine elements, their attributes (if any), and content. When two or more elements apply to the same block of text, you should nest tag pairs appropriately so that they do what you intended. *Nesting* means to place one element inside another. Here's an example of correct nesting:

```
<p>Make sure your pet has plenty of <i><b>fresh water</b></i>
during hot weather.</p>
```

In this case, we want the words "fresh water" to stand out so they are italicized and bolded by using the `<i>` and `<b>` tags. If you placed the `</b>` end tag after the `</p>` end tag (shown below), the words "fresh water during hot weather" would appear bold but only "fresh water" would be italicized. It would look awkward, as shown in Figure 2-2.

```
<p>Make sure your pet has plenty of <i><b>fresh water</i>
during hot weather.</p></b>
```

Figure 2-2

Incorrectly nesting tags

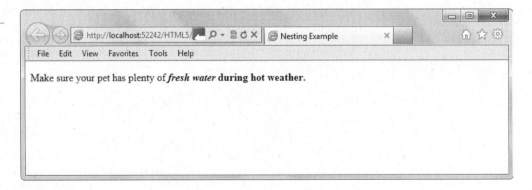

The rule for nesting is that nested tags must be closed before their parent tags. Looking back at the correct example, notice that the paragraph element opens first, followed by the italic element, and then the font element. Then the bold element closes, followed by the italic element, and finally the paragraph element. The italic and bold elements are completely nested within the paragraph element.

UNDERSTANDING ENTITIES

An *entity* is a special character, such as the dollar symbol, the registered trademark (a capital R within a circle), and accented letters. The process of incorporating entities in a Web page is called character encoding. Today's Web editing tools and browsers do a good job of handling special characters that appear on your keyboard, such as those above the number keys. In most cases, those characters render without any problems.

With some browsers, the character you expected doesn't appear and you get a gibberish character or symbol instead. Those situations are easy to handle. Each special character that can be reproduced in a Web page has an entity name and a numerical code. You can use either in a Web page. However, it's generally safer to represent symbols like the trademark using a numbered entity to ensure proper rendering in a wide variety of browsers.

An entity begins with an ampersand (&) and ends with a semicolon (;). For example, the entity ® represents the registered trademark symbol, and its numerical code is ® . When a browser encounters an ampersand, it tries to match the characters that follow with an entity. If the browser finds a match, it displays the special character in place of the entity. Table 2-2 lists a few commonly used entities.

Table 2-2

A sampling of entities for HTML5

Symbol	Description	Entity Name	Code
©	Copyright	&copy;	&#169;
°	Degree	&deg;	&#176;
$	Dollar	&dollar;	&#36;
%	Percent	&percnt;	&#37;
®	Registered trademark	&reg;	&#174;

Another important thing to know about character encoding in HTML5 is that you should use UTF-8 encoding whenever possible, because most browsers use UTF-8. That means you add the following declaration to the head element:

```
<meta charset="UTF-8">
```

The HTML5 specification requires that the whole meta element fits in the first 1,024 bytes of the document, which is why you include it at the top of the page in the head element.

+ MORE INFORMATION

For a list of entities supported in HTML5, go to http://dev.w3.org/html5/html-author/charref.

UNDERSTANDING THE DOCTYPE

The *doctype* is a declaration that is found at the very top of almost every HTML document. When a Web browser reads a doctype declaration, the browser assumes that everything on the Web page uses the language or rules specified in the declaration.

In HTML 4, all <!DOCTYPE> declarations require a reference to a DTD, which stands for Document Type Definition. The DTD is simply a set of rules that help a Web browser turn tags and content into the pages you see on the Web. There are a few different DTDs that an HTML 4 Web page can use. Because of how HTML5 was created, it doesn't require a reference to a DTD.

In HTML 4, the doctype declaration specifies the HTML page's language and DTD, and looks quite complex. Here's an example:

```
<!DOCTYPE html PUBLIC "-//W3C//DTD XHTML 1.1//EN"
    "http://www.example.com/TR/xhtml11/DTD/
    xhtml11.dtd">
```

The new HTML5 doctype, in comparison, is very simple:

```
<!doctype html>
```

The HTML5 doctype is case-insensitive, so the keyword "doctype" can be uppercase or lowercase. This simplified doctype is partially responsible for why HTML5 pages easily lend themselves for viewing in a Web browser on a computer or a mobile device. HTML5 is designed to be broadly compatible with both new and old Web browsers, and the mobile device environment.

EXPLORING THE MARKUP OF A SIMPLE WEB PAGE

An example of markup and content for a simple HTML5 Web page looks like this:

```
<!doctype html>

<html>
  <head>
    <title>78704 Pet Services</title>
  </head>

  <body>
    <p>Your dog is a friend for life. Why not
    provide the best care possible?</p>
  </body>

</html>
```

The blank lines between parts of the page, such as between the doctype declaration and the `<html>` tag, don't appear on a Web page. Neither do indents, such as those for the paragraphs. (Notice that the paragraph elements are indented a bit from the `<body>` tags. Blank lines and indents simply help you read the markup more easily in an editing tool.

Figure 2-3 shows the rendered Web page for the previous HTML markup.

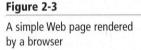

Figure 2-3

A simple Web page rendered by a browser

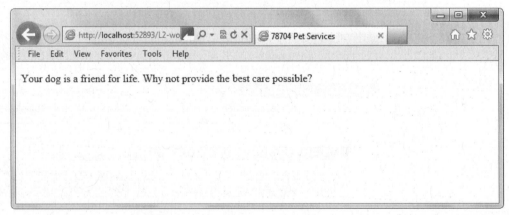

Recall from Lesson 1 that you can use the W3C's validation service at http://validator.w3.org to check and validate HTML code. If a Web page adheres to the specifications perfectly, it is considered **valid**.

 CREATE A SIMPLE WEB PAGE

GET READY. To create a simple Web page and see the effect of missing tags, nesting, and entities, perform the following steps:

1. On your computer or a flash drive, create a subfolder within the My Documents folder that will hold the files you work on in lessons throughout this book. This is your working folder. You can name the subfolder **HTML5** or something similar.

2. Open a Web page editor, app development tool, or even a simple text editor like Notepad and type the following:

```
<!doctype html>
<html>
  <head>
    <title>78704 Pet Services</title>
  </head>
<body>
<h1>Care and Feeding</h1>
    <p>Your dog is a friend for life. Why not provide the best
      care possible?</p>
    <p>Make sure your pet has plenty of <i><b>fresh water</b></i>
      during hot weather. When taking your dog on long walks,
      bring along a collapsible water dish and bottled water.
      You can find specialty water dishes at many pet supply
      stores for $10 or less.</p>
</body>
</html>
```

TAKE NOTE *

You have a lot of choices when it comes to editors and development tools. Notepad is the built-in text editor in Windows, but you can download Notepad++ for free from the Web. Notepad+++ offers features that make it easier to create and edit HTML documents. TextWrangler has a similar feature set and is designed for Macintosh systems. Free HTML editors include HTML-Kit and KompoZer. Development tools include Microsoft Visual Studio, Visual Studio for Web, Microsoft Web Matrix, and Microsoft Expression Web, among many others. All of these applications enable you to create and edit HTML files.

3. Save the file as **L2-pet-orig.html** in the working folder you created in My Documents.

4. Navigate to your working folder and open the HTML page in a Web browser. It should look similar to Figure 2-4.

Figure 2-4

The 78704 Pet Services Care and Feeding Web page

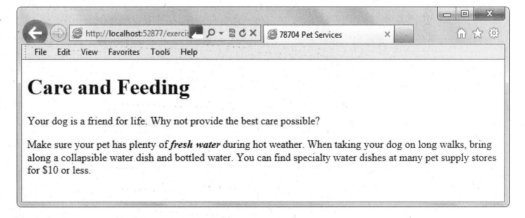

5. To see the effect of a missing tag in a tag pair, delete the </b> end tag after "water." Create a new file to test the changes by saving it as **L2-pet-test.html** and open it in the browser. Now all of the content from "fresh water" to the end of the document is in boldface.

TAKE NOTE *

In Internet Explorer 9, you can press **F12** to open browser mode. This mode enables you to edit pages without leaving the browser. In addition, you can click **Document Mode** on the menu bar and then select an older version of the browser to see how a page renders.

6. To see the effect of improper nesting, move the </i> end tag to appear after the last </p> tag. Save **L2-pet-test.html** again and view it in a browser. Now all of the content from "fresh water" to the end of the document is in boldface and italics, as shown in Figure 2-5.

Figure 2-5

Effects of improper nesting of tags

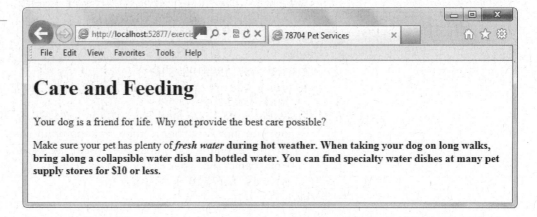

7. Close the **L2-pet-test.html** file in the editor and open **L2-pet-orig.html**.
8. Add a copyright line to the bottom of the page by pressing **Enter** a few times after the closing </p> tag and typing <p>© 2012</p>. Substitute the current year for "2012", if necessary. Press **Enter** to add a blank line. Make sure the copyright line is above the </body> and </html> end tags.
9. Create a new file again by saving L2-pet-test.html as **L2-pet-copyright.html** and view it in the browser. Does the circle C symbol appear as shown in Figure 2-6? If not, change © to **©**, save the file, and then view it again.

Figure 2-6

A copyright symbol appears in the lower-left corner

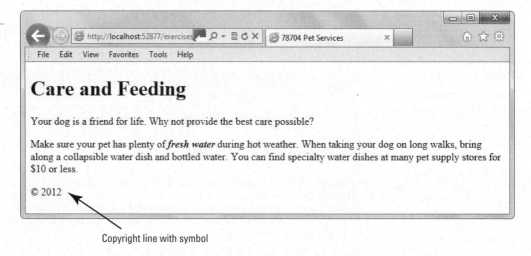

Copyright line with symbol

TAKE NOTE＊

When viewing Web pages that you're editing, it's best to use a variety of Web browsers to ensure your markup renders as expected for the widest audience. Some editing tools let you select a browser for previewing Web pages from a list. If your tool doesn't include that option, you'll need to install three or four different browsers and open your Web pages in each one.

10. Go to the W3C Markup Validation Service Web page at **http://validator.w3.org**. Upload **L2-pet-copyright.html** and click **Check** to have the service check it. Fix any errors reported by the checker that relate to missing tags or typos, if any.

11. You probably received an error message about character encoding. To fix this, open **L2-pet-copyright.html** in your editing tool, insert `<meta charset="UTF-8">` in the head element, on its own line, just before the title.

```
<head>
  <meta charset="UTF-8">
  <title>78704 Pet Services</title>
</head>
```

12. Save the file, upload it to the validation checker again, and check it. The checker should indicate that your file is valid.

13. Leave the editing tool and Web browser open if you're continuing immediately to the next section.

➕ MORE INFORMATION

If you find yourself struggling with the topics in this section, consider taking some tutorials such as those at the W3Schools.com Web site.

■ Choosing and Configuring HTML5 Tags to Display Text Content

THE BOTTOM LINE

HTML5 uses most of the same elements and attributes specified in HTML 4, and has introduced some new tags, modified the preferred usage of others, and no longer supports certain elements. New text-related elements include command, mark, time, meter, and progress. A few of the deprecated elements are basefont, center, font, and strike.

All of the elements covered in the first section in this lesson work well in HTML5, even though they have been used for years in previous versions of HTML. For the most part, HTML5 replaces very little HTML syntax. That means developers can still use most of the same elements they always have. Some elements have the same tag but slightly tweaked functionality, which you'll learn about shortly.

X REF

HTML5 layout, sectioning, and form creation markup is covered in Lesson 3.

HTML5 also includes many new elements that increase the functionality of Web pages or streamline the markup. These include multimedia elements such as audio and video, and elements that make the structure of a Web page seem more intuitive. Structure-related tags include elements for page sections, headers, footers, navigation, and even sidebars. If you create Web forms, new form features make creation and validation much easier. This section, however, focuses on HTML5 markup for text.

Text Elements from HTML 4 with New Meaning or Functionality

Some HTML 4 text-related elements now have slightly different meaning or functionality in HTML5. The elements include `<b>`, `<i>`, `<strong>`, `<em>`, and `<small>`. The `<b>` element should now be used to offset text without conveying importance, such as for keywords or product names. The `<i>` element now indicates content in an alternate voice or mood, like spoken text. The `<strong>` element indicates strong importance, whereas the `<em>` element indicates emphatic stress. The `<small>` element should be used for small print, like a copyright line.

Let's look at some of the text elements carried over from HTML 4 that have slightly different meaning or functionality in HTML5:

- **<b>:** This commonly used element has always represented boldface, and was often used for emphasis or to convey importance. The W3C suggests you now use it to indicate "stylistically offset" text without conveying importance. Use <b> for keywords, product names, and actionable items (such as items you click or press in a list of how-to steps). For example:

  ```
  <p>Click the <b>Check</b> button, and then click
  <b>OK.</b> </p>
  ```

- **<i>:** The italic element is now used for text in an "alternate voice or mood." This could be spoken text, thoughts, or something similar that doesn't convey importance or emphasis. It may also include technical terms and transliterated foreign words. For example:

  ```
  <p><i>He truly has a kind heart,</i> she thought.
  ```

- **<strong>:** The strong element is for strong importance, where the content is more important than nearby words. For example:

  ```
  <p>Courtney wore the <strong>same</strong> outfit to work three
  days in a row.</p>
  ```

- **<em>:** The emphasis element indicates emphatic stress. For example:

  ```
  <p>You should <em>always</em> validate your HTML
  markup before sharing it with others.</p>
  ```

- **<small>:** The small element should be used for small print or side comments. This element is useful for copyright lines or adding a source line to an image. For example:

  ```
  <p><small>Copyright 2012 by XYZ
  Corporation</small></p>
  ```

The intended functionality for some of these elements in HTML5 can be confusing, such as knowing when to use the italic element. The best approach is to strive for consistency within a page or Web site, and watch how other developers use the same elements.

MODIFY TEXT-RELATED TAGS IN A WEB PAGE

GET READY. To modify tags in a Web page, perform the following steps:

1. In your editing tool, open **L2-pet-copyright.html** if it's not already open.

2. In the following paragraph, replace the italic and bold tags with the strong element.

   ```
   <p>Make sure your pet has plenty of <i><b>fresh
   water</b></i> during hot weather.</p>
   ```

   The resulting markup will look like this:

   ```
   <p>Make sure your pet has plenty of <strong>fresh
   water</strong> during hot weather.</p>
   ```

   Note that the strong element will look like the bold element. The W3C prefers that you use <strong> over <b>, although they seem to produce nearly identical results.

3. Add **<small>** start and end tags to the copyright line, nesting them properly within the paragraph tags.

4. Save the file as **L2-pet-modified.html** and view it in a Web browser. See Figure 2-7.

Figure 2-7

Using <strong> and
<small> tags

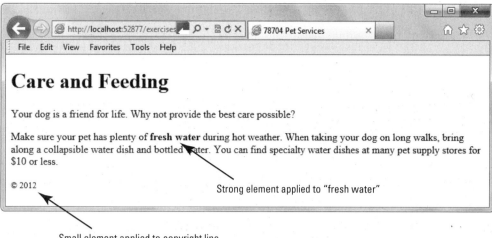

Strong element applied to "fresh water"

Small element applied to copyright line

5. Leave the editing tool and Web browser open if you're continuing immediately to the next section.

New Text Elements in HTML5

New text-related elements in HTML5 include <command>, <mark>, and <time>, along with a few others. The <command> element creates a command button. When the user clicks a command button, a command executes. The <mark> element highlights text on a page, similar to the highlighting feature in Microsoft Word. The <time> element displays a machine-readable time and date, such as 10:10 A.M., CST, July 19, 2012, which is handy for blogs and calendars, and potentially helps search engines provide better results when time and date are part of the search criteria.

Let's take a look at some of the new text elements in HTML5 along with some examples:

- **<command>:** The command element is used to define a command button that users click to invoke a command. The command element has many attributes you can use, such as type, label, title, icon, disabled, checked, and radiogroup. For example:

```
<menu label="Music Genre">

    <command type="radio" radiogroup="musicgenre"
label="Art">

    <command type="radio" radiogroup="musicgenre"
label="Popular">

    <command type="radio" radiogroup="musicgenre"
label="Traditional">

</menu>
```

- **<mark>:** The mark element is very handy for highlighting text on a page. You could use it on a search results page, for example, or to set off a block of text that you want to draw to the reader's attention. For example:

```
<p>Since I started jogging last fall, I have <mark
style="background-color:yellow;">lost 35 pounds</mark>.</p>
```

- **<time>:** The time element indicates content that is a time or date, which can be made machine-readable with the datetime attribute. The time element defines time on a 24-hour clock and a date in the Gregorian calendar. One benefit of making times and dates machine-readable on your Web page is that it helps search engines produce better search results. For example:

`<time datetime="2013">` means the year 2013

`<time datetime="2013-04">` means April 2013

`<time datetime="04-15">` means 15 April (any year)

Two other new elements are meter and progress. The meter element indicates content that's a fraction of a known range, such as disk usage. The progress element indicates the progress of a task towards completion.

 USE THE MARK ELEMENT

GET READY. To use the mark element to highlight text, perform the following steps:

1. In your editing tool, open **L2-pet-modified.html** if it's not already open.

2. Modify the following paragraph by inserting the mark element around the text "friend for life".

   ```
   <p>Your dog is a <mark style="background-color:orange;">
   friend for life</mark>.
   ```

3. Create a new file by saving it as **L2-pet-mark.html** and view it in a Web browser. Figure 2-8 shows the highlighted text.

Figure 2-8

The mark element highlights specific text

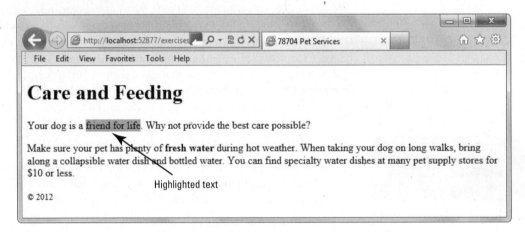

4. Leave the editing tool and Web browser open if you're continuing immediately to the next section.

Text Elements Not Used in HTML5

While new elements become available, the W3C earmarks other elements for eventual removal because their functionality is no longer useful. Removing elements from the list of available HTML elements is referred to as *deprecation*. (The same thing applies to attributes.)

X REF

Lesson 4 explores CSS essentials and the separation of presentation (style) from content.

Deprecation may be due to a new element replacing the functionality of an older element, or the preference of a new method of formatting over an older element. An example of the latter is formatting with Cascading Style Sheets (CSS). Using CSS to change the look and feel of text, images, and other Web content separates style from content. The W3C has been nudging developers toward using CSS to control Web page formatting instead of using local formatting for quite some time, and it's clearly the method to be used in HTML5.

This makes sense because you can easily change styles in CSS that apply across a Web page or even a Web site. Inserting individual styles throughout even a single Web page can be time consuming to modify when a change becomes necessary.

The following HTML elements are considered deprecated and are not supported in HTML5 pages:

- **`<acronym>`:** Defines acronyms in HTML 4 that can be spoken as if they are a single word, such as GUI for graphical user interface. Use the `<abbr>` tag instead.
- **`<applet>`:** Defines an embedded applet. Use the `<object>` tag instead.
- **`<basefont>`:** Defines a default font color, font size, or font family for all the text in a document. Use CSS for applying all fonts.
- **`<big>`:** Makes text bigger relative to the current font size. Use CSS instead.
- **`<center>`:** Center-aligns text and content. Use CSS instead.
- **`<dir>`:** Defines a directory list. Use the `<ul>` tag instead.
- **`<font>`:** Specifies the font face, font size, and font color of text. Use CSS instead.
- **`<frame>`:** Defines a particular frame (a window) within a frameset (see the next bulleted item).
- **`<frameset>`:** Defines a frameset for organizing multiple frames (windows).
- **`<noframes>`:** Displays text for browsers that don't support frames.
- **`<strike>`:** Defines strikethrough text. Use the `<del>` tag instead for small amounts of text, or use CSS for large blocks of text.
- **`<tt>`:** Defines teletype or monospaced text. Use the `<code>` tag or CSS instead.

Just because an element isn't supported doesn't mean it won't work within certain browsers. Many users still use older versions of browsers, and many deprecated elements render well in those browsers. However, a best practice is to create pages assuming Web page visitors use a current or near-current browser, which means using the latest HTML elements. If you know all of your Web page visitors use an older browser version, it's acceptable to use deprecated elements. Regardless, if you need to apply a lot of formatting to any Web page, it's best to use CSS for efficiency.

The following attributes are not used in HTML5, although these attributes are not actually part of any HTML specification:

- **`bgcolor`:** Applies a specified background color to whatever content its associated element describes, which is usually a table or a page. Use the CSS property `background-color` instead.
- **`bordercolor`:** Applies a specified color to the cell of a table. Use the `border-color` CSS property instead.
- **`bordercolorlight`:** Applies a specified color to the upper and left corners of a table cell. Use the `border-color` CSS property instead.
- **`bordercolordark`:** Applies a specified color to the lower and right corners of a table cell. Use the `border-color` CSS property instead.

Like with deprecated elements, you may use these attributes if you know that your Web page visitors use older browsers. Be aware that your attempts to validate your Web page will result in errors, which you can ignore if you're certain your visitors' browsers support the attributes.

➕ MORE INFORMATION

To find out about new features of HTML5, browse the "Learn HTML5 in 5 Minutes!" Web page at http://msdn.microsoft.com/en-us/hh549253 and the W3C "HTML elements" Web page at http://dev.w3.org/html5/markup/elements.html#elements.

⊙ SEE THE EFFECTS OF DEPRECATED ELEMENTS

GET READY. To see the effects of deprecated elements in an HTML5 Web page, perform the following steps:

1. In your editing tool, open **L2-pet-mark.html** if it's not already open.

2. Modify the h1 heading to incorporate the center element, as shown:

   `<h1><center>Care and Feeding</center></h1>`

3. Create a new file by saving it as **L2-pet-temp.html** and view it in a Web browser. Did the element center the heading in your browser?

4. Add the big element to the following content, as shown:

   `<p>Your dog is a <mark style="background-color:orange;">`
   `<big>friend for life</big></mark>.`

5. Save the file and view it in a Web browser. Do you see the effect of the big element? See Figure 2-9 as an example.

Figure 2-9

The effects of the center and big elements

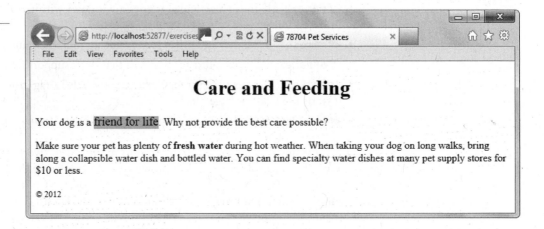

6. Go to the W3C Markup Validation Service Web page at **http://validator.w3.org**. Upload **L2-pet-temp.html** and click **Check** to have the service check it.

7. Notice that the validator displays errors regarding use of the deprecated elements. What can you conclude about using deprecated elements in HTML5? (Deprecated elements don't validate but many of them still render properly in a Web browser.)

8. Close **L2-pet-temp.html** and leave the editing tool and Web browser open if you're continuing immediately to the next section.

■ Choosing and Configuring HTML5 Tags to Display Graphics

THE BOTTOM LINE

Use the img element to display linked images in a Web page. The images can be located with the Web pages HTML files, usually in an images subfolder, or on a different server or Web site. The figure and figure caption elements are new to HTML5, and give you more control of the type of image you are displaying and the ability to include captions. The canvas element is used for drawing, rendering, and manipulating images and graphics dynamically in HTML5. Scalable Vector Graphics (SVG) enables you to create scalable objects that resize to best fit the screen on which they're viewed, whether a PC screen or a smartphone.

You can display different kinds of images on a Web page, most of which fall into two main categories: raster (or bitmap) and vector. A ***raster image*** is made up of pixels, whereas a ***vector image*** is made up of lines and curves based on mathematical expressions. A photograph is a type of raster image and is most often in JPG format. Other raster file formats that work well on Web pages are PNG, GIF, and BMP. A vector image is an illustration, such as a line drawing. Developers often convert vector file formats from programs like Adobe Illustrator or CorelDRAW, which aren't supported by Web browers, into PNG or GIF for Web display. An important difference between the two types of files is that raster images lose quality (they become pixelated) as you enlarge them, but vector images maintain quality even when enlarged.

The primary way to add images to an HTML document is with the `img` element. Like the anchor tag, the `img` tag does nothing by itself and requires attributes and values that specify the image the Web browser should display.

CERTIFICATION READY
What markup do you use to display an external image on a Web page?
2.2

For example, to insert an image named redball.jpg that's in a subfolder called images, type this element:

```
<img src="images/redball.jpg" alt="Red ball graphic" />
```

The image will display as long as the images subfolder is accessible. Both the `src` attribute and the `alt` attribute are required to be fully valid. The value of the `alt` attribute (short for alternate text) displays when a user hovers the mouse pointer over the image; in this case, the phrase "Red ball graphic" would display. The W3C requires the alt attribute for accessibility by people with disabilities. People with limited vision may use a screen reader, which reads aloud the alternate text for each image. Search engines also use the `alt` attribute to identify types of images and what's in them, since search engines can't "see" pixels in images.

As another example, to insert an image named bluelogo.png that's accessible from another Web site, type the following element:

```
<img src="http://www.example.com/mrkt/images/bluelogo.png"
     alt="Company XYZ blue logo" />
```

The `img` element uses several attributes, which are described in Table 2-3.

Table 2-3

`img` element attributes

Attribute	Value	Description
src	URL	Specifies the image's location, such as a path or URL
alt	Text	Specifies alternate text for the image, which displays when the user hovers the mouse pointer or other pointing device over the image
height	pixels	Specifies the height of an image
width	pixels	Specifies the width of an image
ismap	ismap	Specifies an image as a server-side image map
usemap	#mapname	Specifies an image as a client-side image map (which is a picture with defined areas that are clickable links)

Using the `figure` and `figcaption` Elements

Two new graphics-related elements introduced in HTML5 are the `figure` and `figcaption` elements. The `figure` element specifies the type of figure you want to use in an HTML document, such as an illustration or photo. The `figcaption` element provides a caption for the figure.

The **figure element** specifies the type of figure you're adding, such as an image, diagram, photo, and so on. This element provides a major benefit: the ability to easily add multiple images side by side. With HTML 4, doing so requires a good bit of markup. The **figcaption element** is optional. It adds a caption to an image on a Web page, and you can display the caption before or after the image.

The following markup uses the figure element, specifies the width and height of the image, and adds a caption. The result is shown in Figure 2-10:

```
<figure>

    <img src="doghappy.jpg" alt="Happy dog"
    width="100" height="125" />

    <figcaption>Happy dogs are good dogs</figcaption>

</figure>
```

Figure 2-10

Using the figure and figcaption elements to display an image with a caption

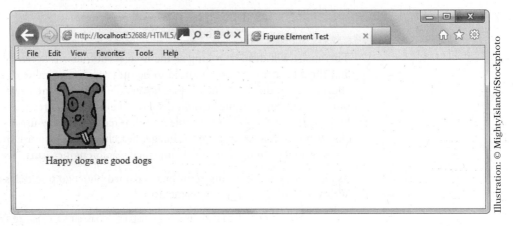

The following markup is for a figure with multiple images that share a single caption, the results of which are shown in Figure 2-11:

```
<figure>

    <img src="doghappy.jpg" alt="Happy dog"
    width="100" height="125" />

    <img src="dogpaws.jpg" alt="Happy dog"
    width="100" height="125" />

    <img src="dogwalk.jpg" alt="Happy dog"
    width="100" height="125" />

    <figcaption>Happy dogs are good dogs</figcaption>

</figure>
```

Figure 2-11

Using the figure and figcaption elements to display multiple images side by side with a single caption

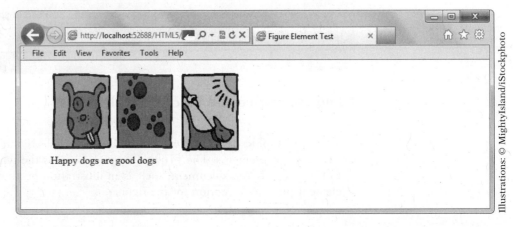

Illustration: © MightyIsland/iStockphoto

Illustrations: © MightyIsland/iStockphoto

> **➕ MORE INFORMATION**
>
> To learn more about displaying images on Web pages, go to http://bit.ly/Kgg1ab. You can find out more about image maps at http://bit.ly/hincW5.

➔ DISPLAY AN IMAGE IN A WEB PAGE

GET READY. To display an image in a Web page, perform the following steps:

1. Locate a JPG, PNG, GIF, or BMP file on your computer to use in this exercise. The image can depict anything you want, but something to do with pets would be most appropriate.

2. In your editing tool, open **L2-pet-mark.html**.

3. Remove the `<mark>` tags from the first paragraph.

4. Insert the following markup after the h1 element, leaving a blank line before and after it, and replacing dogwalk.jpg with your own image file:

```
<figure>

   <img src="dogwalk.jpg" alt="Walking a dog"
   width="100" height="125" />

   <figcaption>Happy dogs are good dogs</figcaption>

</figure>
```

5. Create a new file by saving it as **L2-pet-image.html** and view it in a Web browser. The page should look similar to Figure 2-12.

Figure 2-12

The Web page with an image

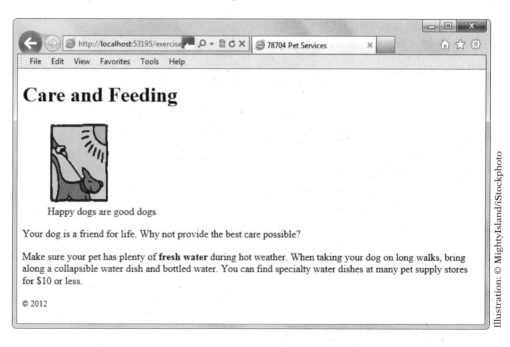

Illustration: © MightyIsland/iStockphoto

6. Leave the editing tool and Web browser open if you're continuing immediately to the next exercise.

➔ USE THE FIGURE AND FIGCAPTION ELEMENTS

GET READY. To display an image in a Web page, perform the following steps:

1. Locate two additional JPG, PNG, GIF, or BMP files to use in this exercise. The image can depict anything you want, but something to do with pets would be most appropriate. You should have three images to work through these steps.

2. In your editing tool, open **L2-pet-image.html** if it's not already open.

3. Replace the markup for the figure that follows the h1 element with the following, replacing the image file names (doghappy.jpg, dogpaws.jpg, and dogwalk.jpg) with your image file names:

```
<figure>

    <img src="doghappy.jpg" alt="Happy dog"
    width="100" height="125" />

    <img src="dogpaws.jpg" alt="Dog paws"
    width="100" height="125" />

    <img src="dogwalk.jpg" alt="Walking a dog"
    width="100" height="125" />

    <figcaption>Happy dogs are good dogs</figcaption>

</figure>
```

4. Save the file as **L2-pet-multpimage.html** and view it in a Web browser. The page should look similar to Figure 2-13.

Figure 2-13

The Web page with multiple images and a caption

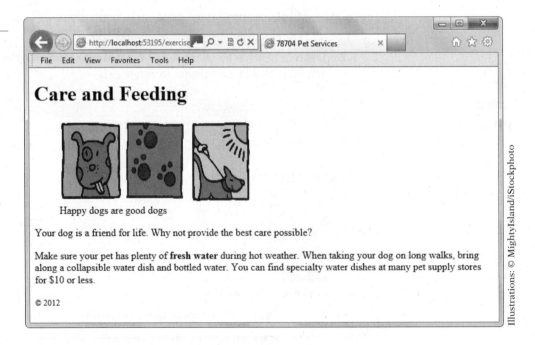

Illustrations: © MightyIsland/iStockphoto

5. Close the **L2-pet-multpimage.html** file. Leave the editing tool and Web browser open if you're continuing immediately to the next exercise.

Creating Graphics with Canvas

The *canvas element* is new in HTML5 and creates a container for graphics, and uses JavaScript to draw the graphics dynamically.

With canvas, the Web page becomes a drawing pad, and you use JavaScript commands to draw pixel-based shapes on a canvas that include color, gradients, and pattern fills. Canvas also enables you to render text with various embellishments, and animate objects by making them move, change scale, and so on.

TAKE NOTE*

Developers use canvas to create online games, rotating photo galleries, stock tickers, and much more. The canvas element graphics and animation functions are intended to provide quality similar to those in Flash movies.

CANVAS BASICS

To use canvas, you first define a canvas in HTML. The basic syntax for the canvas element is as follows:

```
<canvas id="smlRectangle" height="100"
width="200"></canvas>
```

CERTIFICATION READY
What is the basic syntax for the canvas element in an HTML document?
2.2

This element creates your drawing pad. The canvas element requires the id attribute to reference the canvas in JavaScript and to add it to the Document Object Model (DOM). You should also specify the dimensions of the canvas—the height and width—which are in pixels. JavaScript works with the two-dimensional (2D) application programming interface (API) to actually draw items on the canvas.

 USE THE CANVAS TO CREATE A SHAPE

GET READY. To use the canvas element to create a shape, perform the following steps:

1. In your editing tool, type the following markup:

```
<!doctype html>

<html>
  <head>
    <meta charset="UTF-8">
    <title>Canvas Test</title>

<script>
  function f1() {
      var canvas =
      document.getElementById("smlRectangle");
      context = canvas.getContext("2d");
      context.fillStyle = "rgb(0,0,255)";
      context.fillRect(10, 20, 200, 100);
  }
  </script>
  </head>

<body onload = "f1();">

<canvas id="smlRectangle" height="100" width="200 ">
</canvas>

</body>

</html>
```

TAKE NOTE*

You can include JavaScripts inside the head element of your HTML document, or in an external file.

The onload attribute causes the JavaScript function in the script to run. This script first finds the element with the id smlRectangle:

```
var canvas = document.getElementById("smlRectangle");
```

The `context.fillStyle` method fills the rectangle with a blue color using the RGB values 0, 0, 255. The `context.fillRect` method creates a 200-pixel wide x 100-pixel tall rectangle, positioned 10 pixels down and 20 pixels over from the upper-left corner of the canvas and fills it using the color specified by `fillStyle`.

2. Save the file as **L2-canvas.html** and view it in a browser. The shape should appear as shown in Figure 2-14.

Figure 2-14

The Web page with a canvas shape

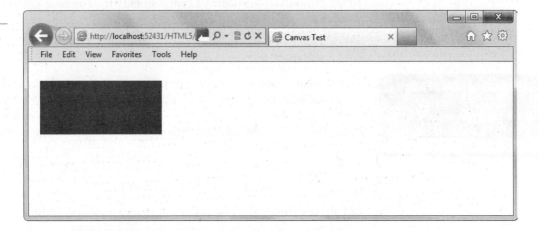

3. If a blue rectangle doesn't appear, go to the W3C Markup Validation Service Web page at **http://validator.w3.org**. Upload **L2-canvas.html** and click **Check** to have the service check it. Fix any errors reported by the checker. Save the file again and view it in a browser.

4. Leave the file, editing tool, and Web browser open if you're continuing immediately to the next exercise.

CREATING AN OUTLINE OF A SHAPE

To create an outline of a rectangle without a fill color, use the `context.strokeRect` method. It uses the same values as `context.fillRect`. To modify the color of the outline (the stroke color), use `context.strokeStyle`. For example, to create a 200 x 100 pixel rectangular outline in red, use these methods in your JavaScript:

```
context.strokeStyle = "red";

context.strokeRect(10,20,200,100);
```

 USE CANVAS TO CREATE THE OUTLINE OF A SHAPE

GET READY. To use the canvas element to create the outline of a shape, perform the following steps:

1. In your editing tool, save **L2-canvas.html** as **L2-canvas-stroke.html**.
2. Replace the `fillStyle` and `fillRect` code lines with the following:

```
context.strokeStyle = "red";

context.strokeRect(10,20,200,100);
```

3. Delete the width and height attributes from the canvas element in the body (after `id="smlRectangle"`).
4. Save the file and view it in a Web browser. The shape should appear as shown in Figure 2-15.

Figure 2-15

The Web page with a canvas shape outline

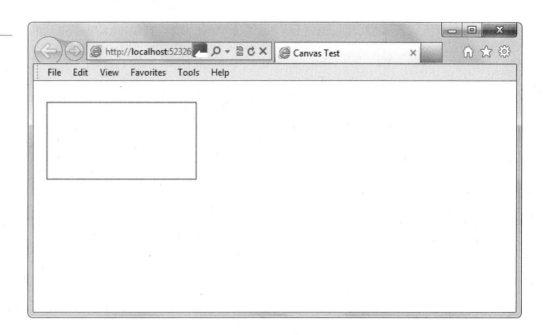

5. Close the file but leave the editing tool and Web browser open if you're continuing immediately to the next exercise.

PROVIDING AN ALTERNATE IMAGE OR TEXT FOR OLDER BROWSERS

Some older browsers cannot render canvas drawings or animation. Therefore, you should add an image, text, or some other HTML content within the canvas element that will display if the drawing cannot. The "backup" content, also referred to as fallback content, won't display if canvas is supported. This example displays an image (smlRectangle.jpg) similar to that which a filled rectangle canvas would create:

```
<canvas id="smlRectangle" height="100" width="200">
   <img
src="http://www.example.com/images/smlRectangle.jpg"
alt="A blue rectangle" />
   </canvas>
```

To display text instead of an image, you would insert text in place of the <img> tag.

 ADD A FALLBACK TO YOUR HTML DOCUMENT

GET READY. To add a fallback to your HTML document, perform the following steps:

1. In your editing tool, open **L2-canvas.html** and save it as **L2-canvas-canvas-fallback.html**.

2. Replace the canvas element with the following:

```
<canvas id="smlRectangle" height="100" width="200">
   Your browser does not support the canvas tag.
</canvas>
```

3. Save the file and view it in the Internet Explorer 9 Web browser. You should see the canvas drawing.

4. Press **F12** to enter browser mode, click **Document Mode** on the menu bar, and select **Internet Explorer 7 standards**.

5. Press **F12** again. An error message appears, stating that it doesn't recognize a property or method. Close the error message. The browser window displays the fallback text, as shown in Figure 2-16.

Figure 2-16

Text displays if the browser doesn't support canvas

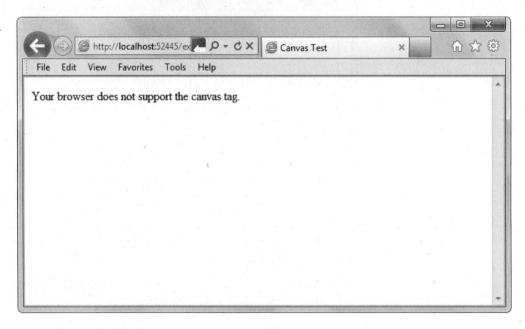

6. Leave the file, editing tool, and Web browser open if you're continuing immediately to the next exercise.

➕ MORE INFORMATION

For more information on the canvas element, visit the Microsoft HTML5 Graphics Web page at http://bit.ly/M8ZNkf. The HTMLCenter Web site at http://www.htmlcenter.com/blog/rgb-color-chart/ lists RGB color codes.

Creating Graphics with SVG

> *Scalable Vector Graphics (SVG)* is a language for describing 2D graphics in Extensible Markup Language (XML). XML is a cousin to HTML, and has played an important part of HTML 4.01 Web pages. SVG technology is not new, but HTML5 now enables SVG objects to be embedded in Web pages without using the `<object>` or `<embed>` tags. (All types of SVG graphics are referred to as objects, and SVG loads into the DOM.)

CERTIFICATION READY
What type of objects can you create with SVG?
2.2

The main purpose of SVG, as its name implies, is to create scalable vector graphic shapes, but you can create images and text as well. Much like canvas, you can apply solid colors, gradients, and pattern fills to SVG objects, and copy and clone objects. You can also use SVG anywhere you would insert a PNG, JPG, or GIF. With SVG, you provide drawing instructions rather than an image file.

One of the major benefits of SVG is its flexibility. Its vector graphic changes size to fit the screen on which it's displayed, whether the screen is on a 32-inch computer monitor or a mobile device like a smartphone. Because only the XML that describes the SVG graphic is transmitted, even large images don't require a lot of bandwidth. This makes SVG handy for use as a Web page background without having to use the repeat property. (Most solid Web page backgrounds are actually a thin line that's repeated using a CSS style.) In addition, SVG can be indexed by search engines because it's created by XML.

You can include attributes such as color, rotation, stroke color and size, and so on, to each SVG object. The following markup can be included in an HTML file to create a purple ball:

```
<svg id="svgpurpball" height="200"
  xmlns="http://www.w3.org/2000/svg">

    <circle id="purpball" cx="40" cy="40"
    r="40" fill="purple" />

</svg>
```

The cs, cy, and r attributes help to define the circle by defining the center x and y points and radius. SVG has a plethora of attributes, which help you create all kinds of shapes. The attributes are available on the W3C Web site at http://www.w3.org/TR/SVG/attindex.html.

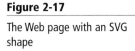 **MORE INFORMATION**

For more information on SVG, visit the Microsoft SVG Web page at http://msdn.microsoft.com/en-us/library/gg589525(v=vs.85).aspx.

 CREATE AN SVG VECTOR GRAPHIC

GET READY. To create a simple SVG vector graphic, perform the following steps:

1. In your editing tool, type the following markup:

```
<!doctype html>
<html>
  <head>
    <meta charset="UTF-8">
    <title>SVG Star</title>
  </head>
<body>
<svg xmlns="http://www.w3.org/2000/svg" version="1.1">
    <polygon points="100,10 40,180 190,60 10,60 160,180"
style="fill:aqua;stroke:orange;stroke-width:5;
fill-rule:evenodd;"/>
</svg>
</body>
</html>
```

The points attribute defines the x and y coordinates for each corner, or "point," of the polygon. The fill-rule determines how the inside of the polygon is filled.

2. Save the file as **L2-SVG.html** and view it in a Web browser. The page should look similar to Figure 2-17. If the page doesn't appear, check it using the W3C Markup Validation Service at **http://validator.w3.org** and fix any errors.

Figure 2-17

The Web page with an SVG shape

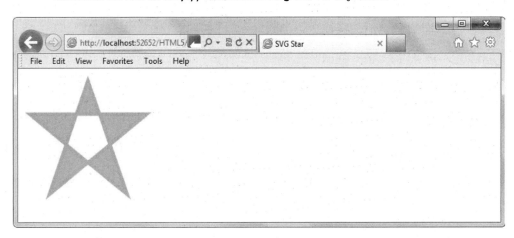

3. Change a few of the polygon point parameter values. Save the file as **L2-SVG-test.html** and view it in a Web browser. For example, changing the first parameter value from 100 to **50** produces the polygon shown in Figure 2-18.

Figure 2-18

Changing even one parameter value changes the shape of the object

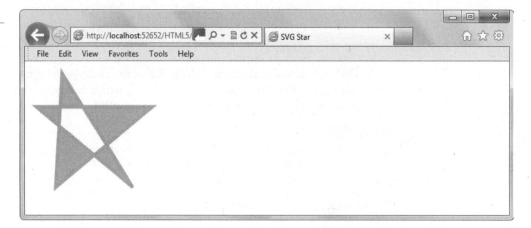

4. Delete `fill-rule:evenodd;`, save the file, and then view it in a Web browser. Compare the polygon to Figure 2-17.

5. Close any open data files. Leave the editing tool and Web browser open if you're continuing immediately to the next exercise.

When to Use Canvas Instead of SVG

There are no hard and fast rules for choosing to use canvas or SVG. Your choice depends mainly on the nature of your project, and your skill level in one or the other.

The following are some considerations that will help you make the right decision:

- If the drawing is relatively small, use canvas.
- If the drawing requires a large number of objects, use canvas. SVG begins to degrade as it continually adds objects to the DOM.
- Generally, use canvas for small screens, such as those on mobile devices. As the size of the screen increases and more pixels are needed, canvas begins to pixelate so use SVG.
- If you must create highly detailed vector documents that must scale well, go with SVG.
- If you are displaying real-time data output, such as maps, map overlays, weather data, and so on, use canvas.

A tip from Microsoft: Think of canvas as being similar to Microsoft Paint. You can draw images using shapes and other tools, and the result is pixel based. Think of SVG as being similar to an Office PowerPoint slide, which uses scalable objects.

➕ **MORE INFORMATION**

For more information on how to choose the best drawing method—canvas or SVG—go to http://msdn.microsoft.com/en-us/library/ie/gg193983(v=vs.85).aspx.

■ Choosing and Configuring HTML5 Tags to Play Media

THE BOTTOM LINE

HTML5 introduces the audio and video elements, which do away with the need for plug-ins or media players to listen to music or watch videos via a Web browser.

The audio element and video element are two of the major changes in HTML5, enabling you to provide multimedia from a Web browser without the need for plug-ins, such as those for Microsoft Windows Media Player, Microsoft Silverlight, Adobe Flash, or Apple QuickTime. That means users can simply open an HTML5-supported browser to listen to music or audio books, enjoy rich sound effects, and watch video clips or movies.

The HTML5 specification includes the <video> and <audio> tags to incorporate multimedia. The following sections cover each in detail.

CERTIFICATION READY
Which HTML5 tags enable you to incorporate multimedia in a Web page?
2.3

Understanding and Using Video Tags

You use the video element along with the src attribute to designate a video file to be played in an HTMLt document. Including he height and width attributes enables you to control the size of the window in which the video displays.

CERTIFICATION READY
What is the markup for using the HTML5 video element?
2.3

The *video element* enables you to incorporate videos in HTML documents using minimal code. The structure for embedding video is simple. The following is an example of the markup for adding an MP4 file to a Web page:

```
<video src="intro.mp4" width="400" height="300">
</video>
```

The src attribute points to the name of the video file (in this case, video.mp4) to be played. The height and width attributes specify the size of window in which the video will display.

Other attributes are available that you can add for control of the video:

- **poster:** Displays a static image file before the video loads
- **autoplay:** Start playing the video automatically upon page load
- **controls:** Displays a set of controls for playing, pausing, and stopping the video, and controlling the volume
- **loop:** Repeats the video

Using all of the controls listed above, the markup would look similar to this:

```
<video src="/videos/intro.mp4"
    width="400" height="300
    poster="78704-splash.jpg"
    autoplay="autoplay"
    controls="controls"
    loop="loop">

</video>
```

Notice that this markup refers to an MP4 video file. Other popular Web video formats also include H.264, OGG, and WebM, although WebM is used less than 10 percent of the time. Along with a video format, you should also specify the *codec*, which is a technology used for compressing data. ***Compression*** reduces the amount of space needed to store a file, and it reduces the bandwidth needed to transmit the file. ***Video compression*** reduces the size of video images while retaining the highest quality video with the minimum bit rate. All of this makes for better performance.

In a nutshell, the main video formats along with codecs (for the last two) are:

- MP4 or H.264
- OGG + Theora with Vorbis audio
- WebM + VP8

A best practice is to use the type attribute to specify the video format. You should also use the codecs attribute to specify the codec(s), if applicable. Sample markup is shown as follows:

```
<video
   width="400" height="300"
   poster="78704-splash.jpg"
   autoplay="autoplay"
   controls="controls"
   loop="loop">

   <source src="intro.mp4" type="video/mp4" />

</video>
```

The `<source>` tag is being used as content of the video element so that the `type` attribute can be set and so that the multiple format option is available.

Not all video formats are supported by all browsers, although MP4/H.264 is the most widely used by both Web browsers and mobile devices. (The HTML5 Video Web page at http://www.w3schools.com/html5/html5_video.asp displays a table showing which video formats work for what browser. The table is updated regularly.) To help make your video viewable by the majority of browsers and devices, you can use the source attribute to include multiple formats in your markup. This example shows the same video available in two formats, and the OGG format specifies codecs:

```
<video
   width="400" height="300" poster="image.png"
   autoplay="autoplay"
   controls="controls"
   loop="loop">

   <source src="video.mp4" type="video/mp4">

   <source src="video.ogg" type='video/ogg;
      codecs="theora, vorbis"'>

</video>
```

➔ **WORK WITH THE VIDEO ELEMENT**

GET READY. To work with the HTML5 video element, perform the following steps:

1. Locate a video clip, and an image file to use as a poster. If you don't have a video clip, search for a public domain MP4 file on the Web and download it. Save the video and image files to your HTML5 folder.

2. In your editing tool, create an HTML file with the following markup. Substitute appropriate file names for your image file and video clip. Change the type attribute, if necessary, and replace sample.mp4 with the name of your video file.

```
<!doctype html>
<html>
  <head>
    <meta charset="UTF-8">
    <title>Video Test</title>
  </head>
<body>
  <video
    width="400" height="300"
    poster="sample.jpg"
    autoplay="autoplay"
    controls="controls">
    <source src="sample.mp4" type="video/mp4" />
  </video>
</body>
</html>
```

3. Save your file as **L2-video.html**.

4. Go to the W3C Markup Validation Service Web page at **http://validator.w3.org**. Upload **L2-video.html** and click **Check** to have the service check it. Fix any errors reported by the checker that relate to missing tags or typos, if any.

5. Open the HTML file in a Web browser. Does the video play automatically? Do the controls appear? You should open the L2-video.html file in a variety of Web browsers as a test.

6. In your editing tool, delete the **autoplay** line and replace controls="controls" with simply **controls**.

7. Save the file again and validate it. It should validate with no errors. That indicates that HTML5 allows you to use a shorthand method of specifying the controls attribute. The same principle applies to the autoplay and loop attributes.

8. Leave the editing tool and Web browser open if you're continuing immediately to the next exercise.

Understanding and Using Audio Tags

The HTML5 audio element works much like the video element but for sound only. To use the audio element, include the <audio> tag and a path to the file on your hard drive or a uniform resource locator (URL) that points to the audio file.

The **audio element** enables you to incorporate audio, such as music and other sounds, in HTML documents. You can include the same control-related attributes as the video element: autoplay, controls, and loop. the following example shows just the controls attribute included:

CERTIFICATION READY
What is the markup for using the HTML5 audio element?
2.3

```
<audio src="sample.mp3" controls="controls">

</audio>
```

TAKE NOTE*

If you use the autoplay attribute so that the audio plays automatically when the Web page loads, use a short clip such as a sound effect. Many Web visitors dislike automatic sound and prefer to have more control.

The three primary types of audio files supported by popular browsers are OGG, MP3, and WAV. However, not every browser supports every audio file format, at least not today. For the most part, MP3 is the best choice for multiple browser compatibility.

To help ensure your audio plays on the majority of browsers and devices, use the source attribute to include multiple formats in your markup. This example shows the same audio file available in two formats:

```
<audio controls="controls">
    <source src="sample.ogg" type="audio/ogg" />
    <source src="sample.mp3" type="audio/mp3" />
</audio>
```

You can find a lot of free audio files, which are also royalty and copyright free, at http://flashkit.com. This is a good resource for learners, and for developers who may need a sound effect for a project. Another source is the Public Domain Sherpa Web site at http://www.publicdomainsherpa.com/public-domain-recordings.html. You can also make your own recordings using your computer and recording software. Windows 7 includes the Sound Recorder, which lets you save audio files in WAV format.

 WORK WITH THE AUDIO ELEMENT

GET READY. To work with the HTML5 audio element, perform the following steps:

1. Locate an audio clip.

2. In your editing tool, create an HTML file with the following markup. Substitute the appropriate file name for your audio clip.

```
<!doctype html>
<html>
    <head>
        <meta charset="UTF-8">
        <title>Audio Test</title>
    </head>
<body>
    <audio src="sample.mp3" controls="controls">
    </audio>
</body>
</html>
```

3. Save your file as **L2-audio.html** and view it in a browser. You should see something similar to Figure 2-19. Because we didn't include the autoplay attribute in this example, you need to click the Play button to start the audio clip.

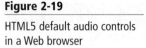

Figure 2-19

HTML5 default audio controls in a Web browser

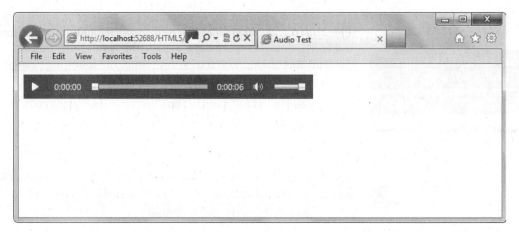

4. If the audio controls don't appear, go to the W3C Markup Validation Service Web page at **http://validator.w3.org**. Upload **L2-audio.html** and click **Check** to have the service check it. Fix any errors reported by the checker that relate to missing tags or typos, if any.

5. Save the file again and open it in a Web browser. Play the audio clip.

6. Close any open files, including the editing tool and Web browser.

➕ MORE INFORMATION

For more information on incorporating multimedia into HTML5 Web pages, and the audio and video elements in particular, go to http://msdn.microsoft.com/en-us/library/ie/hh771805(v=vs.85).aspx.

SKILL SUMMARY

IN THIS LESSON YOU LEARNED:

- Hypertext Markup Language (HTML) uses markup to describe content for display on a Web page.
- An element is the combination of tags and the content they enclose. You may need to use special characters on a Web page, which requires character encoding.
- Every Web page requires the doctype declaration at the top of the page.
- HTML5 uses most of the same elements and attributes specified in HTML 4, and has introduced some new tags, modified the preferred usage of others, and no longer supports certain elements. New text-related elements include command, mark, time, meter, and progress. A few of the deprecated elements are basefont, center, font, and strike.
- Use the img element to display linked images in a Web page. The images can be located with the Web pages HTML files, usually in an images subfolder, or on a different server or Web site.
- The figure and figure caption elements are new to HTML5 and give you more control or the type of image you are displaying and the ability to include captions.
- The canvas element is used for drawing, rendering, and manipulating images and graphics dynamically in HTML5.
- Scalable Vector Graphics (SVG) enables you to create scalable objects that resize to best fit the screen on which they're viewed, whether a PC screen or a smartphone.
- HTML5 introduces the audio and video elements, which do away with the need for plug-ins or media players to listen to music or watch videos via a Web browser.

■ Knowledge Assessment

Fill in the Blank

Complete the following sentences by writing the correct word or words in the blanks provided.

1. An HTML tag that doesn't require an end tag is called a(n) _____ tag.

2. A(n) _____ works with an element to describe data in enough detail for rendering.

3. The _____ is a declaration that is found at the very top of almost every Web page.

4. A _____ element or attribute has been removed from the list of available HTML elements according to the W3C.

5. A _____ image is made up of pixels, whereas a _____ image is made up of lines and curves based on mathematical expressions.

6. New to HTML5, the _____ element specifies the type of figure you're adding, such as an image, diagram, photo, and so on.

7. The _____ element adds a caption to an image on a Web page, and you can display the caption before or after the image.

8. Using the _____ element, the Web page becomes a drawing pad, and you use JavaScript commands to draw pixel-based shapes on a canvas that include color, gradients, and pattern fills.

9. _____ is a language for describing 2D graphics in Extensible Markup Language (XML).

10. The HTML5 _____ element and _____ elements enable you to provide multimedia from a Web browser without the need for plug-ins.

Multiple Choice

Circle the letter that corresponds to the best answer.

1. Which of the following tags are required on every Web page? (Choose all that apply.)
   a. `<html>`
   b. `<head>`
   c. `<title>`
   d. `<body>`

2. Which of the following is the syntax for creating a hyperlink in HTML?
   a. `<link href="http://www.example.com">link</a>`
   b. `<a href="http://www.example.com"> link text</a>`
   c. `<link>http://www.example.com</link >`
   d. `<http://www.example.com>`

3. Which HTML5 element defines a command button that users click to invoke a command?
   a. `<objectbut>`
   b. `<combutton>`
   c. `<command>`
   d. `<cbutton>`

4. Which HTML5 element enables you to highlight blocks of text in an HTML document?
   a. `<mark>`
   b. `<highlight>`
   c. `<emphasis>`
   d. `<yellow>`

5. Which of the following tags are deprecated in HTML5? (Choose all that apply.)
   a. `<big>`
   b. `<center>`
   c. `<font>`
   d. `<time>`

6. Which tag is used with the `<figure>` tag to display an image?
   a. `<img>`
   b. `<src>`
   c. `<fig>`
   d. `<a>`

7. Both canvas and SVG require which of the following?
   a. Microsoft Silverlight
   b. An external drawing program, such as Microsoft Paint
   c. A large amount of storage space or bandwidth
   d. JavaScript

8. When deciding whether to use canvas or SVG, which of the following considerations are true?
   a. If the drawing is relatively small, use SVG.
   b. Generally, use canvas for small screens and SVG for larger screens.
   c. If the drawing requires a large number of objects, use SVG.
   d. If you must create highly detailed vector documents that must scale well, go with canvas.

9. Which of the following is the general format of the `video` element?
   a. `<movie src="file.mp4" width="X" height="Y">`
   b. `<movie href="file.mp4" width="X" height="Y">`
   c. `<video src="file.mp4" width="X" height="Y">`
   d. `<video href="file.mp4" width="X" height="Y">`

10. Which of the following is the general format of the `audio` element?
    a. `<audio src="sample.mp3" controls="controls">`
    b. `<audio href="sample.mp3" controls>`
    c. `<sound src="sample.mp3" controls>`
    d. `<sound href="sample.mp3" controls="controls">`

True / False

Circle T if the statement is true or F if the statement is false.

T F 1. The `canvas` element requires JavaScript to create shapes.

T F 2. Creating an SVG object in HTML5 does not require JavaScript.

T F 3. The audio element can provide playback controls with a single attribute.

T F 4. Deprecated elements cannot render in an HTML5-supported browser.

T F 5. The most popular format for audio files is MP4.

■ Competency Assessment

Scenario 2-1: Correcting Simple Markup Errors

Geraldine, the assistant to the company owner, is learning HTML. Her markup as shown below isn't rendering as she expected. The boldface doesn't stop after "Thursday." The image of the company logo doesn't display, even though it's saved in her images subfolder like all of her other images. The alternate text doesn't display either when she hovers her mouse pointer over the image placeholder. What do you tell her?

```
<!doctype html>
<html>
  <head>
    <meta charset="UTF-8">
    <title>Internal</title>
  </head>
```

```
<body>
<h1>Staff Meeting</h1>
<img src="cologo.jpg" olt="Company logo" />
<p>Report to the <strong>Blue Conference Room</strong> at
<strong>10:00 a.m.</strong> on <strong>Thursday<strong> for an
emergency staff meeting.</p>
</body>
</html>
```

Scenario 2-2: Working with Symbols

Petra is formatting some accounting-related documents to be hosted on the company's intranet. She says the dollar signs and percent symbols look fine when she views them in one browser, but only garbage characters appear when she views the documents on a different browser. What should she do?

Proficiency Assessment

Scenario 2-3: Canvas or SVG?

M.A. is a graphic artist at ClickTick Watches, an upscale wristwatch manufacturer. She has been asked to refresh the company logo and create it using a tool that scales well whether the image is viewed on laptops or smartphones. She has also been tasked with creating interactive graphs for sales staff to use on their slate or tablet devices. She wants to keep her skillset current by learning as much as possible about HTML5 technologies, but doesn't know whether to focus on canvas or SVG for these projects. What do you suggest?

Scenario 2-4: Selecting Appropriate Web Video Formats and Codecs

Sammy is responsible for setting up meetings for employees of Clear Blue Resorts. He wants to post a video from the CEO, who is overseas reviewing possible locations for new resorts, to the intranet for the upcoming employee appreciate party. He knows Clear Blue standardized on Internet Explorer 9, and he has heard that he can easily display video in HTML5 but doesn't know where to start. What do you tell Sammy?

Building the User Interface by Using HTML5: Organization, Input, and Validation

EXAM OBJECTIVE MATRIX

SKILLS/CONCEPTS	MTA EXAM OBJECTIVE	MTA EXAM OBJECTIVE NUMBER
Choosing and Configuring HTML5 Tags to Organize Content and Forms	Choose and configure HTML5 tags to organize content and forms.	2.4
Choosing and Configuring HTML5 Tags for Input and Validation	Choose and configure HTML5 tags for input and validation.	2.5

KEY TERMS

article element

aside element

autofocus attribute

automatic validation

client-side validation

datalist element

email attribute

footer element

form input

global attribute

header element

menu element

nav element

ordered list

pattern attribute

placeholder text

required attribute

section element

semantic markup

server-side validation

table

unordered list

validation

Web form

One of your new tasks as an intern at Malted Milk Media is to create a Web form that restricts what a user can enter into the form fields and validates the input. To prepare to create the Web form, you must first learn how best to organize or structure the markup using new HTML5 elements.

■ Choosing and Configuring HTML5 Tags to Organize Content and Forms

↓
THE BOTTOM LINE

HTML5 introduces several new elements for organizing content and forms. They represent the new semantic markup that's an important part of HTML5.

HTML5 markup introduces many new markup tags for organizing the structure of HTML documents, which makes documents easier to create and modify. The new tags have more intuitive names than similar constructs in previous HTML specifications; the tags are named more appropriately for the part of the page they apply to, such as `<header>`, `<section>`, and `<footer>`.

HTML5 has also streamlined table creation, moving many of the table attributes that affect width, cell padding, and vertical and horizontal alignment to the CSS file.

Understanding Semantic HTML

Semantic markup uses tag names that are intuitive, making it easier to build and modify HTML documents, and for Web browsers and other programs to interpret.

CERTIFICATION READY
What is semantic markup?
2.4

One of the very handy new features of HTML5 is the use of *semantic markup*, which gives better meaning, or definition, to several tags so they make more sense to humans, programs, and Web browsers. As mentioned in Lesson 2, not all HTML tags have been replaced or updated for HTML5, but some new tags introduced in HTML5 make the work of creating Web pages a lot easier.

In HTML 4.01 and prior specifications, a developer creating the structure of an HTML document uses the `<div>` tag frequently throughout. The `<div>` tag often includes a class or ID attribute, which may also include CSS styles such as `background-color`, `height`, and `width`. A simple example of a `<div>` tag is:

```
<div id="header" > This is a header </div>
```

TAKE NOTE*

`class` and `id` are *global attributes*, which means they can be used with any HTML element. You can see the complete list of global HTML attributes at http://dev.w3.org/html5/markup/global-attributes.html.

The `div` element alone doesn't have much meaning without the `id` or `class` attribute. Even the ID can be assigned a value of your choice, such as "header", "header_inner", "slogan", "content", "style", and many more. An example from an HTML 4.01 document is shown as follows:

```
<div id="header">
   <div id="header_inner">
      <img src="images/doghappy.jpg"
        alt="Attaboy Pet Services" />
        <div id="slogan">Happy dogs are good dogs</div>
   </div>
</div>
```

HTML5 uses simpler tags to replace many of the `div` tags, some of which are shown in Figure 3-1.

Figure 3-1

A comparison of document parts marked up in HTML 4.01 and HTML5

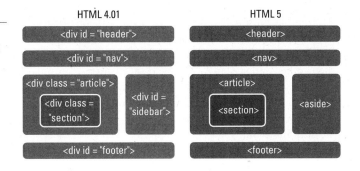

Notice how HTML5's semantic markup gives more specific meaning to parts of an HTML document, making the structure easier to understand.

Using Tags to Add Structure to an HTML Document

New HTML5 elements for structuring and organizing content in an HTML document include header, footer, section, nav, article, and aside.

Now that you understand semantic markup, let's look at several of the new HTML5 elements for organizing documents. Table 3-1 lists new HTML5 structure-related tags and describes them.

Table 3-1

New HTML5 markup tags for organizing content and creating structure

TAG	DESCRIPTION
<address>	Defines an area for contact information for a page or section
<article>	Defines an article, such as a magazine or newspaper article, blog post, or similar content
<aside>	Defines content that's separate from but related to the page content; similar to a sidebar in book chapters and magazine articles
<details>	Contains additional details pertinent to text around it; creates an interactive widget a user can display or hide
<footer>	Defines a footer for a document or section; may include the document author, contact information, copyright information, and links to terms of use
<header>	Defines a header for a document or section; may contain introductory content or navigation links
<hgroup>	Groups headings and subheadings (using the <h1> to <h6> tags) for multi-level headings
<nav>	Defines a block of navigation links
<section>	Defines a section in a document, such as chapters, parts of a thesis, or parts of a Web page whose content is distinct from each other
<summary>	Defines a visible heading for a details element; user can click to display or hide information
<wbr>	Defines a possible line break; when a word is very long, or you're concerned the browser will break a line at the wrong place, you can use the <wbr> element to break the word or line appropriately

TAKE NOTE *

As you learned in Lesson 1, the HTML5 standard won't be finalized for several years, which means changes to the specification are still occurring. The major Web browsers, like Microsoft Internet Explorer and Mozilla Firefox, support many HTML5 elements but not all of them. The "When Can I Use" Web site at http://caniuse.com/ is an excellent source for determining which browsers support specific HTML5 features. The Web site is updated regularly, so you should make it a part of your essential HTML5 resources. In addition, you can test any browser's support for HTML5 by browsing to the HTML5 Test Web site at http://html5test.com.

Let's look more closely at the HTML5 tags shown in Figure 3-1, which are the most commonly used structure-related HTML5 tags.

THE HEADER AND FOOTER ELEMENTS

The *header element* defines a header for a document, section, or article. In HTML 4.01, you use the header div as mentioned in the previous section (`<div id="header">`). The *footer element* defines a footer for a document or section, and typically contains information about the document or section, such as the author name, copyright data, links to related documents, and so on. The `footer` element doesn't automatically appear at the bottom (or foot) of the document—you need to use CSS to instruct the browser where to display the footer. Footers that appear at the bottom of every Web page or document are known as "sticky footers."

An example of an article with a `header` tag and a `footer` tag is as follows:

```
<article>
  <header>
    <h1>Learning HTML5</h1>
    <h2>The New Elements</h2>
  </header>
  <p>New HTML5 tags make Web page and application
  development easier than ever.</p>
  <footer>
    <p>Published: <time datetime="2012-09-
    03"September 3, 2012</time></p>
  </footer>
</article>
```

Like the `div` element, you can use the header and footer elements multiple times in an HTML document, as shown in Figure 3-2.

Figure 3-2

Multiple instances of the header element

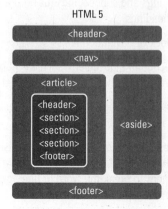

THE SECTION ELEMENT

The *section element* defines a section in a document, such as a chapter, parts of a thesis, or parts of a Web page whose content is distinct from each other. The WC3 specifies uses for the section element to differentiate it from other structure-related elements, mainly that it contain at least one heading and that it define something that would appear in the document's outline. For example, you should use the `section` element to divide different parts of a one-page Web site or to create a portfolio of images. The following is an example of a simple section:

```
<section>
   <h1>Eight Count</h1>
   <p>Hip-hop dance instructors often teach moves
   that have eight counts per set.</p>
</section>
```

CERTIFICATION READY
When should I use the
<section> tag versus
another type of element?
2.4

Table 3-2 lists situations in which you should avoid using the `section` element, and provides the better technique.

Table 3-2

Situations in which you should not use the `section` element

SITUATION	USE
Separate content that is independent from the rest of the content on the Web page or document	article
Plan to syndicate a block of content	article
Create a sidebar	aside
Wrap and position multiple sections that are not related to each other	div
Add a drop shadow to or border around an item	div

TAKE NOTE*

The new HTML5 structure-related tags don't replace the <div> tag entirely, but HTML5 tags greatly reduce the number of <div> tags needed in an HTML document.

Knowing when to use the `<section>` tag versus a different element can be tricky at times. When you're working on an HTML document and are unsure which element to use, browse the W3C HTML5 specification or research the Web to see how other developers have handled a similar situation.

When defining a section header, which may contain h1 through h6 headings, you can use the `hgroup` element to group headings. The `hgroup` element affects organization but not presentation. Consider using `hgroup` when you have a heading and a subheading one right after the other, as follows.

```
<section>
   <hgroup>
      <h1>Hip-Hop Dance Routines</h1>
         <h3>The Eight-Count Method</h3>
   </hgroup>
   <article>
      <p>Hip-hop dance instructors often teach
      moves that have eight counts per set.</p>
   </article>
</section>
```

This markup would appear in a Web page as shown in Figure 3-3.

Figure 3-3

Using hgroup to group headings in an HTML document

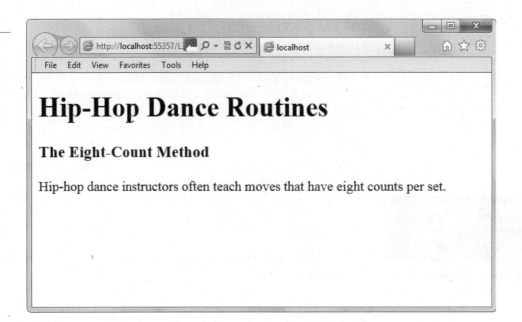

CREATE AN HTML DOCUMENT WITH A HEADER, SECTIONS, AND A FOOTER

GET READY. To create an HTML document using the HTML5 header, section, and footer elements, perform the following steps:

1. Using an HTML editor or app development tool and a Web browser, create a simple HTML document that incorporates the <header>, <section>, and <footer> tags. Include two sections, and be sure to include at least one h1 element within the sections. You can include images if you want. The markup might look like the following:

```
<!doctype html>
<html>
<head>
    <meta charset="utf-8" />
    <title>My Page</title>
</head>
<body>
<header>
    <h1>Selecting a Concert Style</h1>
</header>
<section>
    <h1>Symphonies</h1>
    <p>A symphony is a type of musical composition generally
    performed by a full orchestra.</p>
</section>
<section>
    <h1>Raves</h1>
    <p>A rave is a gathering of people who listen and dance to
    music, especially electronic music, usually performed by a
    live band or live DJs.</p>
</section>
<footer>
    <p>Author: Nathaniel Becker</p>
</footer>
</body>
</html>
```

TAKE NOTE*

Remember, you have several choices of tools to use for creating HTML documents. For the PC, consider the Notepad or Notepad++ text editors, the HTML-Kit or KompoZer HTML editors, or development tools like Microsoft Visual Studio, Visual Studio for Web, or Microsoft Expression Web.

This markup would display in a Web page as shown in Figure 3-4.

Figure 3-4

An HTML document with a header, footer, and section

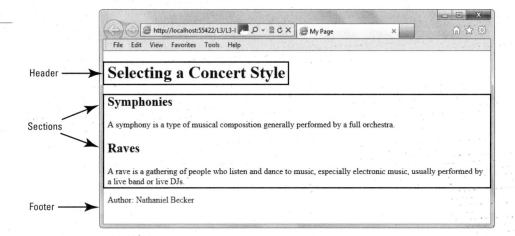

2. Save the file as **L3-MyPage.html**.

3. Validate the document using the W3C Markup Validation Service at http://validator. w3.org. If you need help doing so, refer to Lesson 2.

4. Leave the editing tool and Web browser open if you continue to the next exercise during this session.

THE NAV ELEMENT

The **nav element** defines a block of navigation links. The nav element is useful for creating a set of navigation links as your document's primary navigation, a table of contents, bread-crumbs in a footer, or Previous-Home-Next links.

The W3C mentions that you don't have to use <nav> tags for all navigation links, just major blocks of links. Because <nav> tags are interpreted by screen reader software for the visually challenged, the software can determine if it should make the navigation links available to the user immediately or not, depending on their importance.

The following example shows the <nav> tag in use:

```
<nav>
    <a href="/hiphop/">Hip-Hop</a>
    <a href="/modern/">Modern</a>
    <a href="/swing/">Swing</a>
    <a href="/tap/">Tap</a>
</nav>
```

The links would display in a Web page as shown in Figure 3-5.

Figure 3-5

Simple links using the nav element

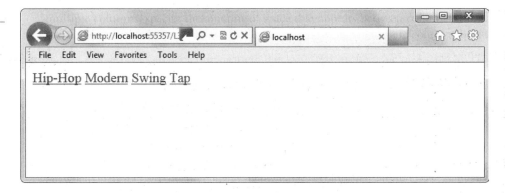

An example of markup for Previous-Home-Next links follows, with vertical bars after each navigation item to separate it from the others visually:

```
<nav>
    <a href="http://www.example.com/Services">Previous</a> |
    <a href="http://www.example.com">Home</a> |
    <a href="http://www.example.com/About">Next</a>
</nav>
<br />
```

The links would appear in a Web page as shown in Figure 3-6.

Navigation is often displayed in a vertical list, which you'll learn how to do later in this lesson.

Figure 3-6

Previous-Home-Next navigation with vertical bars separating each link

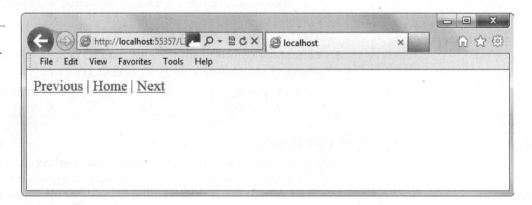

ADD THE NAV ELEMENT TO AN HTML DOCUMENT

GET READY. To add the nav element to an HTML document, perform the following steps:

1. In your HTML editor or app development tool, open the **L3-MyPage.html** file (if it's not already open) and save it as **L3-MyPage-nav.html** to create a new file.

2. Include the following nav tags and content within the <header> tag:

```
<header>
    <h1>Selecting a Concert Style</h1>
    <nav>
      <a href="#symphonies">Symphonies</a> |
      <a href="#raves">Raves</a>
    </nav>
</header>
```

This navigation block will link to the Symphonies and Raves sections in the HTML document.

3. To make the links work, modify the Symphones and Raves <h1> heads as follows:

```
<h1><a id="symphonies">Symphonies</a></h1>
<h1><a id="raves">Raves</a></h1>
```

4. Resave the file as **L3-MyPage-nav.html** and then open it in a Web browser. The navigation links would appear in a Web page as shown in Figure 3-7.

Figure 3-7

Page with newly added navigation links

Navigation links

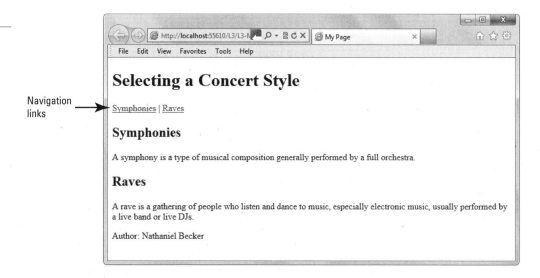

5. Leave the editing tool and Web browser open if you continue to the next exercise during this session.

THE ARTICLE ELEMENT

The *article element* defines a part of an HTML document that consists of a "self-contained composition" that is independent from the rest of the content in the document. Content set off by <article> tags can be distributed in syndication, so think of it as content that makes sense on its own. (Web syndication is the process of making content from one Web site available to many Web sites.)

 TAKE NOTE The W3C encourages use of the article element rather than the section element for any content that could be syndicated

Examples of content suitable for tagging with <article> include a magazine article, a blog entry, or content for an RSS feed. You can also use the article element for About and Contact content, which are independent from the rest of the page on which they reside but aren't necessarily going to be syndicated.

THE ASIDE ELEMENT

The *aside element* is used to set off content that's related to the current topic but would interrupt the flow of the document if left inline. Essentially, the aside element is used for information that lends itself to sidebars and notes. This content might give a more detailed look at a topic, offer related reading links, or display definitions for keywords in the paragraph. The aside element doesn't change the position of content or how the content displays; it simply lets the browser and search engines know that it's related content.

```
<article>
  <header>
    <h1>Learning HTML5</h1>
    <h2>The New Elements</h2>
  </header>
  <p>New HTML5 tags make Web page and application
  development easier than ever. One of the very
  handy new features of HTML5 is the use of
  semantic markup.</p>
  <aside>
      <h4><b>semantic markup</b></h4>
        <p> gives better meaning, or definition,
        to tags so they make more sense to humans,
        programs, and Web browsers</p>
    </aside>
  <p>Not all HTML tags have been replaced or updated
  for HTML5, but some new tags introduced in HTML5
  make the work of creating Web pages a lot
  easier.</p>
<footer>
    <p>Published: <time datetime="2012-09-
    03">September 3, 2012</time></p>
  </footer>
</article>
```

The markup would appear in a Web page as shown in Figure 3-8.

Figure 3-8

An example of an aside element

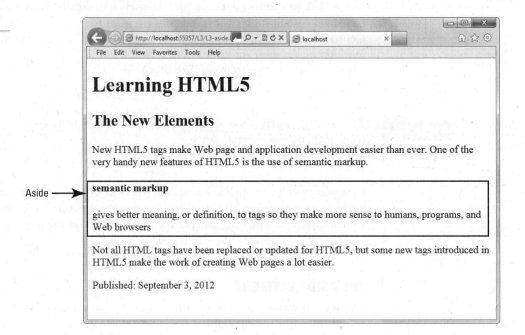

As you can see in Figure 3-8, the aside content doesn't really stand out from the rest of the content. You could add the horizontal rule <hr /> tag before and after the aside content, which would appear in a Web browser as shown in Figure 3-9.

Figure 3-9

Using the `<hr />` tag to add horizontal rules to set off aside content

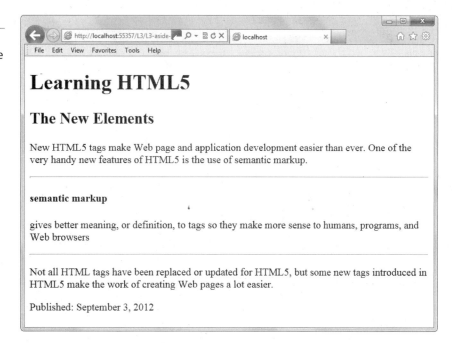

You could also use CSS to adjust the margins of the aside content so it's indented on the left and right. In later lessons, you'll learn CSS layout techniques to display similar content in a box along the left or right side of the corresponding body text.

 ADD THE ASIDE ELEMENT TO AN HTML DOCUMENT

GET READY. To add the `aside` element to an HTML document, perform the following steps:

1. In your HTML editor or app development tool, open the **L3-MyPage-nav.html** file (if it's not already open) and save it as **L3-MyPage-art-aside.html** to create a new file.

2. Include an `aside` element just before the footer, as follows:

```
<aside>
    <hr />
    <p>Note: The U.S. Drug Enforcement Administration is also
    interested in raves. Go to http://www.justice.gov/dea/
    ongoing/raves.html to learn more.</p>
</aside>
```

3. Resave the file as **L3-MyPage-art-aside.html** and view it in a Web browser. The page should look similar to Figure 3-10.

4. Validate the document using the W3C Markup Validation Service at http://validator.w3.org.

5. Close the file, and then leave the editing tool and Web browser open if you continue to the next exercise during this session.

➕ **MORE INFORMATION**

To find out about new features of HTML5, browse the "Learn HTML5 in 5 Minutes!" Web page at http://msdn.microsoft.com/en-us/hh549253 and the W3C "HTML elements" Web page at http://dev.w3.org/html5/markup/elements.html#elements.

Figure 3-10

An HTML document that includes article and aside elements

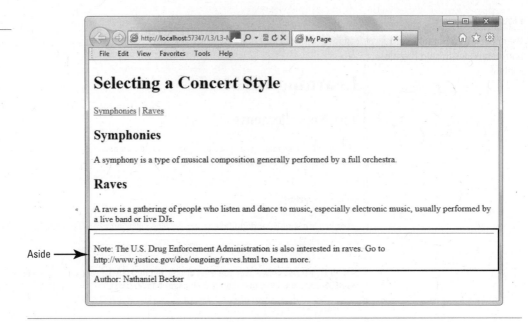

Aside ──→

Using Tags to Create Tables and Lists

Tables and lists give structure to specific information in HTML documents. A table contains rows and columns, and displays data in a grid. In HTML, you can create ordered and unordered lists. Each item in an ordered list is marked by a number or letter. An unordered list is a bulleted list.

This section focuses on how to create tables and lists using HTML elements. HTML5 introduces some new elements for both tables and lists, but most of the tags and concepts are the same as previous specifications. If you've ever created an HTML table or list, you should be able to breeze through this section.

CREATING TABLES

An HTML *table* contains rows and columns, and is used to organize and display information in a grid format. Some developers use tables for layout purposes, such as to position or align content with images, but that's not the best use for tables.

Regarding markup, every HTML table begins with the `<table>` tag. Rows are marked by the `<tr>` tag, column headers use the `<th>` tag, and cells are defined by the `<td>` tag.

The markup for a very basic two-column, five-row table is as follows. Comments have been added to indicate columns and rows, which are informational only and don't appear when the document is viewed in a browser, is shown in Figure 3-11:

```
<table border="1">
  <tr> <!--first row-->
    <th>Quarter</th> <!--first column in first row-->
    <th>Total Sales</th> <!--first row, second column-->
  </tr>
  <tr> <!--second row-->
    <td>Q1</td>
    <td>$4,349</td>
  </tr>
```

```
        <tr> <!--third row-->
          <td>Q2</td>
          <td>$2,984</td>
        </tr>
        <tr> <!--fourth row-->
          <td>Q3</td>
          <td>$3,570</td>
        </tr>
        <tr> <!--fifth row-->
          <td>Q4</td>
          <td>$7,215</td>
        </tr>
      </table>
```

Figure 3-11

A simple table

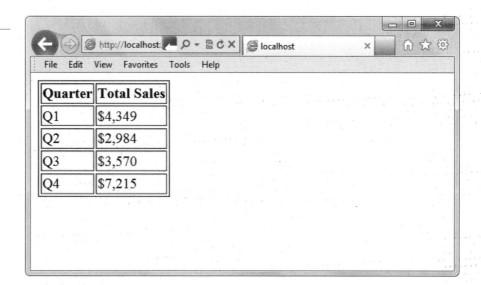

Building on a simple table, you can use the `<caption>` tag to add a caption above or below the table. To apply inline styles using HTML rather than CSS, use the `<col>` tag to apply styles to an entire column. (You'll learn about inline formatting shortly.) The `<colgroup>` tag groups columns within a table so you can apply formatting to the group rather than just a column.

When creating a long table that requires scrolling within a browser, use the `<thead>`, `<tfoot>`, and `<tbody>` tags. The content within the table header and footer will remain on the page while the content marked by `<tbody>` will scroll between them.

The `<thead>` tag creates column headings (bolded by default), and the `<tfoot>` tag is used to display the last row, such as a totals row. The `<tbody>` tag defines all of the content between the header and footer.

The following is an example of the markup for a table with three columns and five rows, the first row being the column headings and the last row the table foot. The markup also includes a caption above the table. The markup is shown rendered by a browser in Figure 3-12:

```
<table>
  <caption>Sales for Employee ID 2387</caption>

    <colgroup
      span="2"
      style="background-color:#EEE8AA;">
    </colgroup>
```

TAKE NOTE *

You must include the **thead** and **tfoot** elements before the **tbody** element so the browser can render the table header and footer before receiving all of the rows of data.

Figure 3-12

A more advanced version of a
simple table

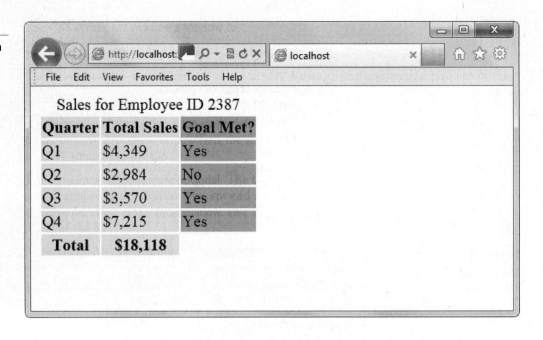

```
        <colgroup
          style="background-color:#00FA9A;">
        </colgroup>

    <thead>
      <tr>
        <th scope="col">Quarter</th>
        <th scope="col">Total Sales</th>
        <th scope="col">Goal Met?</th>
      </tr>
    </thead>
  <tfoot>
      <tr>
        <th scope="col">Total</th>
        <th scope="col">$18,118</th>
      </tr>
  </tfoot>
  <tbody>
      <tr>
        <td>Q1</td>
        <td>$4,349</td>
        <td>Yes</td>
      </tr>
      <tr>
        <td>Q2</td>
        <td>$2,984</td>
        <td>No</td>
      </tr>
      <tr>
        <td>Q3</td>
        <td>$3,570</td>
        <td>Yes</td>
```

```
      </tr>
      <tr>
        <td>Q4</td>
        <td>$7,215</td>
        <td>Yes</td>
      </tr>
    </tbody>
```

Notice in the preceding example the use of background color for grouped columns. This is an example of inline formatting. The `style` attribute uses one or more CSS properties and values, separated by semicolons. For HTML color, you can use either the color name or the hexadecimal code. The hexadecimal code #EEE8AA produces the pale goldenrod color. The hexadecimal code #00FA9A produces the spring green color. An HTML standard color chart is available at http://www.w3schools.com/html/html_colornames.asp.

You could also center the content in a cell, column, or column group using `style="text-align:center"`. To string multiple properties and values in the same style attribute, use syntax similar to `style="color:blue;text-align:center"`. CSS and its many properties are covered in Lessons 4 through 6 of this book.

Table 3-3 summarizes the common elements used to build tables in HTML5.

Table 3-3

Common elements used to build tables

ELEMENT	DESCRIPTION
col	Defines a table column
colgroup	Defines a group of columns in a table
caption	Marks text as a table caption
table	Defines a table
tbody	Defines a group of rows in a table for formatting and scrolling purposes
td	Defines a table cell
tfoot	Defines a group of footer rows in a table for formatting and scrolling purposes
th	Defines a table header cell
thead	Defines a group of heading rows in a table for formatting and scrolling purposes
tr	Defines a table row

TAKE NOTE *

If you've created tables using HTML 4 or earlier, you might be familiar with the `cellpadding`, `cellspacing`, `frame`, `rules`, `summary`, and/or `width` elements. They are deprecated and not supported in HTML5.

CREATE A TABLE

GET READY. To create a table, perform the following steps:

1. Using an HTML editor or app development tool and a Web browser, create a file named **L3-PracTable.html** with the following markup:

```
<!doctype html>

<html lang="en" xmlns="http://www.w3.org/1999/xhtml">
<head>
    <meta charset="utf-8" />
    <title>High-grossing Movies</title>
</head>
<body>
<table border="1">
  <tr>
    <th>Movie</th>
    <th>Gross Proceeds</th>
  </tr>
  <tr>
    <td>Avatar</td>
    <td>$2.7 billion</td>
  </tr>
  <tr>
    <td>Titanic</td>
    <td>$2.1 billion</td>
  </tr>
  <tr>
    <td>The Dark Knight</td>
    <td>$1.0 billion</td>
  </tr>
</table>
</body>
</html>
```

2. Italicize the title of each movie by using the `<i>` tags.

3. Modify the table to add a caption above the table that reads "High-grossing Movies" and a footer that includes the word "Total" and "$5.8 billion".

4. Change the background of the entire table, from column headings through the footer, to khaki, using hexadecimal code **#F0E68C**. To do so, add the following `colgroup` markup between `<table border="1">` and `<thead>`, as follows:

```
<table border="1">
    <colgroup
    span="2"
    style="background-color:#F0E68C;">
    </colgroup>
<thead>
```

5. Save the file and view it in a Web browser. The finished table should look similar to Figure 3-13. Revise your markup if necessary and resave the file.

6. Close the file, and then leave the editing tool and Web browser open if you continue to the next exercise during this session.

Figure 3-13

The final high-grossing movies table

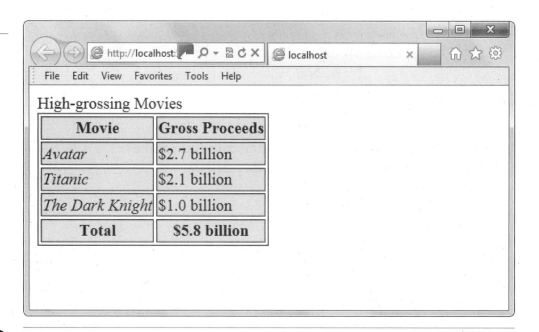

CERTIFICATION READY

How do you create an ordered list and an unordered list?

2.4

CREATING LISTS

Creating lists in HTML5 is simple, especially if you've created them in previous HTML specifications. The rules are nearly identical, although HTML5 modified how one list item should be used and introduces some new attributes.

There are two primary types of HTML lists:

- *Ordered list:* Orders the list entries using numbers, by default. It uses the <ol> tag. You can use the following attributes with an ordered list:
  a. reversed: Uses the value "reversed," which reverses the order of the list, in descending order; this attribute is not supported in most browsers as of this writing
  b. start number: Specifies the start value of the ordered list
  c. type: Specifies the kind of marker to use at the beginning of each list item; the value "1" is the default and displays decimal numbers, the value "A" uses capital letters, the value "a" uses lowercase letters, the value "I" uses uppercase Roman numerals, and the value "i" uses lowercase Roman numerals

- *Unordered list:* Displays list entries in a bulleted list. It uses a <ul> tag.

Items in a list are marked by <li>, which indicates an ordinary list item. Let's look at some examples.

Here is an ordered list, shown in a browser in Figure 3-14:

```
<p>Favorite cupcakes:</p>
<ol>
    <li>Chocolate chip cheesecake</li>
    <li>Strawberry delight</li>
    <li>Italian creme</li>
</ol>
```

Here is an unordered list, and shown in a Web browser in Figure 3-15:

```
<p>Cupcake flavors:</p>
<ul>
    <li>Strawberry delight</li>
    <li>Chocolate chip cheesecake</li>
    <li>Italian creme</li>
</ul>
```

Figure 3-14

An example of an ordered list

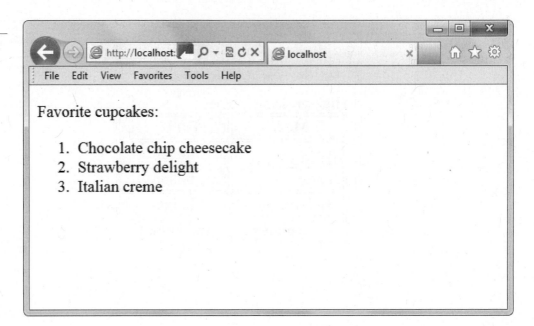

Figure 3-15

An example of an unordered list

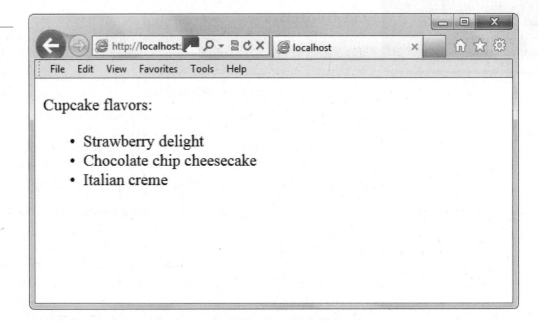

You can change the round bullet symbols in an unordered list by simply adding an attribute to change the nature of the bullets. For square symbols, add `type="square"` to the `<ul>` tag, and for empty circles add `type="circle"`. You can also add the attributes to individual list items (marked by `<li>`) to affect individual points. For example, to display all bullet symbols as filled-in squares:

```
<p>Cupcake flavors:</p>
<ul type="square">
   <li>Strawberry delight</li>
   <li>Chocolate chip cheesecake</li>
   <li>Italian creme</li>
</ul>
```

The markup would appear as shown in Figure 3-16.

Figure 3-16

The bulleted items have
filled-in squares as symbols

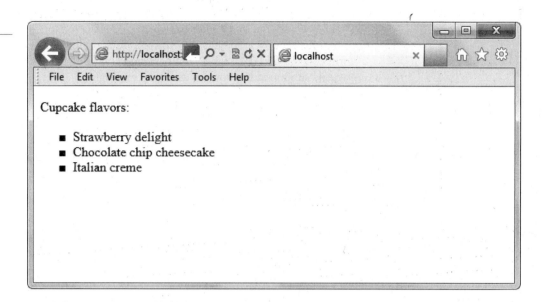

Another type of list is the definition list. It displays items with their definitions below the list
item and indented. The `<dl>` tag defines the list, the `<dt>` tag marks each term in the item,
and the `<dd>` tag defines each description. Here's an example of the markup, and Figure 3-17
shows the rendered list.

```
<dl>
  <dt>Strawberry delight</dt>
    <dd>Strawberry meringue buttercream with
    tiny wild strawberries</dd>
  <dt>Chocolate chip cheesecake</dt>
    <dd>Mini chocolate chips blended with creamy
    cheesecake and a chocolate brownie bottom,
    topped with cream cheese frosting</dd>
  <dt>Italian creme</dt>
    <dd>Italian cream cake topped with cream
    cheese frosting and toasted coconut</dd>
</dl>
```

Figure 3-17

An example of a definition list

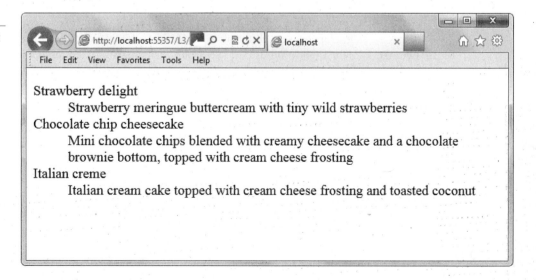

TAKE NOTE

The menu element was deprecated in HTML 4.01 but has been redefined in HTML5.

HTML5 also uses the **menu element**, which presents a list (or menu) of commands, usually with buttons. The W3C prefers that you use the menu element only for context menus, lists of form controls and commands, toolbars, and similar items. The HTML5 menu element is not widely supported by browsers as of this writing.

CREATE AN ORDERED LIST

GET READY. To create an ordered list, perform the following steps:

1. Using an HTML editor or app development tool and a Web browser, enter the following:

```
<!doctype html>
<html>
<body>

  <ol>
     <li>Desktops</li>
     <li>Laptops</li>
     <li>Tablets</li>
     <li>Smartphones</li>
  </ol>

</body>
</html>
```

2. Save the file as **L3-OrderedList.html** and view it in a Web browser.

3. To change the initial markers to capital letters, insert **type="A"** in the <ol> tag, like this: <ol type="A">

4. Save the file and view it in a Web browser. Do the list items now start with A, B, C, and D?

5. To start list numbering at 5, insert **start="5"** in the <ol> tag. Replace the current <ol> tag with this: <ol start="5">

6. Save the file and view it in a Web browser. Do the list items now start with 5 and end with 8?

7. Close the file, and then leave the editing tool and Web browser open if you continue to the next exercise during this session.

■ Choosing and Configuring HTML5 Tags for Input and Validation

THE BOTTOM LINE

Developers use Web forms as the interface for collecting information from Web site and client application users. HTML input elements serve to build a form's interface and ensure that information is collected from users consistently. Validation ensures that the entered information is in the correct format and usable before sending the data to the server.

In HTML, input and validation apply to forms. A **Web form** is a Web page that provides input fields for a user to enter data, which is sent to a server for processing. From there, the information is stored in a database or forwarded to a recipient.

Web forms are used as the interface for many different tasks:

- To log in to a Web site, server, or network
- To collect contact information, such as name, email address, phone number, and mailing address
- To sign up for emails or newsletters from an organization

- To capture user comments after an article on a Web site
- To select preferences on a Web page
- To enter reservation information

Many client applications use some kind of Web form to interact with the user.

You use HTML input elements to build a form's interface and ensure that information is collected from users consistently. Validation ensures that the entered information is in the correct format and usable before sending the data to the server. For example, if you enter "637 Park Street" into a Web address field, which is expecting something like "http://www.example.com", validation will fail and prompt the user to correct the input. Validation also reduces the amount of spam and malicious content that can make its way to the server or the recipient of the form's data.

Understanding Input and Forms

Most Web forms, or at least many fields in most forms, require specifically formatted input. The new HTML5 form and input attributes are intuitive, easy to use, and replace a lot of scripting that was required in HTML 4.01 and previous versions.

Form input is the information a user enters into fields in a Web or client application form. (To keep things simple, we use the term "Web form" most of the time, but it applies to client application as well.) HTML5 introduces several new form and input element attributes, such as `url` for entering a single Web address, email for a single email address or a list of email addresses, and search to prompt users to enter text they want to search for. The new attributes make form development much easier than in the past. What used to take a lot of scripting can be accomplished by HTML5 tags.

On the flip side, many of the new attributes are not yet supported by all of the major browsers. However, if you use a new element or attribute that isn't yet supported, the browser "falls back" to an alternate display, a different form of input, or what have you.

HTML5 introduces two new attributes for the form element—`autocomplete` and `novalidate`. All attributes for the form element are listed in Table 3-4, with the new attributes indicated with a double asterisk.

Table 3-4

Form element attributes used in HTML5

Attribute	Value	Description
accept-charset	character_set	Specifies a set of character encodings the server accepts
action	URL	Specifies the Web address to which form data is sent
autocomplete**	on off	Specifies whether autocomplete is on or off in a form or input field; can be "on" for specific input fields and "off" for the form, or vice versa
enctype	application/x-www-form-urlencoded multipart/form-data text/plain	Specifies the encoding type for form data when submitting the data to a server; used only for method="post"

(continued)

Table 3-4

continued

ATTRIBUTE	VALUE	DESCRIPTION
method	get post	Specifies the HTTP (transmission) method used when sending form data; use "get" for retrieving data and use "post" for storing or updating data or sending email
name	text	Specifies the name of a form, which is used to reference form data after a form is submitted
novalidate**	novalidate	A Boolean attribute that specifies that the form data (user input) should not be validated when submitted; HTML5 also allows Boolean attributes to be set by mentioning the attribute without an equals sign or assigned value
target	_blank _self _parent _top	Specifies where to display the response received after submitting the form _blank loads the response in a new, unnamed browser window _self loads the response in the current window; this is the default, so it's use isn't required _parent loads the response in the parent window (the browser window that opens the form window) _top loads the response in the full browser window

**New in HTML5.

CERTIFICATION READY
Which HTML5-specific attributes do you use for restricting form input?
2.5

HTML5 introduces numerous input element attributes. The attributes for the input element are listed in Table 3-5; new attributes in HTML5 are indicated by a double asterisk.

Table 3-5

Input element attributes used in HTML5

ATTRIBUTE	VALUE	DESCRIPTION
accept	audio/* video/* image/* MIME_type	Specifies file types the server accepts; used only for type="file"
alt	text	Specifies alternate text for images; used only for type="image"; commonly used when creating a custom Submit button from your own image file
autocomplete**	on off	Specifies whether autocomplete is on or off in a form or input field; can be "on" for specific input fields and "off" for the form, or vice versa

(continued)

Table 3-5

continued

ATTRIBUTE	VALUE	DESCRIPTION
autofocus**	autofocus	A Boolean attribute, specifies that a control is to be focused, or selected, as soon as the page loads
checked	checked	Specifies that an input element be pre-selected upon page load; used only for type="checkbox" or type="radio"
disabled	disabled	Disables an input element
form**	form_id	Specifies the form (or multiple forms) an input element belongs to
formaction**	URL	Specifies the Web address of the file that will process the input control when the form is submitted
formenctype**	application/x-www-form-urlencoded multipart/form-data text/plain	Specifies the encoding type for form data when submitting the data to a server; used only for method="post"
formmethod**	get post	Specifies the HTTP (transmission) method used for sending form data to a Web address
formnovalidate**	formnovalidate	A Boolean attribute that prevents validation when submitting input
formtarget**	_blank _self _parent _top framename	Specifies a keyword that indicates where to display the response received after submitting the form
height	pixels	Specifies the height of an input element; used only with input type="image"
list**	datalist_id	Refers to a datalist element that contains predefined content to autocomplete input, such as selecting an item from a drop-down list
max**	number date	Specifies the maximum value for an input element
min**	number date	Specifies the minimum value for an input element
multiple**	multiple	A Boolean attribute that specifies the user may enter multiple values
pattern**	regexp	Provides a format (a regular expression) for the input field; the input element's value is checked against the expression

(continued)

Table 3-5

(continued)

ATTRIBUTE	VALUE	DESCRIPTION
placeholder**	text	Displays a key word or short phrase that describes the expected value of an input field, such as "Email" for an email input field; placeholder disappears when user enters data
readonly	readonly	Restricts an input field to read-only
required**	required	A Boolean attribute that requires an input field to be filled out before submitting the form
size	number	Specifies the width of an input element, in number of characters
src	URL	Specifies the Web address of the image used as a submit button; used only for type="image"
step**	number	Specifies the accepted number of intervals for an input element; can be used with the min and max attributes to create a range of values For example, you are creating a slider bar for input. If you set step="3", each time the user move the slider, the input value increases or decreases by 3
type	button, checkbox, color, date, datetime, datetime-local, email, file, hidden, image, month, number, password, radio, range, reset, search, submit, tel, text, time, url, week	Specifies the type of input element to display
value	text	Specifies the value of an input element
width	pixels	Specifies the width of an input element; used only with input type="image"

**New in HTML5.

EXPLORING FORM CREATION, INPUT ATTRIBUTES, AND VALUES

To create a form, use the `<form>` start and end tags. All of the form's content and fields go between the two `<form>` tags. Most forms also include the `id` attribute in the start tag, as follows:

```
<form id="keyword">
   <content and fields>
</form>
```

The `fieldset` element is used with many forms to group related elements. The `<fieldset>` tag draws a box around individual elements and/or around the entire form, as shown in Figure 3-18.

Figure 3-18

The `fieldset` element groups related elements in a form and adds a border

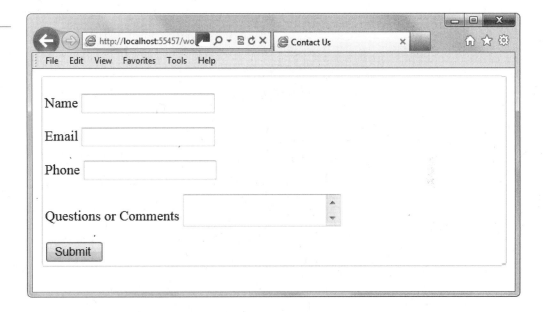

If the form is included in an HTML document with other items, you can use the `<div>` tag at the beginning and end of the form to separate it from other content. Using the `<div>` tag also lets you include inline formatting, if the form uses tags to align fields vertically short and simple and you don't want to create a CSS style sheet. The `<div>` tag uses the `id` attribute and appears before the first `<form>` tag. The `label` element displays the label for each field. An example of the markup for a very simple form is:

```
<div id="contact-form"
  style="font-family:'Arial Narrow','Nimbus Sans
  L',sans-serif;">
   <form id="contact" method="post" action="">
    <fieldset>
       <label for="name">Name</label>
       <input type="text" name="name" />
    </fieldset>
    <fieldset>
       <label for="email">Email</label>
       <input type="email" name="email" />
    </fieldset>
   </form>
</div> <!-- end of contact-form -->
```

The form is shown in Figure 3-19.

Figure 3-19

A very simple form

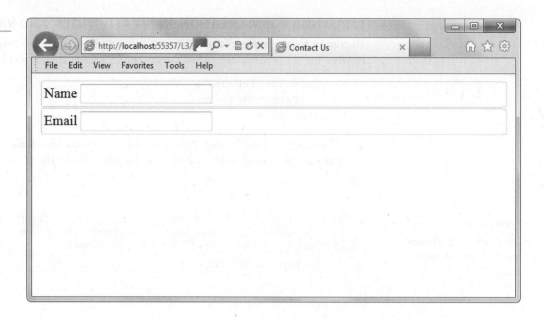

Now let's look at some of the new HTML5 attributes and values. Although this section doesn't address everything listed in Tables 3-4 and 3-5, it does describe and show examples of some of the most commonly used attributes and values.

The *required attribute* requires information in a field when the form is submitted. The *email attribute* (shown in the preceding example) requires the user to enter an email address. The browser will alert the user with an error message to fix these issues.

An example of an input element with the `required` and `email` attributes is:

```
<input type="email" required />
```

To make a form more user-friendly, add placeholder text. *Placeholder text* is text displayed inside an input field when the field is empty. It helps users understand the type of information they should enter or select. When you click on or tab to the input field and start typing, the newly entered text replaces the placeholder text. An example of the `placeholder` attribute is:

```
<input name="fName" placeholder="First Name" />
```

The *pattern attribute* provides a format (a regular expression) for an input field, which is used to validate whatever is entered into the field. For example, let's say you have a required input field for employee ID. Every employee ID begins with two capital letters followed by four digits. You would use a text input field with the required and pattern attributes to ensure that the field (1) is populated when the user clicks the submit button and (2) contains a value that matches the correct format for an employee ID. If the user hovers over the field, the message in the `title` attribute displays, which you add separately. An example of the `pattern` attribute is:

```
<input type="text" id="empID" name="EmployeeID"
  required pattern="[A-Z]{2}[0-9]{4}"
  title="Employee ID is two capital letters followed
  by four digits">
```

You can use the `pattern` attribute with these `<input>` types: `text`, `search`, `url`, `telephone`, `email`, and `password`.

The **datalist element** enables you to present the user with a drop-down list of options to select from. Only the options in the list may be selected. Alternately, you could insert type="text" into the input element to create a text box in which the user enters text. The following example lets the user select from one of three countries:

```
<input id="country" name="country"
size="30" list="countries" />
  <datalist id="countries">
    <option value="United States">
    <option value="Canada">
    <option value="United Kingdom">
  </datalist>
```

The search value for the type attribute enables you to create a search feature for a Web page. An example of the markup is:

```
<form>
  <input name="search" required>
  <input type="submit" value="Search">
</form>
```

Finally, the **autofocus attribute** moves the focus to a particular input field when a Web page loads. An example of autofocus is when you open a search engine Web page and the insertion point automatically appears in the input box so you can type search terms without first clicking in the box. An example of the markup to place the focus on a field named fname when a page loads is:

```
<input type="text" name="fname"
  autofocus="autofocus" />
```

autofocus has historically been handled by JavaScript, and if a user turns off JavaScript in a Web browser, the autofocus feature doesn't work. To work around this issue, the HTML5 autofocus attribute is supported by all major browsers and behaves consistently across all Web sites.

 CREATE A SIMPLE WEB FORM

GET READY. To create a simple Web form, perform the following steps:

1. Using an HTML editor or app development tool and a Web browser, create a simple Web form with the following markup:

```
<!doctype html>
<html lang="en">
<head>
<meta charset="utf-8">
<title>Contact Us</title>
</head>
<body>
  <div id="contact-form">

  <form id="contact" method="post" action="">
  <fieldset>

  <label for="custname">Name</label>
  <input type="text" id="custname" />
```

```
        <label for="email">Email</label>
        <input type="email" id="email" />

        <label for="phone">Phone</label>
        <input type="text" id="phone" />

        <label for="message">Questions or
          Comments</label>
        <textarea name="message"></textarea>

        <input type="submit" name="submit" id="submit"
          value="Submit" />

    </fieldset>
    </form>

    </div><!-- End of contact-form -->

    </body>
    </html>
```

2. Save the file as **L3-WebForm-orig.html**. The rendered version is shown in Figure 3-20.

Figure 3-20

The beginning of a Web form

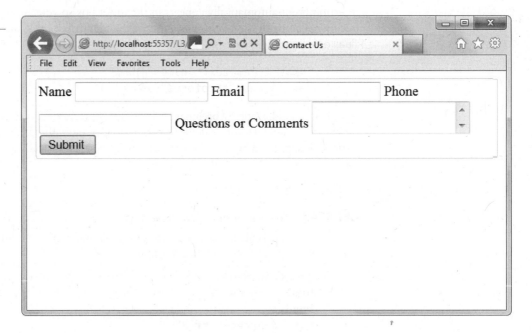

3. The Web form looks unstructured. Ideally, you would use CSS to apply alignment, but because you haven't learned CSS yet, you can apply a workaround to make the fields align vertically. One method is to add `<fieldset>` start and end tags around each label/input pair. This would align the fields vertically and add boxes around them. Using opening and closing `<p>` tags instead of `<fieldset>` tags would accomplish the same thing but without adding boxes. For this exercise, use the `<p>` tags. Figure 3-21 shows the same Web form with `<p>` tags around the label/input pairs, including the comments field.

Figure 3-21

A Web form using <p> tags to align fields vertically

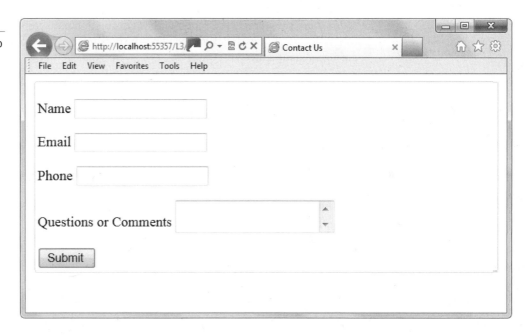

4. Add placeholder text to all fields. The result should look similar to Figure 3-22, if viewed in the Mozilla Firefox Web browser.

Figure 3-22

A Web form with placeholders added to each field

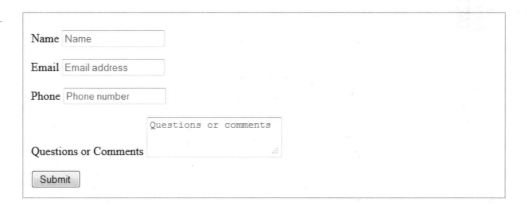

5. Save the file as **L3-WebForm-placeholders.html**.

6. Leave the file and editing tool open if you continue to the next exercise during this session.

➕ MORE INFORMATION

To learn more about HTML5 input element attributes, visit the W3C.org Web site at http://bit.ly/I1PW3P.

Understanding Validation

HTML5 provides new attributes that validate Web form fields as users are entering data or when they click the submit button. The attributes include required, email, and pattern, among others.

Validation is the process of verifying that information entered or captured in a form is in the correct format and usable before sending the data to the server. Some things that are verified during validation are:

- Required fields are empty
- Email addresses are valid
- Dates are valid
- Text does not appear in a numeric field or vice versa

Using HTML 4.01 and previous specifications, you often needed to use a lot of JavaScript or scripting in another language to create custom validity rules and response messages, or to determine if an element is invalid.

CERTIFICATION READY
How does HTML5
validate data entered into
a form by a user?
2.5

In HTML5, several of the input element types you learned about in the last section offer *automatic validation* of input, which means the browser checks the data the user inputs. This is referred to as *client-side validation*, because the input data is validated before submission to the server. (In cases in which the server validates data received from an input form, it's referred to as *server-side validation*.) If the user enters the wrong type of data into a field, such as an email address in a field with the `url` attribute, the browser instructs the user to enter a valid URL. Let's look at examples of the default error messages that are generated during automatic validation.

The `required` attribute avoids the problem of empty fields that need to be populated. When a user skips a required field and clicks the submit button, an error message appears as shown in Figure 3-23. This example uses the Mozilla Firefox Web browser.

Figure 3-23

Error message in the Firefox browser for a required field

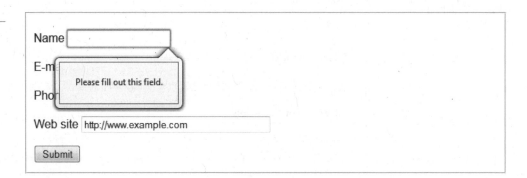

HTML5 also offers validation of Web addresses entered into fields with the `<input type="url">` construct, and numbers entered into fields with the `<input type="number">` construct. If you use the `min` and `max` attributes with `type="number"`, you will receive an error message from the browser if you enter a number that's too small or too large.

Finally, the `pattern` attribute prevents the user from entering data that doesn't follow the pattern expression. In this example, the `pattern` attribute validates a five-digit zip code:

```
<input type= "text" name= "zipcode"
   pattern= "[0-9] {5}"
   title= "Five-digit zip code" />
```

Incorrectly entering data in the Zip Code field in the Firefox browser results in the error message shown in Figure 3-24.

Figure 3-24

Error message in the Firefox browser when entering an incorrect pattern

As mentioned previously, no markup is required to activate HTML5 form validation—it's on by default. To turn it off, use the `novalidate` attribute for specific input fields.

ADD VALIDATION FIELDS TO A WEB FORM

GET READY. To add validation fields to a Web form, perform the following steps:

1. Using an HTML editor or app development tool, open **L3-WebForm-placeholders.html**.
2. Save the file as **L3-WebForm-valid.html**.
3. Add the **required** attribute to the email field, as follows:

```
<p>
    <label for="email">Email</label>
    <input type="email" name="email" required
     placeholder="Email address">
</p>
```

4. Add the **pattern** attribute to the phone field. The expression should restrict entry to area code and phone number, in the format XXX-XXX-XXXX, as follows:

```
<p>
<label for="phone">Phone</label>
<input type="text" name="phone" pattern="[0-9]{3}-
 [0-9]{3}-[0-9]{4}" placeholder="Phone number">
</p>
```

5. Save the file, and then view it in a Web browser. Type text in each input field except the email field and click the **Submit** button. Did you receive an error message prompting you to enter an email address?
6. Type text in each field again including the email field, but this time type a phone number without the area code and then click **Submit**. Did you receive an error regarding the phone number field?
7. Close the file, the editing tool or app development tool, and the Web browser.

SKILL SUMMARY

IN THIS LESSON YOU LEARNED:

- HTML5 introduces several new elements for organizing content and forms. They represent the new semantic markup that's an important part of HTML5.
- Semantic markup uses tag names that are intuitive, making it easier to build and modify HTML documents, and for Web browsers and other programs to interpret.
- New HTML5 elements for structuring and organizing content in an HTML document include header, footer, section, nav, article, and aside. These elements reduce the number of div tags required in a document.
- Tables and lists give structure to specific information in HTML documents. A table contains rows and columns, and displays data in a grid. In HTML, you can create ordered and

unordered lists. Each item in an ordered list is marked by a number or letter. An unordered list is a bulleted list.

- Developers use Web forms as the interface for collecting information from Web site and client application users. HTML input elements serve to build a form's interface and ensure that information is collected from users consistently.
- Most Web forms, or at least many fields in most forms, require specifically formatted input. The new HTML5 form and input attributes are intuitive, easy to use, and replace a lot of scripting that was required in HTML 4.01 and previous versions.
- Validation ensures that information entered in an input field of a Web form is in the correct format and usable before sending the data to the server.
- HTML5 provides new attributes that validate Web form fields as users are entering data or when they click the submit button. The attributes include required, email, and pattern, among others.

■ Knowledge Assessment

Fill in the Blank

Complete the following sentences by writing the correct word or words in the blanks provided.

1. An HTML _____ contains rows and columns, and is used to display information in a grid format.

2. Class and ID are _____ attributes, which means they can be used with any HTML element.

3. An _____ list orders the list entries using numbers, by default.

4. An _____ list displays list entries in a bulleted list.

5. The HTML5 _____ element presents a list (or menu) of commands, usually with buttons.

6. Form _____ is the information a user enters into fields in a Web or client application.

7. The _____ attribute requires information in a field when the form is submitted.

8. _____ text is displayed inside an input field when the field is empty. It helps users understand the type of information they should enter or select.

9. _____ is the process of verifying that information entered or captured in a form is in the correct format and usable before sending the data to the server.

10. The _____ attribute moves the focus to a particular input field when a Web page loads.

Multiple Choice

Circle the letter that corresponds to the best answer.

1. Which HTML5 element defines subdivisions in a document, such as chapters, parts of a thesis, or parts of a Web page whose content is distinct from each other?
   a. aside
   b. section
   c. header
   d. article

2. Which HTML5 element defines a part of an HTML document that consists of a "self-contained composition" that's independent from the rest of the content in the document and may be syndicated?
   a. aside
   b. section
   c. header
   d. article

3. Which HTML5 element is used to set off content that's related to the current topic but would interrupt the flow of the document if left inline?
   a. aside
   b. section
   c. header
   d. article

4. Which HTML5 attribute provides a format (a regular expression) for an input field, which is used to validate whatever is entered into the field?
   a. pattern
   b. autofocus
   c. required
   d. placeholder

5. Which of the following does validation not check and return an error for, by default, if invalid?
   a. Required fields are empty
   b. Valid email addresses
   c. Email address to the wrong recipient
   d. Text in a numeric field or vice versa

6. Which of the following is a practical use for a Web form?
   a. To collect contact information from a user
   b. To capture user comments after an article on a Web site
   c. Both a and b
   d. Neither a nor b

7. Which of the following are new form attributes in HTML5? (Choose all that apply.)
   a. autocomplete
   b. target
   c. method
   d. novalidate

8. What pattern attribute expression would you use to enter a product code that consists of three digits, separated by a hyphen, and then a single lowercase letter?
   a. [a-z]{1}-[0-9]{3}
   b. [0-9]{3}-[a-z]{1}
   c. [A-Z]{3}-[0-9]{1}
   d. [0-9]{1}-[a-z]{3}

9. Which of the following displays a key word or short phrase that describes the expected value of an input field, and then disappears when a user enters data?
   a. label
   b. placeholder
   c. title
   d. email

10. What is the format for the HTML5 tag that validates an email address?
    a. `<input label="email" name="URL">`
    b. `<form id="email">`
    c. `<label for="email">Email</label>`
    d. `<input type = "email" name = "email">`

True / False

Circle T if the statement is true or F if the statement is false.

T | F 1. In a table, the `tfoot` element must appear before the `tbody` element.

T | F 2. You can use numbers or letters for each item in an ordered list.

T | F 3. You can specify the height of an input element using the size attribute.

T | F 4. The label element displays the caption, or title, for a table.

T | F 5. The `nav` element defines a block of navigation links.

■ Competency Assessment

Scenario 3-1: Markup for a Newsletter Article

Sally Rowe, the document controller at Malted Milk Media, wants to publish a series of articles on the company intranet regarding document security and versioning. She needs to create a skeleton of the HTML5 markup for an article that will appear in the monthly online newsletter created by one of the Web developers. Each article will have a title and subtitle, several paragraphs of text, and her name and the article date in the footer. What should her article markup look like?

Scenario 3-2: Displaying Long Tables in HTML

Vince generates accounting reports for the VP of Finance at Momentum Strategies, a PR firm geared toward political campaigns. Vince regularly prints tables that are two- or three-pages long and delivers hard copies to senior management staff. He wants to publish them to a secure area of the company intranet, but the rows of data separate from the column headings and totals line at the end. He wants to know how to present the tables properly in HTML5. What do you tell him?

■ Proficiency Assessment

Scenario 3-3: Creating a Glossary of Terms

Waylon is a student working on a term paper. His instructor requires each student to format the paper for display on the Web. Waylon wants to include a glossary of terms at the end of the paper but can't produce the right "look" using an unordered list. Which markup would be better suited for Waylon's glossary?

Scenario 3-4: Using Proper Input Types in a Web Form

Margie is creating and testing a Web form that includes an email field, a Web address field, and a zip code field, among others. When she has a few co-workers test the form, she finds they often enter the email address in the Web address field by mistake, and sometimes enter too many or too few numbers in the zip code field. She doesn't want to use a pattern expression because she says it's too complicated. What other input types can Margie use?

Understanding CSS Essentials: Content Flow, Positioning, and Styling

EXAM OBJECTIVE MATRIX

SKILL/CONCEPTS	MTA EXAM OBJECTIVE	MTA EXAM OBJECTIVE NUMBER
Understanding CSS Essentials	Understand the core CSS concepts.	3.1

KEY TERMS

absolute positioning

block flow

bounding box

Cascading Style Sheets (CSS)

class

CSS3

declaration

float positioning

font

font-family property

hidden overflow

inline flow

monospace

rules

sans serif

scrolling overflow

selector

visible overflow

A designer at your company, Malted Milk Media, has mocked up the design for an online application for a new client, Trusty Lawn Care, Inc. You have been asked to work on the project, and you need a clear understanding of what CSS can do for you and how to make the most of it.

■ Understanding CSS Essentials

THE BOTTOM LINE

CSS is a crucial tool for achievement of much of the appearance and even behavior of modern mobile applications as well as Web sites. To build the "front end" of an app or Web site, and especially to keep its appearance correct and "fresh" as functional changes are made to the app or Web site during its life-time, you need to understand CSS well and how CSS co-operates with other tools including HTML and JavaScript. You'll also be in a far better position to estimate the effort required for particular projects when you fully digest concepts of user interface "style" as CSS uses them.

Think of Trusty Lawn Care's Web site. Near the top are the words "Trusty Lawn Care": that's a title or heading. The detailed appearance of that heading might show individual letters in *italics*, **bold**, or even color; the letters will have a particular size, and be chosen from a specific font; and a wealth of more subtle special effects is also within the reach of advanced Web developers. All these elements of presentation, as opposed to content, are part of the style of the Web site. ***Cascading Style Sheets*** (***CSS***) is a language that defines style of HTML elements.

What does "cascading" mean here? One of the original principles of HTML is that the appearance of an element is controlled not only by CSS but also by the way the end user configures his or her browser or desktop. A vision-impaired end user can, for example, request that content be displayed in a particularly large font size. In HTML theory, definition of appearance *cascades* between these different style sheets.

CERTIFICATION READY
What is the purpose of CSS?
3.1

TAKE NOTE ✱ It's common for Web designers to call the file that holds CSS rules a style sheet or "the CSS." Some style coders and many programmers say "CSS source" or "CSS file" to refer to the same.

As you learned in previous lessons, HTML's responsibility is to structure content; CSS's responsibility is to format that content. ***CSS3*** is the version of CSS that corresponds to HTML5, and most modern Web browsers support CSS3. The exciting basis of this book is that modern tools leverage the same standards to construct mobile applications: HTML, CSS, and JavaScript let you build apps, too.

The good thing about CSS3 is that it's backward compatible with previous versions of CSS, so you can start using CSS3 with your existing Web pages without having to change anything. CSS3 generally adds features and functionality rather than changing how CSS has always been used.

Some of the significant additions to CSS3 are selectors, the box model, 2D and 3D transformations, animations, and multiple column layout. CSS3 also lets you create rounded borders, add shadows to boxes and text, use multiple images in a background, and use any font you like, whether it's on the user's computer or not.

These topics are covered in this lesson or Lessons 5 and 6 of this book. Much like HTML5, CSS3 is still under development at the time of this writing. However, because most browsers already support CSS3, many developers are already incorporating CSS3 into their Web sites and applications.

Using the Appropriate Tools

You can create CSS files entirely from a simple text editor like Notepad. However, many HTML editors and application development tools provide a debugging feature that helps you quickly find errors in your markup and code. These tools also usually include a button to open a Web browser rather than having to do so manually.

As you begin to work with CSS, decide which editing tools you need: you can work with markup and source code using anything from the Notepad program built into Windows to an Integrated Development Environment (IDE) specific to a particular mobile environment.

Just like when working with HTML, at any one time, you'll have at least two applications open:

- An editor (open to a CSS source and an HTML document), which might be Notepad, Microsoft Visual Studio, Microsoft Expression Blend, Expression Studio, notepad++ for Windows or textwrangler for Mac OS, Microsoft Web Matrix, or a number of other tools.
- A Web browser, such as Internet Explorer 9, Firefox, etc.

X REF

In Lesson 2 you learned the basics of editing HTML source and viewing the resulting display. Use the same skills to work with CSS.

You can use whatever you're comfortable with, but Notepad has its limitations and wasn't designed as a full-featured editor. Many HTML editors and application development tools include time-saving features like debugging, line numbers, and a button to open a Web browser.

Exploring the Link Between HTML and CSS

The `<link>` element links an HTML file to a CSS file. This section briefly covers fundamental CSS styling and how HTML and CSS files are linked.

When you create an HTML page and want to pull styles from a CSS file, you must include a `<link>` element to the CSS file in the HTML page. (You can reference more than one CSS file in an HTML page.) An example of correct syntax for a `<link>` is as follows:

```
<link href = "filename.css" rel = "stylesheet"
type = "text/css">
```

An HTML file might have a name like `myproject.html` or `file1.htm`; a typical CSS filename is `myproject.css`. Their contents also look quite different: HTML source is organized around tags, while, as you'll see below, CSS is a sequence of ***rules***.

Commercial organizations often enforce specific filesystems. You might, for example, develop a CSS source that fulfills specific requirements. During your development, you refer to your work as `... href = "mytheme.css" ...` The larger team might not even make explicit, though, its assumption that it expects a reference such as `... href = "styles/ mytheme.css" ...`

It's important to recognize that if you misspell the CSS file name, or "stylesheet," or "text/css" within the HTML page markup, the resulting Web page doesn't apply any of the styles in the CSS file. The HTML page treats the link to the CSS as simply missing. The default behavior for all leading Web browsers is *not* to complain or warn about the misspelling.

CERTIFICATION READY
How is content created with HTML and then styled with CSS?
3.1

A SIMPLE USE OF CSS WITH HTML

GET READY. There are a number of ways to style an HTML page with CSS styles. Here is a basic way to start:

1. Use a text editor or app development tool to create a file in your home directory called **e1.html** with the following content:

```
<!doctype html>
<html>
  <head>
    <title>Trusty Lawn Care, Inc.</title>
      <link href = "e1.css" rel = "stylesheet"
        type = "text/css">
  </head>
<body>
  <h1>Trusty Lawn Care, Inc.</h1>
  <p id = "slogan">We keep you in green.</p>
  <p>Trusty Lawn Care can keep your lawn looking lush and vigor-
  ous all season. We use only natural fertilizers, mulches, and
  soils to boost the health of your turf.</p>
</body>
</html>
```

2. Create a second file, in the same folder as the **.html** source; name it as **e1.css** and use the following content:

```
#slogan {
    font-size: 20px;
    color: green;
    font-style: italic;
}
```

3. Open the **e1.html** file in a Web browser. The page should look like Figure 4-1.

Figure 4-1

Simplest possible home page for Trusty Lawn Care

In this example, the HTML file (e1.html) defines content and structure: it has the words "Trusty Lawn Care, Inc.", it identifies five words as part of a slogan, and so on. The CSS file (e1.css) provides style to that content. To make certain characters green, the CSS file doesn't use green paint or green light, but instead the word "green" to communicate to the browser how to color the slogan. The files are linked together using the <link> element in the HTML file.

TAKE NOTE*

You can specify color using a name or a hexadecimal value. For example, to use the standard blue color, the color name is "blue" and the hexadecimal value is #0000FF. You can see a list of color names and their values at http://www.w3schools.com/cssref/css_colornames.asp.

CERTIFICATION READY
What are essential CSS styling principles?
3.1

Let's try creating a Web page and CSS file and then modifying the CSS file to see how the changes affect the Web page. You'll be able to understand for yourself how HTML and CSS work together to produce displays in your Web browser or mobile application.

 CREATE A BASIC WEB PAGE AND CSS FILE

GET READY. To explore basic CSS styling, perform the following steps:

1. Create a Web page named **e1.html** and a CSS file named **e1.css** using the markup shown previously.

2. Point your Web browser to **e1.html** to display the rendered page.

3. Edit **e1.css** to make the slogan appear in a larger font, such as **25px**. Change the color from green to **#00CC00**. Change its style from italic to **bold**. After you make each change, confirm that the corresponding display updates as you expect. You final Web page should look similar to Figure 4-2.

Figure 4-2

The modified Trusty Lawn Care Web page

4. Close the HTML and CSS files. Leave the editing tool and Web browser open if you're continuing immediately to the next section.

It's essential that you are comfortable with CSS basics. If you find yourself struggling with the basics while working through the lessons and exercises, consider taking some CSS tutorials online such as those offered on the W3Schools.com Web site.

Separating Content from Style

In HTML documents, it's standard practice to maintain HTML files, which contain content, and simply reference a separate CSS file, which contains code for styling the content in the HTML files. This enables you to change styles in only one file (the CSS file) and see those style changes made throughout all associated HTML files automatically. When working on a small, standalone HTML file in which the styles probably won't change, it's acceptable to include CSS styling code within the HTML file itself.

You can create pages as "pure" HTML, that is, with a single HTML source file and no CSS file. HTML has the ability to specify italicization, color, and more. Simple Web sites sometimes don't use CSS, or they use it in an inline syntax.

TAKE NOTE ✱

Even something as simple as coloring a text block green can be done in several distinct ways. Manuals and references often switch between these different styles with little explanation. You might see any of "<div style = 'color:green' ..." in HTML, or "div {color:green ..." in CSS, or "<style ...> div {color:green ...</style>" in HTML, or possibly even more unusual combinations. The first is often called "in-line", to underline that the CSS specification appears in the same HTML expressions which define structure and content.

CERTIFICATION READY
How do Web sites manage "content" and "style"?
3.1

However, separating HTML and CSS into different files is itself a fundamental concept you need to understand. "Separation of content and style" is a phrase often repeated by those who work on Web sites and mobile apps. Content is managed as HTML and style as CSS. This division of labor often mirrors the organization of project teams: different people are responsible for content and style. The separation of HTML and CSS helps make it possible for two people to work simultaneously without interfering with each other.

In addition, separation of content and presentation helps you conform more closely with HTML5, which is becoming the new standard for Web pages and applications.

This lesson shows correspondences between CSS and a Web page. Keep in mind that the Web page depends on a larger configuration, typically including at least an HTML file and a browser. Don't think you can learn CSS in complete isolation from these other parts. A second correspondence is between CSS and the display of a particular mobile app built with that CSS. While your purpose in learning and working with CSS might be to develop apps, all the instruction of this chapter will be in terms of Web pages. The tools for mobile apps are changing rapidly, and aren't as well standardized as the Internet Explorer (IE) Web browser. Therefore, all examples will be shown with Release 9 of IE. All you learn about CSS applies equally well for programming your apps.

Understanding Selectors and Declarations

Once these basics are comfortable for you, you are in a position to look more deeply at CSS source files. A CSS file typically contains a sequence of style specifications or rules and might include an initial @import rule. The order of the rules will be significant in later lessons.

Each individual rule has two primary parts: a selector and one or more declarations. The *selector* is usually the HTML element you want to style. The **declaration** is the style for a specific selector. A declaration has a property, which is a style attribute, and a value. The general syntax of a declaration consists of a property keyword followed by a colon and space, and then a value followed by a semi-colon terminator. A declaration is within curly brackets. These concepts are illustrated in Figure 4-3.

Figure 4-3

Describing a selector and declaration

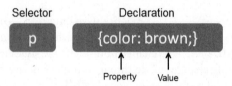

Consider this example:

```
/* This is the content of the file e1.css. */
p {color: brown;}
#slogan {
    font-size:20px;
    color: green;
    font-style: italic;
}
```

Content between /* and */ in a CSS file is called a comment. It's a note inserted by the developer for informational purposes only and it doesn't affect the CSS or Web page. Comments can appear anywhere in a style sheet.

This example has two rules, one for "p" and one for #slogan. The first rule applies to all content within all paragraph tags (or type) <p> on the Web page. The second rule applies only to the unique HTML element with ID "slogan." The selector part of a rule can be quite complicated; for now, think of selectors as one of the following three:

- HTML tags, like <p> above. CSS rules also commonly select such tags as <h...>, <table>, <a>, and so on.
- ID selectors, like #slogan above. For these, the symbol # is a prefix that determines that selection is by ID.
- Class selectors, like the example that follows.

Notice that an ID should be unique within a particular HTML instance. Several elements may share a class, though. **Class** is an attribute a Web author uses to provide structure to a document beyond the meaning HTML builds in with elements such as paragraph, header, and so on. We might choose to label some content on a page "opinion" and other "fact." These kinds of categories are conveniently implemented as classes, because CSS can manage content in terms of its class definitions. The following markup illustrates the use of a class.

This is the content of an HTML file, named e2.html:

```
<!doctype html>
<html>
  <head>
    <title>A class example</title>
    <link href = "e2.css" rel = "stylesheet"
    type = "text/css">
  </head>
<body>
  <h1>About States</h1>
  <p class = "fact">Alaska is the largest U.S. state
  in area.</p>
  <p class = "opinion">New Jersey deserves its
  nickname "Garden State."</p>
  <p class = "fact">A single congressman represents
  Wyoming in the national House of
  Representatives.</p>
</body>
</html>
```

This is the content of the associated CSS file, named e2.css:

```
p {color: black;}
/* The prefix for a class selector is a period: '.' */
.opinion {color: gray;}
```

With these two files in place, opening e2.html produces a display that looks like Figure 4-4.

Figure 4-4

Use of a class selector to specify a paragraph's color

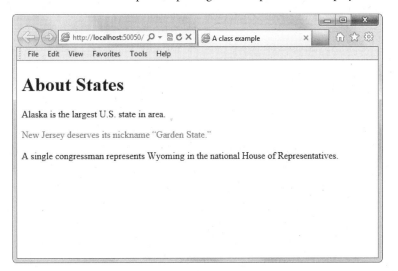

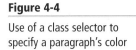

How do you remember the syntax for different selectors? Here's a mnemonic that works for some: the prefix for a class is period—that's because in school, a class fills up one period. The prefix for an ID is a '#', sometimes called the "number sign." A common ID is your Social Security number—number, ID.

Be careful with IDs. You probably understand that they need to be unique within your HTML. They can also appear in JavaScript and CSS. Many teams find they have to take special pains to keep IDs unique across all these different forms of source. If there's a slip—if someone introduces an ID that duplicates another already in use by a single page—it can be difficult to debug the subsequent errors.

Understanding Fonts and Font Families

Typography has to do with the appearance of letters, numbers, and other characters. Typography is a large and involved subject, well beyond the scope of this lesson. It is important, though, to recognize some of its vocabulary.

A *font* is a set of characters of a particular size and style. Graphic artists often have strong beliefs about the readability and visual appeal of different fonts, and you might be asked to arrange a display or parts of a display in specific fonts, or in fonts with particular characteristics. *Monospace* is often used for technical material such as formulas, numbers, codes, and so on. Serifs are the details at the ends of particular letters; look at the "d," "p," and "t" in this sentence for examples of serif characters. *Sans serif* fonts are simply type styles drawn without serifs, such as the Arial font. See examples in Figure 4-5.

Figure 4-5

Examples of a serif and a sans serif font

Serif   Sans serif

The primary way to specify fonts in a CSS file is to use the font-family property. The ***font-family property*** can declare either a specific font, like Garamond or Arial, or a wider family that includes many different fonts, such as "serif." Particularly when developing for mobile handsets, it's safest to specify a broad family, like monospace or sans-serif, because it is hard to predict which particular fonts will be available on a particular handset.

For example, when you include font-family: monospace in a CSS file, you tell the browser to choose characters where each letter occupies the same width on a line, whether the letter itself is as wide as "m" or as narrow as "i." You aren't specifying a specific monospace font; you are specifying only the monospace family.

 EXPERIMENT WITH FONT FAMILIES

GET READY. To understand the basics of font control, perform the following steps:

1. Open the **e1.html** and **e1.css** files from the previous exercise in in your editing tool. Save them as **e3.html** and **e3.css**, respectively.

2. Change **e1.css** to **e3.css** in the link element in the e3.html file and then save the file.

3. Within **e3.css**, add a new rule for #slogan that declares font-family: monospace:

```
p {color: brown;}
#slogan {
    font-family: monospace;
    font-size:20px;
    color: green;
    font-style: italic;
}
```

4. Save the CSS file and then view the HTML file in your Web browser. The results are shown in Figure 4-6.

Figure 4-6

Applying the monospace font family

5. In the CSS file, change the rule to `font-family: sans-serif;`.
6. Save the CSS file, and then view the HTML file in your Web browser. The results are shown in Figure 4-7.

Figure 4-7

Applying the sans serif font family

7. Change the rule to `font-family: Garamond;`, save the CSS file, and then view the HTML file in your Web browser. The results are shown in Figure 4-8.

Figure 4-8

Applying a specific font to the slogan element

8. Close the **e3.html** and **e3.css** files. Leave the editing tool and Web browser open if you're continuing immediately to the next section.

Prior to CSS3, developers had to use Web-safe fonts and/or fonts the developer knew was installed on a Web page visitor's system. The list of Web-safe fonts is relatively short and doesn't offer much variety. Using anything other than Web-safe fonts usually meant creating images for titles and headings, and using other workarounds.

CSS3 provides the @font-face rule, which enables developers to use any font they choose. To do so, you first create a font-face rule by assigning a name to the font. The font must be located on your Web server, or you can include a URL to where the font is located if it's on a different Web server. Here's an example of a rule for a font named Euphemia that's located on your own Web server :

```
@font-face
{
font-family: TrustyHomePage;
src: url('Euphemia.ttf'),
}
```

Just like with images, you (or a client you work for) must own a legal copy of the font to use it in any Web pages you create.

➕ MORE INFORMATION

To learn more about CSS style essentials, visit the Microsoft's Web page on Cascading Style Sheets at http://bit.ly/IKmcZd. You can also take free CSS tutorials on the W3schools.com Web site at http://www.w3schools.com/css/default.asp.

Managing Content Flow

You can manage the flow of content in an HTML document using inline flow and block flow properties in CSS.

CERTIFICATION READY
How do Web sites manage content flow?
3.1

"Flow" or display style is a fundamental HTML concept. It has to do with filling horizontal lines from left to right across the display, and separation of lines from top to bottom as one moves down the display.

Consider these two alternatives for display of a visual element:

- Inline flow: Fills only as much width as required
- Block flow: Fills as much width as is available

Control of the geometry of your user interface, and particularly the horizontal extent of the display, is important. It is correspondingly important to understand flow. A few examples will help.

Inline flow "fits." It forces no new lines before or after the inlined element, but simply places the element between the content before and after the inlined element.

Look at this paragraph:

This is a paragraph in which a word appears in **bold** and another word is *italicized*.

CERTIFICATION READY
What is the difference between inline flow and block flow?
3 .1

In a typical HTML coding, the words "bold" and "italicized" appear as <b> and <i> elements, respectively. These elements are inline: they occupy only as much space in the lines of text as necessary, and they are not forced to new lines.

In *block flow*, in contrast to inline flow, an element is separated from other elements by new lines above and below, and fills from left to right the horizontal extent where it appears.

The paragraph you're reading now is itself a block-flow element: above it and below it are new lines, and the paragraph fills its extent from left to right.

Display flow is under your control. List items, for example, default to block flow. With CSS, though, you can "inline" them to achieve a different and distinctive appearance. While they remain list items, with list item's other usual attributes and behavior, a change in display style allows them to appear one after the other in a *horizontal* sequence, left to right.

Warm up your editor. It's time to try out a few small segments of CSS for yourself.

TAKE NOTE * The beginning of this lesson went to pains to explain how HTML and CSS files work together as a team to achieve design effects. For the next example and subsequent examples, though, the CSS styling is collapsed into the HTML source file. HTML recognizes the `<style>` element, which makes this possible. When learning CSS attributes, it is generally much, *much* more convenient to work within a single source file, so all except the simplest sections of the lesson are implemented within a single HTML source. Keep in mind that most commercial work will be structured in terms of separate HTML and CSS sources.

EXPLORE INLINE FLOW AND BLOCK FLOW

GET READY. To explore inline flow and block flow, perform the following steps:

1. Create the file **e4.html** with the following contents:

```
<!doctype html>
<!-- This is the content of the file e4.html.-->
<html>
  <head>
    <title>Block and inline flow</title>
        <link href = "e4.css" rel = "stylesheet"
        type = "text/css">
<style type = 'text/css'>
   .toolbar li {
   }
</style>
  </head>
<body>
<h1>Block and inline flow</h1>

<p>Here are choices you can make:</p>
<ul class = "toolbar">
    <li>Automobile</li>
    <li>Bicycle</li>
    <li>Scooter</li>
    <li>Taxi</li>
    <li>Walk</li>
</ul>
</body>
</html>
```

2. When you display this source in your browser, you see something like Figure 4-9.

Figure 4-9

Default appearance of list elements

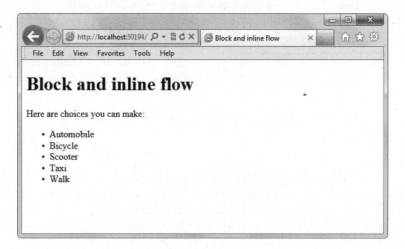

3. Update the source of e4.html so that the `<style>` segment looks like

```
<style type = "text/css">
  .toolbar li {
      display:inline;
      background-color: #EEE;
      border: 1px solid;
      border-color: #F3F3F3 #BBB #BBB #F3F3F3;
      margin: 2px;
      padding: .5em;
  }
</style>
```

4. Save the file and refresh your browser. The list display updates, as shown in Figure 4-10. Notice how this example illustrates that control of flow is useful for visual effects.

Figure 4-10

Appearance of list elements re-styled with inline flow

5. Close the **e4.html** file. Leave the editing tool and Web browser open if you're continuing immediately to the next section.

➕ MORE INFORMATION

To learn more about the CSS display property and managing content flow, visit the W3schools.com CSS display Property Web page at http://www.w3schools.com/cssref/pr_class_display.asp.

CERTIFICATION READY

How are individual elements positioned on an HTML page using CSS?

3 .1

CERTIFICATION READY

How is float positioning used?

3 .1

X REF

Managing content flow and using columns for readability are covered in detail in Lesson 6.

Positioning Individual Elements

HTML and CSS support a number of ways to specify where individual HTML elements appear within a display. The two most important for our purposes are float positioning and absolute positioning.

The default positioning method for all elements is "static", that is, immediately after the document's previous element. To place any element in any other position, use CSS to change the default to either float or absolute.

APPLYING FLOAT POSITIONING

Float positioning often is useful when a layout is in columns, at least in part. To float an element is to have it move as far as possible either to the right or left; text then "wraps" around the element.

Simple columns are constructed by floating several different elements in turn. Suppose you need to produce four-column layout of textual content. Style each of the pieces of content that should appear in successive columns as float positioned; each element "floats" to the side, but is kept separate from the ones before and after it. Note that in this kind of column, text which overruns the bottom of one column does not flow to the top of the next one.

 USE FLOAT POSITIONING WITH MULTI-COLUMNS

GET READY. To apply float positioning to multiple columns, perform the following steps:

1. Create the file **e5.html** with the following contents:

```
<!doctype html>
<!-- This is e5.html. -->
<html>
<head>
<title>Float positioning</title>
<style type = 'text/css'>
#col1 {
    float: left;
    width: 150px;
    background-color: lightskyblue;
}
#col2 {
    float: left;
    width: 120px;
    background-color: yellow;
}
</style>
</head>
<body>
<h1>Float positioning</h1>
<p id = "col1">Lorem ipsum dolor sit amet,
    consectetuer adipiscing elit. Integer pretium dui
    sit amet felis. Integer sit amet diam. Phasellus
    ultricesviverra velit.

<p id = "col2">Lorem ipsum dolor sit amet,
    consectetuer adipiscing elit. Integer pretium dui
    sit amet felis. Integer sit amet diam. Phasellus
    ultrices viverra velit.
```

```
<p id = "col3">Lorem ipsum dolor sit amet,
    consectetuer adipiscing elit. Integer pretium dui
    sit amet felis. Integer sit amet diam. Phasellus
    ultrices viverra velit.

</body>
</html>
```

TAKE NOTE * This section and following section do not always present complete HTML and CSS mark-up; they instead show only crucial lines. This kind of abbreviation is common in reference materials and everyday communications among developers. You are expected to embed such a line in the larger source file in the correct position. This is the equivalent of a lesson in cleaning an automobile's spark plugs, which assumes you already know how to start the engine, open the hood, hold a wrench, and so on.

TAKE NOTE * The "Lorem ipsum" text is called filler or dummy text, commonly used in design circles. While it has the appearance of Latin, it in fact is not meaningful. It's just standard text that looks like content in its sequence and frequency of characters. It's easy to generate dummy text in Word, for example, by typing **=lorem()** into a blank document and pressing the **Enter** key.

2. Display **e5.html**, as shown in Figure 4-11. Note how content appears in columns, indicated by the background colors which appear behind the text.

Figure 4-11

Multiple columns with the float attribute applied

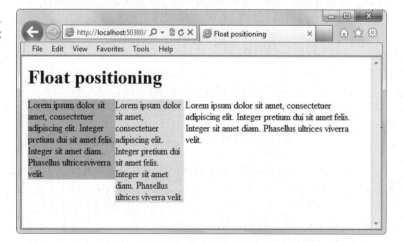

3. In the browser, col1 and col2 appear as two fixed-width columns, and col3 fills up any remaining space. If you change the two CSS float attributes from left to right, how does the display appear?

4. Make the change.

5. Were you correct? Did display of the updated HTML source look as you expect?

6. Close the **e5.html** file. Leave the editing tool and Web browser open if you're continuing immediately to the next section.

APPLYING ABSOLUTE POSITIONING

With *absolute positioning*, an element is removed from its position within the body of a document and placed at a geometric position in the display. "Geometric position" here means a location a definite distance from two sides of the display—the top and the right-hand sides, for example.

USE ABSOLUTE POSITIONING WITH MULTI-COLUMNS

GET READY. To apply absolute positioning to multiple columns, perform the following steps:

1. Create **e6.html** by opening **e5.html** saving a copy as **e6.html**.

2. Replace the comment at the top with:

   ```
   <!-- This is e6.html. -->
   ```

   Replace the content within the <head> tags with the following:

   ```
   <title>Absolute positioning</title>
   <style type = 'text/css'>
   #col1 {
       position: absolute;
       bottom: 100px;
       right: 100px;
       background-color: lightskyblue;
   }
   #col2 {
       background-color: yellow;
   }

   </style>
   ```

3. Within the body element, change the <h1> heading to:

   ```
   <h1>Absolute positioning</h1>
   ```

4. Display **e6.html**, as shown in Figure 4-12. In this example, the col2 (yellow background) and col3 (no colored background) paragraphs appear "normal," near the top of the display. Col1, however, ends at a position locked to the lower-left of the displaying window.

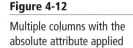

Figure 4-12

Multiple columns with the absolute attribute applied

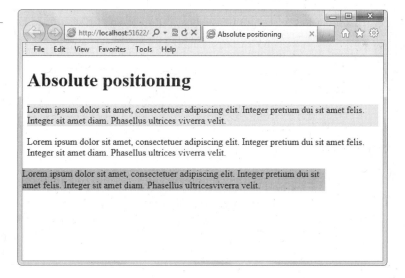

5. Resize the window and see how the three different paragraphs adjust.

6. Close the **e6.html** file. Leave the editing tool and Web browser open if you're continuing immediately to the next section.

Absolute positioning generally hasn't been used in Web work as much as float positioning. Mobile applications often have a display window of a known, definite, and relatively small size, though. For mobile applications, in contrast to the majority of Web applications, it is relatively common to use absolute positioning.

➕ MORE INFORMATION

To learn more about CSS float, go to http://www.w3schools.com/css/css_float.asp. You can get additional information about the CSS position property at http://www.w3schools.com/css/css_positioning.asp and http://www.w3schools.com/cssref/pr_class_position.asp.

Managing Content Overflow

Another crucial concept in HTML design is the bounding box. This section explains overflow in relation to bounding boxes.

When you view letters and characters on a page, look at them as marks rather than letters. Each HTML element occupies a rectangle. The word "rectangle," for example, isn't particularly rectangular: the "t" and "l" stick out above, and "g" dangles below. For the purpose of HTML layout, though, "rectangle" fits within a small rectangle (or ***bounding box***) that includes all the letters of the word along with their background, as shown in Figure 4-13. CSS styling is expressed in terms of this box.

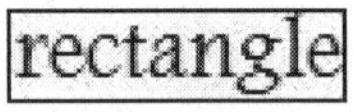

Figure 4-13

Bounding box example

rectangle

In particular, CSS makes it possible to limit the width of an element. What happens if the element doesn't fit in the space CSS defines for it? CSS's `overflow` rule controls this.

UNDERSTANDING SCROLLING OVERFLOW

When an element overflows its box, and its overflow is set to scroll, all the content of the element stays within the box; none of the overflow appears outside the box. This is referred to as ***scrolling overflow***.

Content has to stay inside the box, but it doesn't fit; what can resolve such a conflict? Pretend that the box looks down into a larger area, and that the viewer can move around in this larger area by moving scrollbars. That is a way for the viewer to reach all the content. You can achieve this using the `scroll` value with the `overflow` property.

Experience this for yourself with the following experiment. Use your editor to experiment with the powerful mechanism of scrolling.

 WORK WITH SCROLLING OVERFLOW

GET READY. To practice scrolling overflow, perform the following steps:

1. Create **e7.html** with the following contents:

```
<!-- This is the content of e7.html. -->
<!doctype html>
<html>
<head>
<title>Scroll overflow</title>
<style type = "text/css">
#col1 {
width: 200px;
height: 200px;
background-color: lightskyblue;
overflow: scroll;
}
```

CERTIFICATION READY
Which CSS property controls content overflow?
3 .1

CERTIFICATION READY
Which CSS overflow property value prevents scrolling overflow?
3 .1

```
#col3 {
background-color: yellow;
}

</style>
</head>
<body>
<h1>Scroll overflow</h1>

<p id = 'col1'>Lorem ipsum dolor sit amet, consectetuer
    adipiscing elit. Integer pretium dui sit amet felis. Integer
    sit amet diam. Phasellus ultrices viverra velit. Pellentesque
    habitant morbi tristique senectus et netus et malesuada fames
    ac turpis egestas. Vestibulum tortor quam, feugiat vitae,
    ultricies eget, tempor sit amet, ante. Donec eu libero sit
    amet quam egestas semper.
</p>
<p id = 'col2'>Lorem ipsum dolor sit amet, consectetuer adipi-
    scing elit. Integer pretium dui sit amet felis. Integer sit
    amet diam. Phasellus ultrices viverra velit.
</p>
<p id = 'col3'>Lorem ipsum dolor sit amet, consectetuer adipi-
    scing elit. Integer pretium dui sit amet felis. Integer sit
    amet diam. Phasellus ultrices viverra velit.
</p>
</body>
</html>
```

2. This source renders as a display similar to Figure 4-14.

Figure 4-14

Display of scrollbars created as overflow controls.

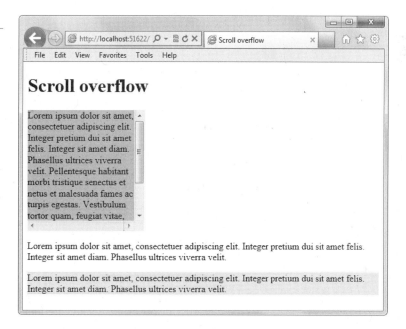

3. Experiment with the source to see how HTML renders under different circumstances. For example, what happens with a width of 400 px?

4. How does the display look when you delete half of the text of col1 from e7.html?

5. Don't save your changes to e7.html. Leave the Web browser open and the e7.html file open in your editing tool if you're continuing immediately to the next section.

UNDERSTANDING VISIBLE OVERFLOW AND HIDDEN OVERFLOW

Visible overflow writes over the content that follows it. *Hidden overflow* makes overflow invisible.

CERTIFICATION READY
Which CSS overflow property values show visible overflow and hide visible overflow?
3.1

Think again of the situation the last section introduced: your display assigns a fixed area to a particular piece of content—but that content is so long that it doesn't fit in its assigned space. The last section demonstrated how scrollbars give the user a chance to see all the content without taking up additional display space. Two other tactics for this situation are to use the overflow property with the visible and hidden values, respectively. You'll understand these alternatives best when you experiment for yourself with them and the displays they produce.

WORK WITH VISIBLE OVERFLOW AND HIDDEN OVERFLOW

GET READY. To practice visible overflow and hidden overflow, perform the following steps:

1. Open the **e7.html** file from the previous exercise (if it's not already open).

2. Change the overflow of e7.html from scroll to visible.

3. Save the file and view it in your Web browser, as shown in Figure 4-15.

Figure 4-15

Visible overflow writes over the content that follows it

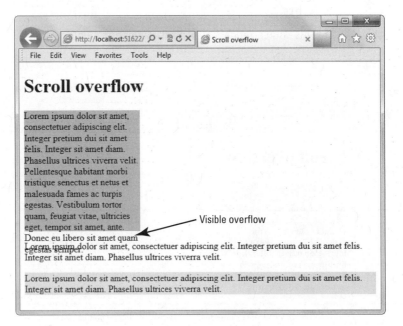

4. Study the details of this display. Visible is the default value of overflow. With visible set, the elements of the HTML display are laid out in order—then any overflow simply overlays other elements.

5. Note that background-color does not apply to the overflow content: col1 has a light sky blue background, but the overflow text reverts to a default background.

6. Now change the overflow of e7.html from scroll to hidden.

7. Save the file and view it in your Web browser, as shown in Figure 4-16. With hidden overflow, the overflow simply becomes invisible.

Figure 4-16

Hidden overflow is simply invisible

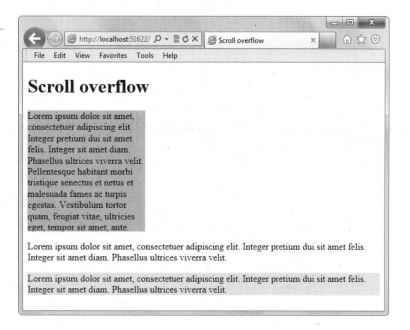

8. Close the editing tool and the Web browser.

Hidden overflow keeps a design under control: it guarantees that overflow won't "pollute" a nice design with pieces out of place. On the other hand, hidden can lead to surprises. If a vision-impaired end user, for instance, specifies a larger font than you expected, use of hidden overflow might make crucial elements of your design completely invisible and inaccessible; in the worst case, your end user might face a screen with no visible controls or ways to navigate back "home."

➕ **MORE INFORMATION**

For more details about CSS overflow, visit the W3schools.com CSS overflow Property Web page at http://www.w3schools.com/cssref/pr_pos_overflow.asp. You can also search for **msdn css content flow**, **msdn css positioning**, and **msdn css overflow** using your favorite search engine.

SKILL SUMMARY

IN THIS LESSON YOU LEARNED:

- CSS is a crucial tool for achievement of much of the appearance and even behavior of modern mobile applications as well as Web sites. To build the "front end" of an app or Web site, and especially to keep its appearance correct and fresh as functional changes are made to the app or Web site during its lifetime, you need to understand CSS well and how CSS co-operates with other tools including HTML and JavaScript. You'll also be in a far better position to estimate the effort required for particular projects when you fully digest concepts of user interface "style" as CSS uses them.

(continued)

- You can create CSS files entirely from a simple text editor like Notepad. However, many HTML editors and application development tools provide a debugging feature that helps you quickly find errors in your markup and code. These tools also usually include a button to open a Web browser rather than having to do so manually.
- The `<link>` element links an HTML file to a CSS file.
- In HTML documents, it's standard practice to maintain HTML files, which contain content, and simply reference a separate CSS file, which contains code for styling the content in the HTML files. This enables you to change styles in only one file (the CSS file), and see those style changes made throughout all associated HTML files automatically.
- When working on a small, standalone HTML file in which the styles probably won't change, it's acceptable to include CSS styling code within the HTML file itself.
- A CSS file typically contains a sequence of style specifications or rules and might include an initial `@import` rule.
- Typography has to do with the appearance of letters, numbers, and other characters.
- You can manage the flow of content in an HTML document using inline flow and block flow properties in CSS.
- HTML and CSS support a number of ways to specify where individual HTML elements appear within a display. The two most important for our purpose are float positioning and absolute positioning.
- The HTML bounding box is a rectangle that includes all the letters of a block of text along with its background. CSS styling is expressed in terms of this box. The bounding box is not visible on Web pages by default.

Knowledge Assessment

Fill in the Blank

Complete the following sentences by writing the correct word or words in the blanks provided.

1. HTML has responsibility for content, and CSS for _____.
2. An HTML source file refers to an external CSS source file with the _____ element.
3. A CSS source file consists of zero or more individual _____.
4. An individual CSS rule has two parts: a _____ and one or more declarations.
5. An individual declaration within a CSS rule consists of a _____, followed by a colon, then a value, and a semi-colon terminator.
6. The most common CSS selectors are: element or type, id, and _____.
7. The two visible HTML content flows are _____and block.
8. To make HTML elements appear in columns, it is common to apply _____ positioning.
9. Suppose an element is subject to overflow: it might grow beyond the size allocated for it on the screen. To give it scrollbars which make it possible for an end user to see the entire element, declare the overflow property to have the _____ value.
10. The most common values for the float property are _____ and _____.

Multiple Choice

Circle the letter that corresponds to the best answer.

1. Which of the following best summarizes a useful pattern for commercial development?
   a. Web pages are written in HTML
   b. Designers need to learn Java or Ruby to layout displays
   c. CSS takes responsibility for visual style
   d. CSS defines structure, and HTML assigns colors and fonts

2. Which of the following codes a comment within CSS?
   a. `<!-- … -->`
   b. `/* … */`
   c. `# …d.`
   d. `// ...`

3. How many different rules within a single valid CSS source file can declare the style of a paragraph `<p>` element?
   a. 0
   b. 1
   c. 1 or 2, depending on whether HTML5 is used
   d. 0 or more

4. Sometimes colors are expressed with English words and sometimes they are expressed with symbolic numbers. Which of the following means "blue"?
   a. `009`
   b. `#0000FF`
   c. `!008000`
   d. `(128, 128, 128)`

5. A paragraph appears on an important display coded as "`<p id = 'introduction'>Trusty Lawn Care takes . . .`". You've been told this paragraph must appear in the Tahoma font. Which of the following will best help you define an appropriate rule?
   a. `p {font: Tahoma;}`
   b. `#introduction {font-family: Tahoma;}`
   c. `.introduction {font: Tahoma;}`
   d. `.p {font-family: Tahoma;}`

6. Someone has set up a Web page with HTML that links to three different CSS source files. The name of one of the source files is misspelled in the HTML. Which of the following is a Web browser most likely to display?
   a. It shows a display as though the link to the CSS with a misspelled name is simply missing.
   b. It shows the misspelled name of the CSS source along with an error message.
   c. It shows as much of the display as possible, using the last CSS correctly linked in place of the CSS with a misspelled name.
   d. It displays a warning that the CSS can't be found and asks whether you want to continue anyway.

7. The anchor tag `<a >` is the HTML element defined for definition of hyperlinks, among other things. Name the default content flow for an anchor.
   a. Inline
   b. Block
   c. Hidden
   d. Visible

8. Your team is constructing an application that embeds a long license statement end-users must have a chance to read and approve. You want to limit the amount of space on the screen the license fills up, at the same time as you make every word of it available to end users who choose to read all of it. Which of the following is most likely to help you code this?
   a. {position: scrolling;}
   b. {fixed: scrolling;}
   c. {overflow: scrolling;}
   d. {overflow: scroll;}

9. The latest CSS standard that is still under development but widely used is:
   a. CSS8
   b. CSS5
   c. CSS3
   d. CSS2

10. When HTML links to CSS you have written, which is most likely to be a useful part of the link?
   a. type = 'text/css'
   b. CSS = "SOME_NAME.css"
   c. type = "style/CSS"
   d. Web = "style/css"

True / False

Circle T if the statement is true or F if the statement is false.

T F 1. A CSS source file includes two different rules for the font of an h1 element. Your Web browser applies the rule one closer to the top of the source file, and ignores the one that appears closer to the bottom.

T F 2. Overflow for a particular element is defined through CSS to scroll. There happens to be no overflow, because the content of the element is unusually short at the moment. Even in this case, the scrollbar is visible.

T F 3. You've been asked to layout a design with columns. Float positioning is more likely than absolute positioning to be useful for this situation.

T F 4. If you use the latest CSS standard in your coding, end users who rely on old Web browsers will be warned that your pages present security risks.

T F 5. Before you can test the CSS you write, you need to make sure a Python compiler is installed on your computer.

■ Competency Assessment

Scenario 4-1: Basic Workflow

Your team is developing an application. You have responsibility for "styling the layout." What files are you likely to update?

Scenario 4-2: Client Consultation

A customer has defined a rather rigid layout in which one news item area occupies a fixed location within the display. The news item has the potential to overrun the area assigned to it. Quickly create sample displays that show for the customer how the layout works with scrollbars for the news item, or with the news item simply truncated if it overruns its assigned "box."

Proficiency Assessment

Scenario 4-3: Theatrical Dialogue

An application already in use displays dialogue for different actors. The display seen by a particular actor has his or her lines in normal font, while everything spoken by others is italicized. This was originally implemented by putting each speech in its own paragraph, with successive paragraphs labled "paragraph1", "paragraph2", and so on. CSS then styled the paragraphs by speaker. Show your team a more efficient and easily maintained way to use CSS to achieve the same result.

Scenario 4-4: International Cooperation

You're a member of a distributed development team. A public-relations firm in Virginia is responsible for copy that will appear on a Web site; at the same time, a Belgian consultancy is providing fashionable typography, while coders in Egypt make sure that the lay-out has the correct appearance and color scheme. How would you outline the file structure of this project?

Understanding CSS Essentials: Layouts

EXAM OBJECTIVE MATRIX

Skills/Concepts	MTA Exam Objective	MTA Exam Objective Number
Arranging User Interface (UI) Content by Using CSS	Arrange user interface (UI) content by using CSS.	3.2
Using a Flexible Box to Establish Content Alignment, Direction, and Orientation	Arrange user interface (UI) content by using CSS.	3.2
Using Grid Layouts to Establish Content Alignment, Direction, and Orientation	Arrange user interface (UI) content by using CSS.	3.2

KEY TERMS

block-level element

border

content

flexbox

flexbox item

Flexbox Box model

grid item

grid layout

Grid Layout model

grid template

inline element

margin

media queries

padding

parent/child relationship

user interface (UI)

vendor prefix

Stacey, the Web site manager at Malted Milk Media, heard you're working with the client application development team and are learning about HTML5 and CSS3. Stacey is also sharpening her HTML5 skills and would like to begin incorporating flexbox and grid layouts into the Malted Milk Web site once the specifications are more widely used. She would like you to gather facts on flexbox and grid layouts, including current browser compatibility, and create a brief cheat sheet of their CSS properties.

■ Arranging User Interface (UI) Content by Using CSS

↓ THE BOTTOM LINE

User interfaces can be clean and simple or they can be more complex with several sections, buttons, and controls. Designing an interface that renders well on large PC screens and small mobile devices used to require a lot of markup and code. Today, the CSS Flexbox Box model and the Grid Layout model reduce the amount of code required for cross-device compatibility. Flexboxes hold text, images, and other content, and the browser automatically adjusts the size of the box depending on the screen size being used to view the HTML document. The same principle applies to grid layouts, which are simply columns and rows that control the layout of content in an HTML document. Because the CSS specifications are not yet final, you'll need to use vendor-specific prefixes before CSS property names to make everything work.

A *user interface (UI)* is the portion of a Web site or application with which a user interacts. The UI has a layout, which can range from ultra simple with just a button or two to highly complex with many parts, and each part can contain one or more buttons, menus, toolbars, forms, and so on.

With such a wide range of layouts, creating UIs that work well for Web sites and applications viewed on mobile devices is challenging. Positioning and autosizing of UI elements has become central to good design. For example, relative positioning of UI elements is appropriate for many Web pages, and Web developers have used the float property for years to achieve flexibility in their designs. (You learned about the float property in Lesson 4.) But relative positioning doesn't work for most mobile Web applications because it results in inappropriate overlapping of elements or elements appearing in the wrong places.

A combination of absolute positioning and flexible boxes (containers) works much better for mobile Web applications and parts of Web pages in general. For example, a UI element that should always appear in the same place on the screen, such as a header or footer, should use absolute positioning. For flexibility, the CSS3 Flexbox Box model is ideal for items that should resize or reposition themselves (horizontally or vertically) depending on the size of the screen. Another UI-related model is the CSS3 Grid Layout model, which gives you greater control over complex layouts than the flexbox model. This lesson focuses on the Flexbox Box and Grid Layout models.

Before we dive into this lesson's topics, you need to understand a few things about CSS3 and browser compatibility. Like HTML5, the CSS3 specification is still in draft format and undergoing modifications. The names of some properties can change from one version of the CSS3 draft specification to the next, and new property values can be introduced while others are removed.

To help ensure that CSS3 styles work during this transition phase, many of the major Web browsers offer alternative property names. These workarounds simply add a *vendor prefix*, which is a keyword surrounded by dashes, to the front of a CSS3 property name. Keep the following in mind as you work with CSS3 properties:

- Internet Explorer uses the `-ms-` prefix.
- Firefox supports the `-moz-` prefix.
- Opera supports the `-o-` prefix.
- Chrome and Safari support the `-webkit-` prefix.

For example, a CSS3 property you'll learn about in this lesson is the `flexbox` property. To apply the flexbox style to elements and view them in Firefox, you currently need to use the `-moz-flexbox` property.

CERTIFICATION READY
How is CSS used to control the arrangement of a UI?
3.2

A best practice is to include all four vendor prefixes for CSS3 features that are still emerging. That way, your Web page has the best chance of being viewed properly regardless of which major browser is used. However, including all four vendor prefixes in your code makes your code longer, and it doesn't guarantee the CSS3 feature will work within all of the browsers. If a browser simply doesn't support the feature or the vendor prefix property, the feature will not display properly. The "When Can I Use" Web site at caniuse.com helps you determine which browsers support specific CSS3 and HTML5 features.

TAKE NOTE*

Another best practice, especially during the transition to CSS3, is to use generic font families to prevent potential viewing problems across different browsers. A monospace font family, either serif or sans serif, is the best way to avoid unexpected results. However, CSS3 also offers the ability to use any font you want. The key is to learn when to use monospace and when it's OK to use a fancier font. You'll learn more about typography and Web fonts in Lesson 7.

Using Flexbox for Simple Layouts and Using Grid for Complex Layouts

Flexboxes are designed for toolbars, menus, forms, and similar elements in Web pages and applications. Grids are better suited to more complex designs.

CERTIFICATION READY
What is the purpose of the CSS Box model?
3.2

Years ago, the W3C created specifications for a simple box model, called the CSS Box model. This model describes the boxes that surround content in an HTML document, whether the document becomes a Web page or a Web application. Think of every part of an HTML document as being in a box. Each box must conform to rules defined by the box model.

The CSS Box model is shown in Figure 5-1. The parts of the CSS Box model are margin, border, padding, and content.

Figure 5-1

The traditional CSS Box model

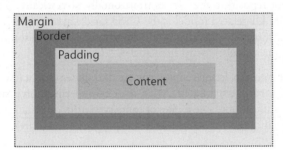

The *margin* is transparent and sits at the outermost edge of a box, providing space between the box and other boxes in the document. The *border* surrounds the box itself. A border can be transparent, or it can be colored and have a pattern like a dashed line. The *padding* is the space between the border of the box and its content. Padding generally takes on the same color as the box's background color. The *content* is whatever is displayed in the box, such as text and images. You use the border, margin, padding, height, and width CSS properties to modify the various parts of the box model.

A major issue with the CSS Box model is that different Web browsers apply the CSS properties differently. For example, although the W3C states that the height and width properties define the height and width of a box's *content*, older versions of Internet Explorer apply the same properties to the height and width of the border, which includes the padding and content.

TAKE NOTE ✱ Web page and Web application designers often resort to using hacks (customized CSS property values) to force Internet Explorer to use CSS tags that other browsers will ignore. The concept is similar to the vendor prefixes for CSS properties mentioned in the preceding section.

Two other concepts to understand about the CSS Box model are block-level and inline elements. A **block-level element** creates boxes that contribute to the layout of the document. Sections, articles, paragraphs, lists, and images are examples of block-level elements. **Inline elements** are designed for laying out text and don't disrupt the flow of the document. Applying boldface and the new HTML5 mark element are examples of inline elements.

Finally, the **parent/child relationship** is important to understand when working with the CSS. Essentially, a parent box can contain one or more boxes. The boxes contained within a parent box are referred to as child boxes. Figure 5-2 shows a simple example of a parent box with a nested child box. A child can inherit CSS styles from a parent, which means styles applied to a parent also apply to a child. Not all CSS properties are inheritable; when applying styles, you need to check the CSS specification to determine property inheritance.

Figure 5-2

Parent and child boxes

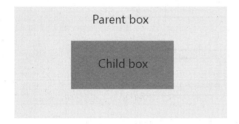

CERTIFICATION READY
What is the Flexbox
Box model?
3.2

What CSS has lacked since its inception is an easy way to arrange elements horizontally and vertically in an HTML document—to use CSS to control layout that renders well in various browsers and when viewed from different screen sizes. The CSS3 Flexbox Box and Grid Layout models address this concern.

The CSS **Flexbox Box model** is a layout mode for using flexible boxes in user interfaces. The model is part of the CSS3 draft specification. A **flexbox** offers flexible layouts for UI design. You can create Web pages and mobile applications with elements, controls, toolbars, menus, and forms that resize and reposition automatically when the user changes the size of the browser window. The browser takes the available space into account and calculates the dimensions for the user, which enables relative sizes and positioning.

For example, Figure 5-3 shows a horizontal toolbar with icons in a flexbox. The parent flexbox is indicated by the shaded background and the icons are the child boxes. When a user increases the size of the screen horizontally, the flexbox expands too, distributing an even amount of space between the children.

Figure 5-3

A flexible toolbar

You can lay out the contents of a flexbox dynamically in any direction, whether left, right, up, or down. You can also swap the order of boxes and flex their sizes and positions to fill the available space. A multi-line flexbox wraps content into multiple lines, much like a word processor handles text in a paragraph.

TAKE NOTE ✱ Flexbox layout is similar to block layout, but flexbox doesn't use columns or floats. In addition, whereas block layout typically lays out content vertically (and inline layout tends to lay out content horizontally), a flexbox resizes in either direction.

CERTIFICATION READY
What is the Grid Layout model?
3.2

Where the Flexbox Box model is suitable for simple things like buttons, toolbars, and many forms, you can use the CSS *Grid Layout model* for more complex layouts. The grid layout model lets you control the design of sections or entire HTML-based documents using CSS3. As the name implies, a grid layout uses rows and columns to make the design look cleaner and structured (see Figure 5-4).

Figure 5-4

An illustration of a grid layout

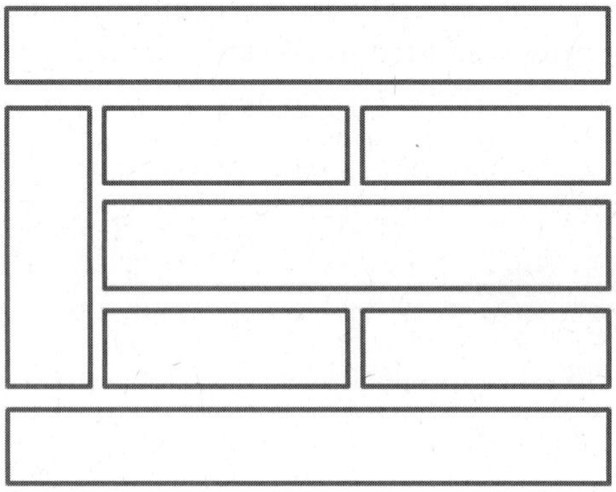

Grid layout also offers modularity, so you can easily drop elements into a grid, or move parts of a grid to a different area of a document. Grids are much more flexible and easier to work with than using HTML tables or even columns or floats to structure layout.

TAKE NOTE ✱ The New York Times Web site (www.nytimes.com) is an example of a grid layout, as are most online newspaper sites.

▪ Using a Flexible Box to Establish Content Alignment, Direction, and Orientation

↓ **THE BOTTOM LINE**

Both a flexbox and its contents can be configured to change size, horizontally and vertically, when the screen on which they're displayed changes size. You can also reverse the direction and order of flexboxes with one line of code.

CERTIFICATION READY
How is flexbox used to establish content alignment, direction, and orientation?
3.2

You define an element as a flexbox using the CSS properties `display:flexbox` or `display:inline-flexbox`, which are described as follows:

- `flexbox`: Sets the flexbox as a block-level element
- `inline-flexbox`: Sets the flexbox as an inline-level element

A box within a box is a child box, which can be flexible or not. A child box is referred to as a *flexbox item*.

Flexbox also introduces nine other properties, as listed in Table 5-1. You'll learn how to use many of these properties and values in the following sections.

Table 5-1

Flexbox properties and values

PROPERTY	VALUE(S)	DESCRIPTION
flex	pos-flex neg-flex preferred-size none	Makes child boxes flexible by height and width
flex-align	start end center baseline stretch	Sets the default alignment for child boxes; if the orientation of the parent box is horizontal, flex-align determines the vertical alignment of the child boxes, and vice versa
flex-direction	row row-reverse column column-reverse	Controls the direction of child boxes in the parent box; also affects the flex-pack property
flex-flow	flex-direction flex-wrap	Sets the flex-direction and flex-wrap properties at the same time
flex-item-align	auto start end center baseline stretch	Overrides the default alignment of child boxes styled with the flex-align property
flex-line-pack	start end center justify distribute stretch	Sets child box alignment within the parent box when extra space exists
flex-order	number	Assigns child boxes to groups and controls the order in which they appear in a layout, beginning with the lowest numbered group
flex-pack	start end center	Justifies the alignment of child boxes within a flexbox to ensure all whitespace in the parent box is filled
flex-wrap	nowrap wrap wrap-reverse	Determines whether child boxes automatically create a new line and wrap onto it or overflow the flexbox

Use the preceding table as a reference when learning how to create flexboxes and flexbox items.

+ MORE INFORMATION

For more information on flexbox, visit the W3C "CSS Flexible Box Layout Module" at http://www.w3.org/TR/css3-flexbox/.

Work with Flexboxes and Flexbox Items

A flexbox can include child boxes that are flexible by height and width. The flex property makes child boxes flexible. The `flex-flow` property sets the `flex-direction` and `flex-wrap` properties of a flexbox (the parent box) at the same time.

Let's take a look at flexbox in action. Assume a company provides three main types of services, which are displayed and briefly described in three paragraphs on a Web page. The three paragraphs form three containers of information, as shown in Figure 5-5.

Figure 5-5

A parent flexbox with three child boxes (flexbox items)

Notice the extra space to the right of the last child box, labeled Child 3. You can modify the CSS that controls the boxes so all three child boxes automatically expand in size uniformly to fill the available space in the flexbox. You could also modify one child box, such as Child3, to make it flexible to fill the space, as shown in Figure 5-6.

Figure 5-6

Modifying the third child box to fill the available space

APPLYING PROPORTIONAL SCALING WITHIN A FLEXBOX

The W3C specifies the `flex` property, which controls the height and width of flexbox items. Whereas the `display: flexbox` property creates a flexible parent box, the `flex` property is what gives the flexible nature to child boxes.

The `display: flexbox` property is used without additional values.

The `flex` property can take on a positive and/or negative flex value, a preferred size, and the `none` keyword, as shown:

```
flex: pos-flex neg-flex preferred-size none
```

The positive and negative flex values indicate flexibility. Contrary to the use of the word "negative," both are actually positive numbers, like 1, 2, 3, and so on. (You can also use 1.0, 2.0, 3.0, etc.)

If space is left over in the flexbox when the screen size increases, the flexbox items expand to fill up the space based on the positive flex value. A value of 1 means each flexbox item will take up one equal part of the available space, a value of 2 means each item will take up two equal parts, and so on. If the flexbox items overflow the parent box because they are collectively wider than the parent, the browser uses the negative flex value to determine the height or width of each item.

If you don't specify a positive flex value, it defaults to 1. Omission of a negative flex value defaults to 0.

The preferred-size value can be any value that's valid for the CSS `height` and `width` property, such as 100px. If you don't specify a preferred-size value, the default is 0px. You can also set the preferred-size value to `auto`, which uses the value of the `width` or `height` property as the preferred size.

The keyword `none` is equivalent to `0 0 auto`.

TAKE NOTE *

The `flex` property value may need some additional explanation. Let's say you have a flexbox with three child boxes. The flex value for child1 and child2 is 1 and the value for child3 is 2. A child with a flex of 2 is twice as flexible as a child with a flex of 1. This doesn't necessarily mean that child3 will be two times as wide as child1 and child2. The flex value is a calculation based on available space for stretching or shrinking; the change is assigned based on the portion of flexibility compared to the other child boxes.

CERTIFICATION READY
How does a flexbox
provide proportional
scaling of elements?
3.2

The power of flexbox items is that they can freely scale or dynamically adjust their main size. The items increase or decrease in size based on the available space in the flexbox in which they reside.

In the following CSS code and HTML markup, the flexbox contains four flexbox items. Each child has a flex value of `1` and is set to `auto`. When the user changes the size of the browser window, the child boxes should expand and contract along with the parent box.

```
<!doctype html>
<html>
<head>
  <meta charset="utf-8">
  <title>Flexible Child Box Example</title>
  <style>
    div { display: flexbox;
        outline: 2px solid silver
        }
    p { flex: 1 auto; margin: 1em;
        font-family: sans-serif;
        color: white;
        background: tomato;
        font-weight: bold;
        text-align: center;
        }
  </style>
</head>

<body>
  <div>
    <p>This is the child1 box.</p>
    <p>This is the child2 box.</p>
    <p>This is child3.</p>
    <p>This is child4.</p>
  </div>
</body>
</html>
```

Figure 5-7 shows the before and after effects of resizing the browser window.

Figure 5-7

Flexible child boxes in a parent box

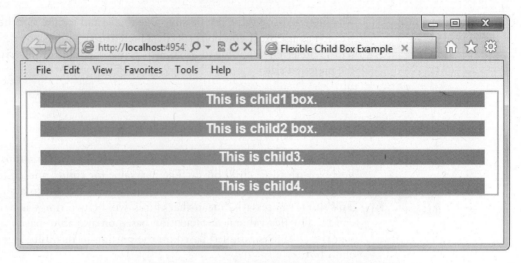

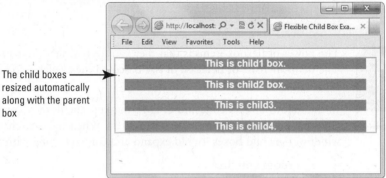

The child boxes resized automatically along with the parent box

→ CREATE A FLEXBOX WITH FLEXBOX ITEMS

GET READY. To learn how to create a flexbox with flexbox items that have a fixed height but a flexible width, perform the following steps:

1. In an editing tool or app development tool, create an HTML file that includes the following CSS code and markup:

```
<!doctype html>
<html>
<head>
  <meta charset="utf-8">
  <title>Flexible Child Box Example</title>
  <style>
    div { display: flexbox;
          outline: 2px solid silver }
    p { flex: 1 auto; margin: 1em;
        font-family: sans-serif;
        color: white;
        background: limegreen;
        height: 25px;
        padding: 1em;
        font-weight: bold;
        font-size: xx-large;
        text-align: center;
    }
  </style>
</head>
```

```
<body>
  <div>
    <p>This is the child1 box.</p>
    <p>This is the child2 box.</p>
    <p>This is child3.</p>
  </div>
</body>
</html>
```

The `display: flexbox` CSS property creates the parent box—the flexbox. A silver outline is created for the flexbox, which simply helps you see the flexbox in the browser window for purposes of this exercise. The paragraph (p) styles apply to the flexbox items (the child boxes). The `flex` property applies flexibility to each child box. The items have a preferred width of 75 pixels. If space is left over in the flexbox when the screen size increases, the flexbox items expand horizontally to fill up the space.

TAKE NOTE * The use of an outline around the flexbox (parent box) is to make it easier to identify the borders of the flexbox. You don't have to include an outline around flexboxes in your applications or Web pages.

2. Save the file as **L5-flexbox-exercise.html** and open it in a Web browser. The display should look similar to Figure 5-8.

Figure 5-8

Creating a flexbox with flexbox items

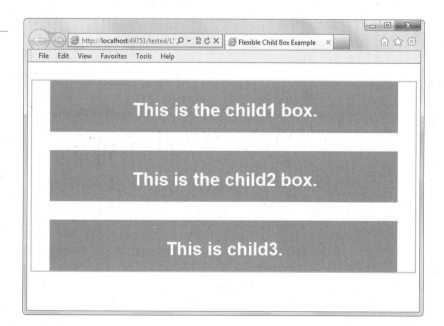

3. Resize the browser window, making it narrower and wider, by dragging the right edge of the window toward the center of the screen and then back toward the right. Notice how the flexbox items expand and shrink along with the flexbox.

4. Close the file but leave the editing tool and Web browser open if you complete the next exercise in this session.

Alternatively, you can use the CSS `flex` function with the CSS `height` or `width` property to control the height and width of flexbox items. The `flex` property and `flex` function behave the same but use slightly different syntax—a function includes values within parentheses.

The next exercise shows you how to use the `flex` function and introduces the `flex-wrap` property. The `flex-wrap` property determines whether child boxes automatically create a new line and wrap onto it (as shown in Figure 5-9). The `flex-wrap` property uses the `nowrap`, `wrap`, and `wrap-reverse` values.

Figure 5-9

An example of wrapping using the flex-wrap: wrap property

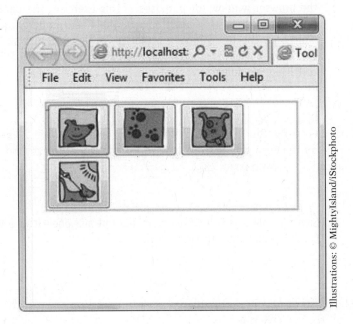

Illustrations: © MightyIsland/iStockphoto

As you'll see, the CSS code uses vendor prefixes (`-ms-`, `-moz-`, `-o-`, and `-webkit-`), which are required to make the `flex-wrap` property work. Remember, vendor prefixes are frequently used during the transition to CSS3 to make the code compatible with as many browsers as possible.

→ CREATE FLEXBOX ITEMS WITH THE FLEX FUNCTION

GET READY. To create flexbox items with the `flex` function and use the `flex-wrap` property, perform the following steps:

1. In an editing tool or app development tool, create an HTML document with the following markup:

```
<!doctype html>
<html>
<head>
    <meta charset="utf-8" />
    <title>Flex Function Example</title>
<style>
    div {
    display: flexbox;
    display: -ms-flexbox;
    display: -moz-flexbox;
```

```
      display: -o-flexbox;
      display: -webkit-flexbox;
      flex-wrap: wrap;
      -ms-flex-wrap: wrap;
      -moz-flex-wrap: wrap;
      -o-flex-wrap: wrap;
      -webkit-flex-wrap: wrap;
      height: 200px;
      padding: 1em;
      color: white;
      outline: 2px solid silver;
      }
    div>div {
      width: 75px;
      width: -ms-flex(1 75px);
      width: -moz-flex(1 75px);
      width: -o-flex(1 75px);
      width: -webkit-flex(1 75px);
      margin: 1em;
      height: 100px;
      background-color: #b200ff;
      font-family: sans-serif;
      text-align: center;
      line-height: 100px;
      font-size: xx-large;
      }
  </style>
  </head>

  <body>
    <div>
      <div>Service 1</div>
      <div>Service 2</div>
      <div>Service 3</div>
    </div>
  </body>
</html>
```

As in the last exercise, the `display: flexbox` property creates the parent box. The second set of div styles (div>div, which is simply a shorthand way to apply styles to a group of HTML elements without assigning classes) apply to the flexbox items: the `width` property along with the `flex` function control the width of the flexbox items, which have a preferred width of 75 pixels but will fill any available space when the screen size increases. The `flex-wrap` property with the `wrap` forces flexbox items to wrap within the flexbox.

2. Save the file as **L5-flexfunction-exercise.html** and open it in the Web browser. Be sure to maximize the window. The file should look similar to Figure 5-10.

Figure 5-10

Flexbox items in a parent flexbox

3. Reduce the width of the browser window slightly by dragging the right edge of the window toward the center of the screen. Notice that as the flexbox (indicated by the silver outline) shrinks, the flexbox items uniformly shrink in size. Figure 5-11 shows the flexbox with flexbox items after reducing the size of the browser window.

Figure 5-11

The flexbox and the flexbox items shrink when the size of the browser window is reduced

4. Decrease the size of the window further until the flexbox items wrap.
5. Open the file in each of the other major Web browsers to see if the file renders appropriately.
6. Close the file but leave the editing tool and Web browser open if you complete the next exercise in this session.

TAKE NOTE *

A good way to determine whether your Web browser can render flexbox properties is to use the controls on the Flexin Web page at http://ie.microsoft.com/testdrive/HTML5/Flexin/Default.html. Click each control to see if the sample flexbox and flexbox items change. For example, some browsers render horizontal justification correctly and others don't. The same applies to flexing child items.

A few other properties you might use fairly often with flexboxes are:

- `flex-pack`: Justifies the alignment of child boxes within a flexbox and minimizes whitespace in the parent box. This property accepts one of four values: `start`, `end`, `justify`, or `center`.
- `flex-align`: Sets the default alignment for child boxes, but with a twist. If the orientation of the parent box is horizontal, flex-align determines the vertical alignment of the child boxes, and vice versa.

After a flexbox's children have finished flexing and if space is still available in the flexbox, the children can be aligned with the `flex-pack` and `flex-align` (or `flex-item-align`) properties. The most important thing to remember is that you apply the `flex-pack` property to the parent flexbox in your CSS code, and apply `flex-align` to the child items.

CHANGING THE DIRECTION OF CHILD ITEMS IN A FLEXBOX

The `flex-direction` property affects the direction of child boxes in the parent box. It uses the `row`, `row-reverse`, `column`, and `column-reverse` values.

The `flex-flow` property sets the `flex-direction` and `flex-wrap` properties at the same time. The following example uses the `flex-flow` property with the column value.

```
<!doctype html>
<html>
<head>
  <meta charset="utf-8">
  <title>Flex-flow Example</title>
  <style>
   div {
     display: flexbox;
     display: -ms-flexbox;
```

```
        display: -moz-flexbox;
        display: -o-flexbox;
        display: -webkit-flexbox;
        flex-flow: column;
        -ms-flex-flow: column;
        -moz-flex-flow: column;
        -o-flex-flow: column;
        -webkit-flex-flow: column;
        height: 400px;
        padding: 1em;
        outline: 2px solid silver;
        color: white;
        font-family: sans-serif;
        font-weight:bold;
    }

      p {
        width: 100px;
        margin: 1em;
        height: 100px;
        background-color: dodgerblue;
        text-align: center;
        line-height: 100px;
      }
    </style>
  </head>

  <body>
    <div>
      <p>Child1</p>
      <p>Child2</p>
      <p>Child3</p>
    </div>
  </body>
</html>
```

The result of rendering this code and markup in the Web browser is shown in Figure 5-12.

Figure 5-12

Three child boxes in numerical order

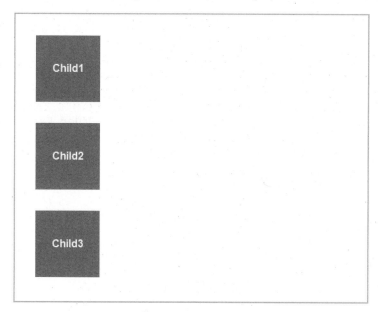

To reverse the order of the child boxes, change each of the `flex-flow` column values to `column-reverse`, as follows:

```
flex-flow: column-reverse;

-ms-flex-flow: column-reverse;

-moz-flex-flow: column-reverse;

-o-flex-flow: column-reverse;

-webkit-flex-flow: column-reverse;
```

Compare Figure 5-13 to Figure 5-12 to see the effects of the reverse value.

Figure 5-13

The same child boxes in reverse order

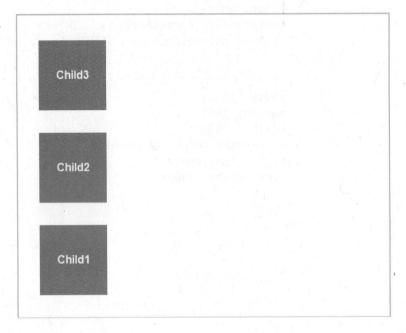

🡒 **REVERSE THE ORDER OF FLEXBOX ITEMS**

GET READY. To create a flexbox that reverses the order of the flexbox items, perform the following steps:

1. In an editing tool or app development tool, create an HTML document with the following markup:

```
<!doctype html>
<html>
<head>
  <meta charset="utf-8">
  <title>Flexbox Items Reverse Order Example</title>
  <style>
    div {
      display: flexbox;
      display: -ms-flexbox;
      display: -moz-flexbox;
      display: -o-flexbox;
      display: -webkit-flexbox;
      flex-flow: column;
      -ms-flex-flow: column;
      -moz-flex-flow: column;
      -o-flex-flow: column;
```

```
        -webkit-flex-flow: column;
        height: 400px;
        padding: 1em;
        outline: 2px solid silver;
        color: white;
        font-family: sans-serif;
        font-weight: bold;
    }

    p {
        width: 300px;
        margin: 1em;
        height: 100px;
        background-color: olive;
        text-align: center;
        line-height: 100px;
    }
    </style>
    </head>

    <body>
        <div>
            <p>Rock</p>
            <p>Paper</p>
            <p>Scissors</p>
        </div>
    </body>
</html>
```

2. Save the file as **L5-reverseorder-exercise.html** and open it in the Web browser. Adjust the size of the Web browser window so the display looks similar to Figure 5-14.

Figure 5-14

A flexbox with flexbox items in a vertical orientation

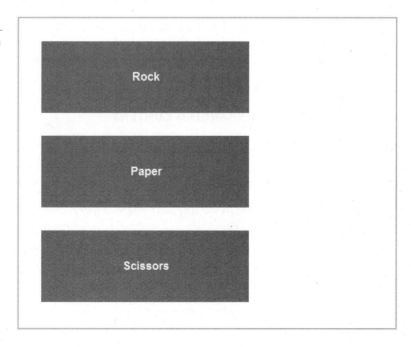

3. Open the file in each of the other major Web browsers to see if the file renders appropriately.

4. In the HTML file, reverse the order of the columns by using the `flex-flow: column-reverse` value, as follows:

```
flex-flow: column-reverse;
-ms-flex-flow: column-reverse;
-moz-flex-flow: column-reverse;
-o-flex-flow: column-reverse;
-webkit-flex-flow: column-reverse;
```

5. Resave the file and open it in the Web browser. The display should look similar to Figure 5-15.

Figure 5-15

The flexbox items are in reverse order

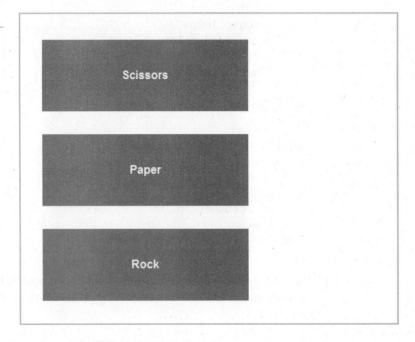

6. Open the file in each of the other major Web browsers to see if the file renders appropriately.

7. Close the file but leave the editing tool and Web browser open if you complete the next exercise in this session.

ORDERING AND ARRANGING CONTENT

You can control the order and arrangement of the contents of a flexbox using the `flex-order` property. This property rearranges child items within a flexbox. To do so, the property assigns child boxes to groups, and then controls the order in which they appear in a layout, beginning with the lowest numbered group.

Let's see how the `flex-order` property works. The following CSS code and markup creates three child boxes in a flexbox:

```
<!doctype html>
<html>
 <head>
  <meta charset="utf-8">
  <title>Flexible Order Example</title>
  <style media="screen">
     div {
       display: flexbox;
       display: -ms-flexbox;
```

```
        display: -moz-flexbox;
        display: -o-flexbox;
        display: -webkit-flexbox;
        flex-flow: row;
        -ms-flex-flow: row;
        -moz-flex-flow: row;
        -o-flex-flow: row;
        -webkit-flex-flow: row;
        height: 200px;
        padding: 1em;
        background-color: palegoldenrod;
        font: bold 100%/1 sans-serif;
      }
    div>div {
      width: 100px;
      margin: 1em;
      height: 100px;
      background-color: dodgerblue;
      text-align: center;
      color:  white;
      font-size:  x-large;
      line-height: 100px;
      }
    </style>
  </head>

  <body>
    <div>
      <div>Keys</div>
      <div>Phone</div>
      <div>Wallet</div>
    </div>
  </body>
</html>
```

Opening the file in the browser displays the results shown in Figure 5-16.

Figure 5-16

Three child boxes in a flexbox with a horizontal orientation

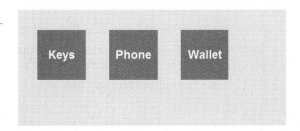

TAKE NOTE*

The preceding HTML style element includes the media=screen attribute, which is a media query. *Media queries* enable you to adapt an HTML document to end-user devices. HTML media element types include aural, braille, handheld, print, projection, screen, tty, and tv. The same syntax can also be used with the @media and @import CSS rules. The @media all rule indicates that the CSS should be applied to all output media.

The flex-order property places child boxes into ordered groups. The default group is 0. You declare groups and assign a number to them in CSS using the flex-order property, and any child items not explicitly assigned to a group remain in group 0, and declared groups appear before group 0. So, to reorder the child boxes so that the Keys and Wallet boxes appear before the Phone box, add this code to the bottom of the style section:

```
div>div:first-child,
    div>div:last-child {
        flex-order: 1;
        -ms-flex-order: 1;
        -moz-flex-order: 1;
        -o-flex-order: 1;
        -webkit-flex-order: 1;
        }
```

Opening the file in the Web browser produces the results shown in Figure 5-17.

Figure 5-17

Reordering child boxes in a parent box

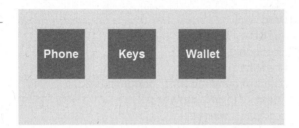

EXPLORE THE FLEX-ORDER PROPERTY

GET READY. To explore the `flex-order` property, perform the following steps:

1. In an editing tool or app development tool, create an HTML document based on the code shown previously for Figure 5-16.
2. Save the file as **L5-flexorder-exercise.html**.
3. Add the following code to the end of the style section:

```
div>div:first-child,
    div>div:last-child {
        flex-order: 1;
        -ms-flex-order: 1;
        -moz-flex-order: 1;
        -o-flex-order: 1;
        -webkit-flex-order: 1;
        }
```

4. Save the file and view it in the Web browser. It should look like Figure 5-17.
5. Open the file in each of the other major Web browsers to see if the file renders appropriately. Note which browsers support the `flex-flow` and `flex-order` properties.
6. Close the file but leave the editing tool and Web browser open if you complete the next exercise in this session.

■ Using Grid Layouts to Establish Content Alignment, Direction, and Orientation

THE BOTTOM LINE

Grid layouts are similar to spreadsheets in that they use columns, rows, and cells, but you can create many different types of layouts that, in the end, don't look like a spreadsheet at all.

Grid layouts are best suited for more complex layouts than flexbox can easily handle. Game interfaces are good candidates for grids, as are newspaper layouts (see Figure 5-18). A grid layout enables you to position rows and columns for precise control over your layout, with a fraction of the CSS code as would be required using older techniques. Another benefit of grids are their modularity. To move blocks of content from one part of a page or application to another, you simply move some code lines in CSS.

Figure 5-18

A newspaper layout using a grid

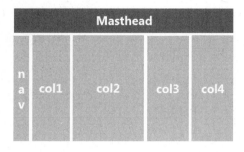

You define a grid element (layout) using the `display:grid` or `display:inline-grid` CSS property. This creates the container for the layout.

Child elements of a grid are called **grid items**, which you position and size according to:

- **Grid tracks:** The columns and rows of the grid; you define grid tracks using the `grid-rows` and `grid-columns` properties
- **Grid lines:** The horizontal and vertical lines that divide columns or rows
- **Grid cells:** The logical space used to lay out grid items, similar to a cell in a spreadsheet

The grid properties and their values are listed in Table 5-2.

CERTIFICATION READY
How is grid layout used to establish content alignment, direction, and orientation?
3.2

Table 5-2

Grid properties and values

PROPERTY	VALUE(S)	DESCRIPTION
`grid-columns` or `grid-rows`	length *percentage* *fraction* max-content min-content minmax (min, max) auto	Specifies parameters for one or more columns or rows in a grid
`grid-template`	*string+* none	Provides a visualization of the grid element's structure and defines the grid cells
`grid-cell`	*string* none	Positions a child item inside a named grid cell
`grid-column` or `grid-row`	[*integer* or *string* start] [*integer* or *string* end] auto	Places child items in a grid
`grid-column-span` or `grid-row-span`	*integer*	Defines the dimensions of a grid cell by specifying the distance (in lines) from the starting line to the ending line

(continued)

Table 5-2

(continued)

PROPERTY	VALUE(S)	DESCRIPTION
grid-column-sizing or grid-row-sizing	track-minmax	Changes the size of implicit columns or rows, which are auto-sized by default
grid-flow	none rows columns	Creates additional columns or rows as needed to accommodate content
grid-column-align or grid-row-align	start end center stretch	Controls a child item's alignment within a cell

With all of the available properties, you might guess that you can specify the structure of the grid element and position and size grid items in multiple ways.

Creating a Grid Using CSS Properties for Rows and Columns

The CSS properties `display:grid` (or `display:inline-grid`), `grid-columns`, and `grid-rows` are used to create grid structures. The size of columns and rows can be fixed or flexible.

The primary properties that create a grid are `display:grid` (or `display:inline-grid`), `grid-columns`, and `grid-rows`.

You can define columns and rows to have a fixed size, which doesn't resize when the screen size changes, or a fractional size relative to the grid. Fractional sizes are defined using `fr`, so a row defined as `2fr` will be twice the size of a row defined as `1fr`. The value `1fr` stands for "one fraction." You can also use the "auto" value to make columns or rows fit their content.

The following CSS code and HTML markup provide an example of a grid layout. The `-ms-` vendor prefix is included at the beginning of all grid-related constructs because, as of this writing, only Microsoft Internet Explorer 10 supports grid layouts. This is shown in Figure 5-19.

CERTIFICATION READY
What are the CSS properties for grid rows and columns?
3.2

Figure 5-19

A simple grid layout

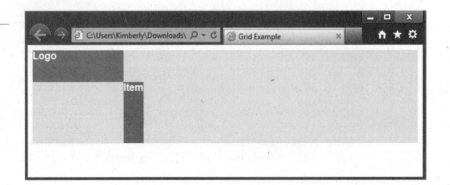

```html
<!doctype html>
<html>
<head>
  <meta charset="utf-8">
  <title>Grid Example</title>
  <style type="text/css">
    #grid {
      background: palegoldenrod;
      border: silver;
      display: -ms-grid;
      color: white;
      font-family: sans-serif;
      font-weight: bold;
      -ms-grid-columns: 150px auto 2fr;
      -ms-grid-rows: 50px 6em auto;
    }
    #logo {
      background: dodgerblue;
      -ms-grid-row: 1;
      -ms-grid-column: 1;
    }
    #item {
      background: olive;
      -ms-grid-row: 2;
      -ms-grid-column: 2;
    }
  </style>
</head>

<body>
  <div>
    <div id="grid">
      <div id="logo">Logo</div>
      <div id="item">Item</div>
    </div>
  </div>
</body>

</html>
```

In this example, the grid structure has three columns and three rows. The first column is a fixed width of 150 pixels. The second column adjusts its width to fit the column's content, as indicated by the auto keyword. The third column is two fraction units of the remaining space in the grid.

The first row is 50 pixels tall, the second row is 6 ems tall, and the third row adjusts to fit the content of the row.

CREATE A SIMPLE GRID LAYOUT

GET READY. To create a simple grid layout, perform the following steps:

1. In an editing tool or app development tool, create an HTML document based on the code shown previously for Figure 5-19.

2. Save the file as **L5-grid-exercise.html**.

3. Open **L5-grid-exercise.html** in Internet Explorer 10. Rendering the HTML file in any other browser will produce unexpected results. The layout should look like Figure 5-19.

4. Add another item to the grid so a cell appears in the third row and third column. To do so, insert the following at the end of the style section:

```
#item2 {
    background: orange;
    -ms-grid-row: 3;
    -ms-grid-column: 3;
    }
```

5. Insert the following after the item div in the body section:

```
<div id="item2">Item2</div>
```

6. Save the file again and view it in a Web browser. The layout should look like Figure 5-20.

Figure 5-20

A third item added to the grid

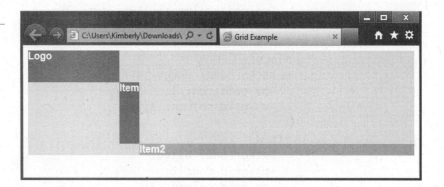

7. Close the editing tool and the Web browser.

+ MORE INFORMATION

For more information on grid layouts, visit the "CSS Grid Layout" page at http://www.w3.org/TR/css3-grid-layout/.

Understanding Grid Templates

A grid template uses alphabetical characters to represent the position of items in a grid. You use the alpha characters with the grid-template, grid-rows, and grid-columns properties to create a grid into which data flows.

CERTIFICATION READY
What is a grid template?
3.2

The W3C's CSS Grid Template Layout Module presents another approach to grid layouts by creating a **grid template**, which is like an empty table into which data can be flowed. A grid template uses alphabetical characters to represent the position of items in a grid.

You use the grid-position property and assign an alphabetical character as a position value. The following examples show the grid-position property defined for four items:

```
news { grid-position: a; }
weather { grid-position: b; }
sports { grid-position: c; }
events { grid-position: d; }
```

After assigning positions, you create a layout using strings of characters. A string equals a row, and each character in the string is a column. For example, to create a grid with one row with four columns that size to fit the content, you would use the following syntax:

```
div { grid-template: "abcd"; grid-rows: auto;
grid-columns: auto;}
```

Although this example used the `auto` keyword, you can use any of the values for `grid-rows` and `grid-colums` as listed in Table 5-2.

The specification for grid template layouts is very much in draft format and isn't supported by any Web browsers at the time of this writing. However, you might come across grid templates on the MTA 98-375 exam. Therefore, you should check the latest W3C CSS Grid Template Layout Module specification when preparing to take the exam.

SKILL SUMMARY

IN THIS LESSON YOU LEARNED:

- User interfaces can be clean and simple or more complex with several sections, buttons, and controls.
- Designing an interface that renders well on large PC screens and small mobile devices used to require a lot of markup and code. Today, the CSS Flexbox Box and Grid Layout models reduce the amount of code required for cross-device compatibility. Because the CSS specifications are not yet final, you'll need to use vendor prefixes before CSS property names to make everything work.
- Flexboxes are designed for toolbars, menus, forms, and similar elements in Web pages and applications. Grids are better suited to more complex designs.
- Both a flexbox and its contents can be configured to change size, horizontally and vertically, when the screen on which they're displayed changes size. You can also reverse the direction and order of flexboxes with one line of code.
- A flexbox can include child boxes that are flexible by height and width. You use the `flex` property to work with child boxes. The `flex-flow` property sets the `flex-direction` and `flex-wrap` properties of a flexbox (the parent box) at the same time.
- Grid layouts are similar to spreadsheets in that they use columns, rows, and cells, but you can create many different types of layouts that, in the end, don't look like a spreadsheet at all.
- You use the CSS properties `display:grid` (or `display:inline-grid`), `grid-columns`, and `grid-rows` to create grid structures. The size of columns and rows can be fixed or flexible.
- Flexboxes and grids are designed to scale proportionally.
- The `flex-order` property enables you to change the order of child items in a flexbox, rearranging them in any order you like without having to change them in the HTML markup.
- A grid template uses alphabetical characters to represent the position of items in a grid. You use the alpha characters with the grid-template, grid-rows, and grid-columns properties to create a grid into which data flows.

■ Knowledge Assessment

Fill in the Blank

Complete the following sentences by writing the correct word or words in the blanks provided.

1. A _____ is the portion of a Web site or application with which a user interacts.

2. In the original W3C CSS box model, the _____ is the space between border and the content of the box.

3. In the W3C CSS box model, a _____ -level element creates boxes that contribute to the layout of the document.

4. Flexbox children are called _____ and are laid out using the flexbox model.

5. Child elements of a grid are called _____.

6. _____ offers flexible layouts for UI design, mainly to create controls, toolbars, menus, and forms that resize and reposition automatically when the user changes the size of the browser window.

7. The _____ relationship describes how a parent box can contain one or more child boxes.

8. A _____ is like an empty table into which data can be flowed.

9. An _____ element is designed for laying out text and doesn't disrupt the flow of a document. Examples include boldface and the new HTML5 mark element.

10. Where the flexbox model is suitable for simple things like buttons, toolbars, and many forms, you can use the _____ model for more complex layouts.

Multiple Choice

Circle the letter that corresponds to the best answer.

1. The original W3C CSS Box model does *not* include which of the following?
   a. margin
   b. border
   c. toolbar
   d. padding

2. Which of the following is best suited for buttons and toolbars?
   a. Flexbox Box model
   b. CSS Box model
   c. Grid Layout model
   d. none of the above

3. You are using CSS to create a flexbox in an HTML document for work. Everyone at work uses the Internet Explorer Web browser. Which prefix should be used with the CSS property names to ensure compatibility while viewing the HTML document?
   a. -moz-
   b. -ms-
   c. -webkit-
   d. -o-

4. Which flexbox property makes child boxes flexible by height and width?
   a. flex
   b. flex-child
   c. flex-wrap
   d. flex-align

5. You want to ensure that extra space in a browser window is distributed equally to the size of all child boxes in a flexbox. Which CSS property should be used?
   a. flex-align
   b. flex-wrap
   c. flex-order
   d. flex-pack

6. Which flexbox property assigns child items to groups to control arrangement within a flexbox?
   a. flex
   b. flex-group
   c. flex-direction
   d. flex-order

7. Which of the following places child items in a grid?
   a. grid-columns
   b. grid-column
   c. grid-flow
   d. grid-pack

8. Which of the following enables you to adapt an HTML document to end-user devices?
   a. Media queries
   b. The CSS Box model
   c. The grid-template property
   d. @import

9. Which of the following is the best use of a grid layout?
   a. Menu
   b. Toolbar
   c. Footer
   d. Game interface

10. What is the primary purpose of a grid template?
    a. To style a grid
    b. To create a table that will hold data
    c. To ensure your grid has equal numbers of columns and rows
    d. none of the above

True / False

Circle T if the statement is true or F if the statement is false.

T | F 1. A flexbox is defined by an element with the CSS properties display:boxflex or display:inline-boxflex.

T | F 2. A parent box can contain one or more child boxes.

T | F 3. You cannot reverse the order of child boxes within a flexbox.

T | F 4. A flexbox requires an outline or background color.

T | F 5. An appropriate use for a grid layout is for an online newspaper or a game.

■ Competency Assessment

Scenario 5-1: Distinguishing between the Flexbox Box Model and the Grid Layout Model

A co-worker named Cynthia is confusing the W3C CSS Flexbox Box model with the Grid Layout model. What do you tell her to clarify both?

Scenario 5-2: Understanding Flexboxes and Flexbox Items

Miss Takeet is a teacher at Barely Tall Academy, a private pre-school. She wants to develop a memory game to help her students learn about African animals. The game will include a lot of boxes that contain images and questions. She has decided to use a flexible layout but has no experience with HTML5 or CSS, and she's growing frustrated trying to understand flex-boxes and flexbox items. What do you tell Miss Takeet?

■ Proficiency Assessment

Scenario 5-3: Working Around Browser Incompatibility

Ed says that no matter how carefully he checks his CSS code and HTML markup, and has validated his document at the W3C Markup Validation Service Web page, the document doesn't render as expected in his Web browser. Some of the flexbox properties simply don't work. What do you tell Ed?

Scenario 5-4: Understanding the Flex Property

Ed is back with another issue. He is experimenting with the flex property to create portions of a Web page. He wants one child box to be double the size of the other child box on the same row. He says he's using a flex value of 2 for the second box but it doesn't render twice as large as the first child box. What do you tell him in order to help him better understand the flex property?

Managing Text Flow by Using CSS

EXAM OBJECTIVE MATRIX

SKILLS/CONCEPTS	MTA EXAM OBJECTIVE	MTA EXAM OBJECTIVE NUMBER
Managing the Flow of Text Content by Using CSS	Manage the flow of text content by using CSS.	3.3
Understanding and Using Regions to Flow Text Content between Multiple Sections	Manage the flow of text content by using CSS.	3.3

KEY TERMS

content container

content source

CSS Exclusions

CSS Regions

flow-from

flow-into

hyphenation

iframe

multi-column layout

named flow

positioned float

Stacey, the Web site manager at Malted Milk Media, has enjoyed learning about HTML5 and CSS3 with your help. She has one last request: She would like to learn more about content flow techniques using CSS3. She would like you to prepare an electronic presentation on CSS Regions, multi-column layout, hyphenation, and CSS Exclusions, and present the information during a lunch-time seminar for staff next week.

■ Managing the Flow of Text Content by Using CSS

 THE BOTTOM LINE   Content flow has, historically, been a manual procedure in HTML documents. Today, CSS Regions, CSS Exclusions, and multi-column layouts help you flow content dynamically.

Complex page layout for print publications like magazines, newspapers, and books has been finely tuned by software manufacturers such as Adobe and Microsoft. Adobe InDesign, Microsoft Publisher, and even Microsoft Word 2010 handle the flow of content between columns efficiently. InDesign and Publisher in particular are adept at flowing content between areas of a document that aren't contiguous (touching), such as those separated by images, boxes of content, or pages. Desktop publishing software makes it easy to connect content in different areas, so that changes made to one area allows content to reflow properly to other connected areas.

In HTML documents, content flow has been a challenge for Web and application designers for years. Displaying a complex layout in HTML requires the same flexible placement of boxes as desktop publishing software, but the tools to accomplish this type of content flow have only recently become available.

Microsoft and Adobe collaborated with the W3C to create the concept of CSS Regions for Web-based content flow. CSS Regions allows developers to dynamically flow content across multiple boxes, or containers, in HTML documents with fluid layouts. The content adjusts and displays properly whether a user views the document on a large computer monitor or on a small tablet screen.

Although CSS3 enables you to use multi-column layout to separate content into columns (see Figure 6-1), CSS Regions offer better control of content flow in more complex layouts. You combine CSS Regions with CSS layout techniques, such as columns, flexboxes, and grid layouts.

Figure 6-1

A Web layout with columns

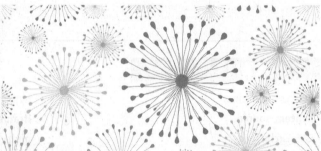

Illustration: © Megan Tamaccio/iStockphoto

Lorem ipsum dolor sit amet, consectetur adipiscing elit. Mauris id dui nisl, vitae congue est. Nulla molestie sollicitudin ligula, eu suscipit lorem. Sed molestie posuere suscipit. Nullam ornare est sed nunc lacinia a lobortis enim mollis.

Ut tempus enim sit amet lorem feugiat sit amet eleifend velit pretium. Nulla facilisi. Phasellus ultricies lobortis gravida. Praesent pharetra ligula vitae nunc lacinia quis accumsan eros tincidunt. Sed tellus massa, euismod ullamcorper vitae felis.

Morbi viverra scelerisque suscipit. Quisque purus metus, ullamcorper eu scelerisque eu, mollis a ipsum. Sed ut augue accumsan leo pulvinar ultrices at et ipsum. Curabitur sit amet mi eu justo congue condimentum. Sed nec orci.

Content flow

Hyphenation, which breaks words between syllables at the end of lines, is also important to fluid layouts, enabling full justification of standalone paragraphs and those in columns. Positioned floats, now called CSS Exclusions, enable you to completely wrap text around images, shapes, and containers of text.

This lesson covers CSS Regions, CSS3 multiple columns, CSS3 hyphenation, and positioned floats to help you learn how to flow and present content in dynamically adjusting HTML layouts.

➕ **MORE INFORMATION**

For more information on CSS regions, hyphenation, and multi-column layout, Microsoft and Adobe both offer resources worth checking out. Browse the Adobe "CSS3 regions: Rich page layout with HTML and CSS3" Web page at http://adobe.ly/kN7MUy. For more information from Microsoft, visit the Microsoft "CSS" Web page at http://bit.ly/rZLwOr.

■ Understanding and Using Regions to Flow Text Content between Multiple Sections

THE BOTTOM LINE

CSS Regions lets you flow content between neighboring or distant areas in an HTML document. CSS Regions are defined areas (regions) of an HTML document where content can flow. When there's too much content to fit in one region, the remaining content automatically flows into the next region. This is similar to how page layout programs work.

In a typical HTML document, you can display content in different sections or areas, but each area is independent. If you want overflow text to move from one area to another, you generally have to do so manually. This approach doesn't work well when a user resizes the screen or uses accessibility tools such as a screen magnifier. This method also doesn't lend itself to automatic switching from portrait to landscape orientation on tablets and smartphones. One solution is CSS Regions.

CSS Regions are defined areas (regions) of an HTML document where content can flow. Similar to a page layout program, when there's too much content to fit in one region, the remaining content automatically flows into the next region. (See Figure 6-2.) If a user resizes the screen on which the document is viewed, or views the document on a smaller or larger screen, the content resizes and automatically reflows through the regions.

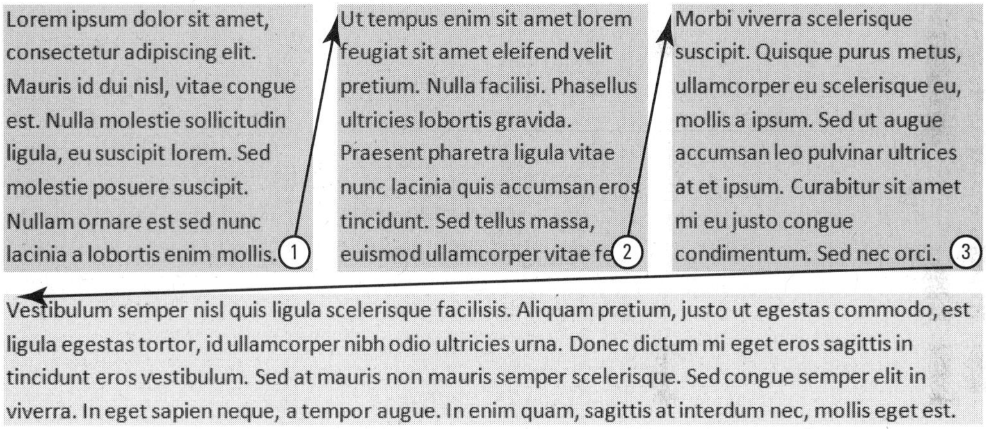

CERTIFICATION READY
What are CSS Regions?
3.3

Figure 6-2

Content flow with CSS Regions

Lorem ipsum dolor sit amet, consectetur adipiscing elit. Mauris id dui nisl, vitae congue est. Nulla molestie sollicitudin ligula, eu suscipit lorem. Sed molestie posuere suscipit. Nullam ornare est sed nunc lacinia a lobortis enim mollis. ①

Ut tempus enim sit amet lorem feugiat sit amet eleifend velit pretium. Nulla facilisi. Phasellus ultricies lobortis gravida. Praesent pharetra ligula vitae nunc lacinia quis accumsan eros tincidunt. Sed tellus massa, euismod ullamcorper vitae fe ②

Morbi viverra scelerisque suscipit. Quisque purus metus, ullamcorper eu scelerisque eu, mollis a ipsum. Sed ut augue accumsan leo pulvinar ultrices at et ipsum. Curabitur sit amet mi eu justo congue condimentum. Sed nec orci. ③

Vestibulum semper nisl quis ligula scelerisque facilisis. Aliquam pretium, justo ut egestas commodo, est ligula egestas tortor, id ullamcorper nibh odio ultricies urna. Donec dictum mi eget eros sagittis in tincidunt eros vestibulum. Sed at mauris non mauris semper scelerisque. Sed congue semper elit in viverra. In eget sapien neque, a tempor augue. In enim quam, sagittis at interdum nec, mollis eget est.

The regions don't have to be next to each other within the document, and you can control the order in which the flowed content appears. Figure 6-3 shows non-contiguous content flow between regions. This type of flow is sometimes called "story threading" and makes it possible to add pull quotes and sidebars to a document without disrupting the flow of the content.

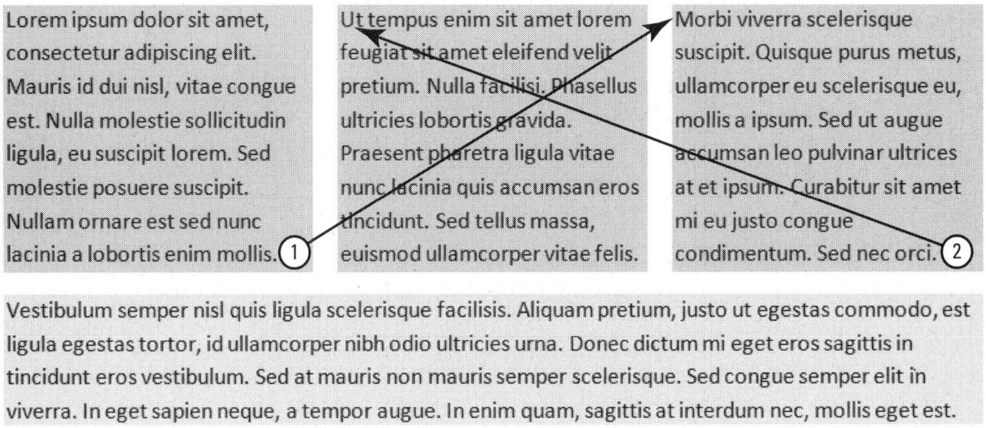

Figure 6-3

Non-contiguous content flow between regions

Lorem ipsum dolor sit amet, consectetur adipiscing elit. Mauris id dui nisl, vitae congue est. Nulla molestie sollicitudin ligula, eu suscipit lorem. Sed molestie posuere suscipit. Nullam ornare est sed nunc lacinia a lobortis enim mollis. ①

Ut tempus enim sit amet lorem feugiat sit amet eleifend velit pretium. Nulla facilisi. Phasellus ultricies lobortis gravida. Praesent pharetra ligula vitae nunc lacinia quis accumsan eros tincidunt. Sed tellus massa, euismod ullamcorper vitae felis.

Morbi viverra scelerisque suscipit. Quisque purus metus, ullamcorper eu scelerisque eu, mollis a ipsum. Sed ut augue accumsan leo pulvinar ultrices at et ipsum. Curabitur sit amet mi eu justo congue condimentum. Sed nec orci. ②

Vestibulum semper nisl quis ligula scelerisque facilisis. Aliquam pretium, justo ut egestas commodo, est ligula egestas tortor, id ullamcorper nibh odio ultricies urna. Donec dictum mi eget eros sagittis in tincidunt eros vestibulum. Sed at mauris non mauris semper scelerisque. Sed congue semper elit in viverra. In eget sapien neque, a tempor augue. In enim quam, sagittis at interdum nec, mollis eget est.

Flowing Content through Containers Dynamically

To implement CSS Regions, you need to specify a content source and content containers. You accomplish both tasks using the `flow-into` and `flow-from` CSS properties.

A *content source* may be one or more blocks of text in the same or a separate HTML document that holds the content you want to flow through a layout. The content is referred to as a "content stream."

You also need *content containers*, which are the areas into which content is flowed. An HTML document with content containers acts as a master page, like a template, in which each container is sized and positioned where you want content to appear, but each container is initially empty.

Within the content source, the element that contains the content to be flowed is assigned the *flow-into* CSS property. The value of this property is called a *named flow*.

The following example begins with some CSS code for a content source. The `flow-into` value is "main," which is the named flow. Because the content will actually appear in another place (in the content containers), this source element itself will not be displayed on the HTML page.

```
<style>
#source {
    flow-into: main;
}

.region {
    flow-from: main;
    background: #9ACD32;
}
</style>

<body>
<div id="source">
    <p>Lorem ipsum dolor ...</p>
</div>
    <div id="region1" class="region"></div>
    <div id="region2" class="region"></div>
    <div id="region3" class="region"></div>
</body>
```

TAKE NOTE＊

The W3C defines CSS Regions in the CSS Regions specification, which is a work in progress as of this writing. So, like with flexboxes and grids as described in Lesson 5, you should use vendor prefixes with property names. You'll see use of the vendor prefix in the next step-by-step exercise.

Continuing in the same sample, the *flow-from* CSS property creates the content container, which is a CSS Region. The value for the `flow-from` property must match the named flow value of the `flow-into` property—this is how the content source and content container are associated. (The example in this section includes the content source in the same HTML document as the content containers for convenience. In a real-world application, you would most likely use a separate HTML document for source and containers.)

When a browser renders the page with the content containers, the content flows into the containers and displays on the screen as shown in Figure 6-4. If you resize the screen, the content reflows as shown in Figure 6-5.

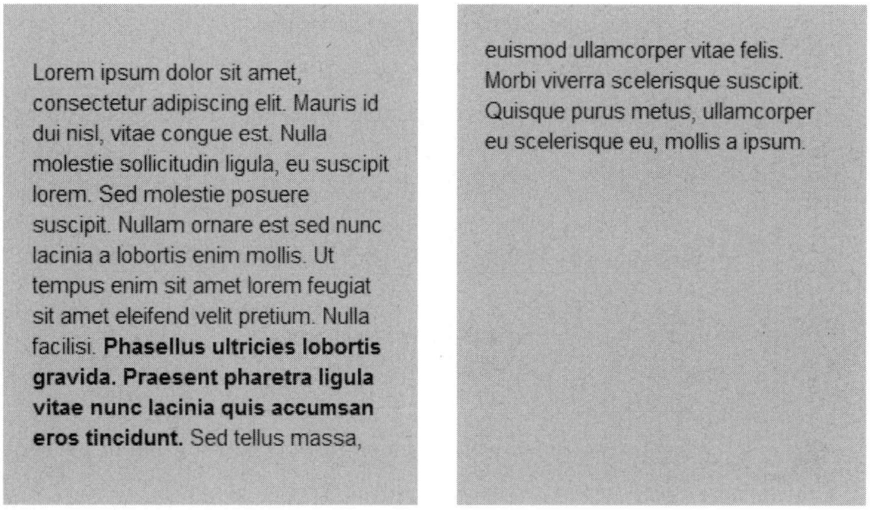

Figure 6-4

Content flow into containers

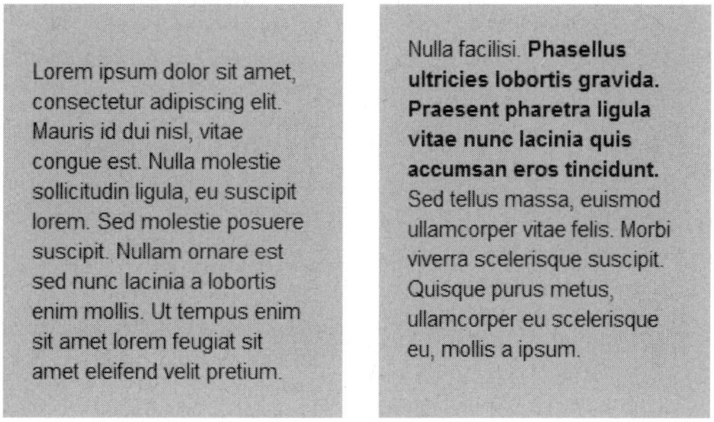

Lorem ipsum dolor sit amet, consectetur adipiscing elit. Mauris id dui nisl, vitae congue est. Nulla molestie sollicitudin ligula, eu suscipit lorem. Sed molestie posuere suscipit. Nullam ornare est sed nunc lacinia a lobortis enim mollis. Ut tempus enim sit amet lorem feugiat sit amet eleifend velit pretium. Nulla facilisi. **Phasellus ultricies lobortis gravida. Praesent pharetra ligula vitae nunc lacinia quis accumsan eros tincidunt.** Sed tellus massa,

euismod ullamcorper vitae felis. Morbi viverra scelerisque suscipit. Quisque purus metus, ullamcorper eu scelerisque eu, mollis a ipsum.

Figure 6-5

Resizing the screen reflows the content

Lorem ipsum dolor sit amet, consectetur adipiscing elit. Mauris id dui nisl, vitae congue est. Nulla molestie sollicitudin ligula, eu suscipit lorem. Sed molestie posuere suscipit. Nullam ornare est sed nunc lacinia a lobortis enim mollis. Ut tempus enim sit amet lorem feugiat sit amet eleifend velit pretium.

Nulla facilisi. **Phasellus ultricies lobortis gravida. Praesent pharetra ligula vitae nunc lacinia quis accumsan eros tincidunt.** Sed tellus massa, euismod ullamcorper vitae felis. Morbi viverra scelerisque suscipit. Quisque purus metus, ullamcorper eu scelerisque eu, mollis a ipsum.

You can also have multiple sources and assign the flow-into property to multiple elements. The content will be pulled from the source in the order in which it appears in the Document Object Model (DOM). This is referred to as the document order.

TAKE NOTE *

The DOM was introduced in Lesson 1 but should be revisited here. The DOM is a W3C specification that describes the structure of dynamic HTML and Extensible Markup Language (XML) documents in a way that allows a Web browser to manipulate. The DOM allows programs and scripts to update content, structure, and styles on the fly—anything in an HTML or XML file can be modified.

OVERFLOWING TEXT

In order for CSS Regions to work, content flow can't affect the height of a region—you need to define region heights in your CSS so they are not flexible. A region receives as much content as it can hold and then flows the remaining content into the next region.

If there is still content left over after all regions are filled, one of three situations can occur. The overflow content in the last region will:

- Be truncated
- Continue overflowing and be visible
- Continue overflowing but be hidden

You can control how the last region handles overflow content using the `region-overflow` and `overflow` properties.

`region-overflow` is set to either auto or break. Using the auto value, you can specify the `overflow` property as visible or hidden. For example, if you want overflow content to continue to flow and be visible, you would use the following syntax:

```
.region {
    region-overflow:auto;
    overflow:visible;
}
```

Figure 6-6 shows visible content flowing past the end of the last region.

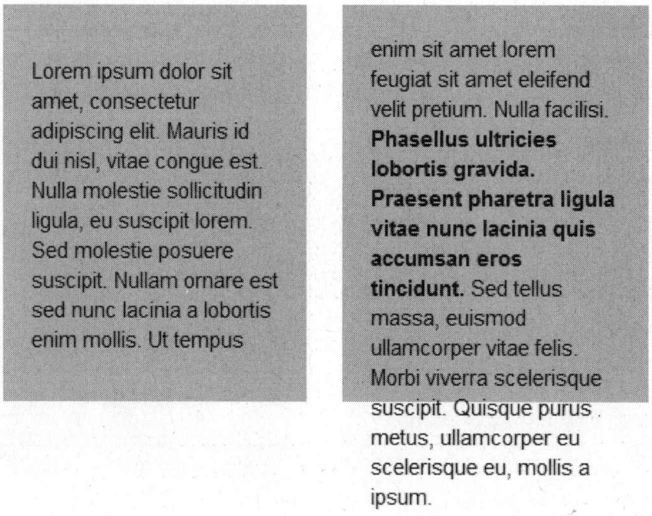

Figure 6-6

Overflow content is visible

Lorem ipsum dolor sit amet, consectetur adipiscing elit. Mauris id dui nisl, vitae congue est. Nulla molestie sollicitudin ligula, eu suscipit lorem. Sed molestie posuere suscipit. Nullam ornare est sed nunc lacinia a lobortis enim mollis. Ut tempus

enim sit amet lorem feugiat sit amet eleifend velit pretium. Nulla facilisi. **Phasellus ultricies lobortis gravida. Praesent pharetra ligula vitae nunc lacinia quis accumsan eros tincidunt.** Sed tellus massa, euismod ullamcorper vitae felis. Morbi viverra scelerisque suscipit. Quisque purus metus, ullamcorper eu scelerisque eu, mollis a ipsum.

Using the break value for `region-overflow` will prevent content from overflowing the last region, truncating the content at that point. The syntax is:

```
.region {
    region-overflow:break;
}
```

MICROSOFT'S IMPLEMENTATION OF CSS REGIONS

Microsoft's method of implementing CSS Regions varies a bit from the W3C version described previously. Microsoft uses *iframes*, which are like mini boxes on a Web page that contain external content embedded in an HTML document, as the content source. You must also use the `-ms-` vendor prefix with the `flow-into` and `flow-from` properties.

For example, the following shows an iframe element with a unique ID, which you would add to a master page:

```
<iframe id="main-data-source" src="source.html" />
```

Then you would create the named flow using a CSS selector that specifies the data source:

```
#main-data-source { -ms-flow-into: main; }
```

To create content containers, assign a class name to the elements you want to use as containers:

```
<div class="region"></div>
<div class="region"></div>
```

TAKE NOTE* The use of **region** in both instances is not a mistake! Just like applying any CSS rule, you can identify regions using a shared classname (as in this example) or list them using individual IDs (as in the first example).

Then create a CSS selector that specifies the data source from which to accept the content flow:

```
.region { -ms-flow-from: main; }
```

If you compare this Microsoft-specific code and markup to the general example shown previously, you should be able to see the similarities fairly easily.

There are a few more things to be aware of regarding the Microsoft version of CSS Regions, which might appear on the 98-375 exam:

- **msRegionUpdate**: Allows you to manipulate regions dynamically
- **msRegionOverflow**: Handles content overflow, similar to the **region-overflow** property
- **msGetRegionContent**: A script method defined by Microsoft as returning "an array of Range instances corresponding to the content from the region flow that is positioned in the region"

It's possible you'll see these constructs when researching or developing CSS Regions for use in Windows 8 or Internet Explorer 10.

 CREATE CSS REGIONS

GET READY. To create CSS Regions, perform the following steps:

1. In an editing tool or app development tool, create an HTML document that includes the following content:

```
<!doctype html>
<html>
<head>
    <meta charset="utf-8" />
    <title>CSS Regions Example</title>
<style type="text/css">
```

```
            body, html { height:100%; width:100%; }
            body{
                font-family: serif;
                color: black;
                font-size: large;
        }

            #source{
                -webkit-flow-into: main;
            }

            .region{
                -webkit-flow-from: main;
                margin: 0 25px 0 0;
                background: #EEE8AA;
                padding: 20px;
            }

            #region1{
                width: 20%;
                height: 50%;
                float: left;
            }

            #region2{
                width: 20%;
                height: 50%;
                float: left;
            }

            #workarea{
                position: relative;
                padding: 25px;
            }
        </style>
    </head>

    <body>

    <div id="source">
        <p>Lorem ipsum dolor . . . mollis a ipsum.</p>
    </div>

    <div id="workarea">
        <div id="region1" class="region"></div>
        <div id="region2" class="region"></div>
    </div>

    </body>
    </html>
```

The ellipsis (. . .) in the Lorem ipsum paragraph means some content has been omitted for presentation purposes. In your HTML document, include a paragraph of dummy text that's 8 to 10 lines long.

2. Save the file as **L6-regions-exercise.html.**

3. Apply inline boldface on some paragraph text that's about halfway through the paragraph text.

4. Save the file again.

5. Notice that the CSS code uses the -webkit- vendor prefix. You must use a command-line flag to enable CSS Regions in the browser. To do so, select **Start**, type **the browser name** in the search box, right-click **the browser name** in the results list, and then select Properties. The **Properties** dialog box opens. In the Target field, cursor to the end of the field, enter a space, and then type --**enable-css-regions**.

6. Click **OK**.

7. Open **L6-regions-exercise.html** in the Web browser. Size the browser window so that content appears in both containers and the bolded content is in the container on the left. The results should look similar to Figure 6-7.

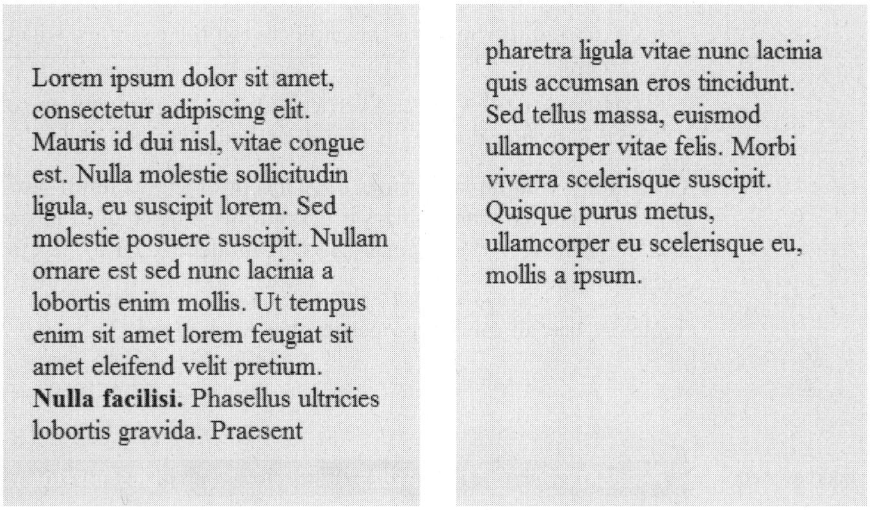

Figure 6-7

Content flowing into CSS Regions containers

Lorem ipsum dolor sit amet, consectetur adipiscing elit. Mauris id dui nisl, vitae congue est. Nulla molestie sollicitudin ligula, eu suscipit lorem. Sed molestie posuere suscipit. Nullam ornare est sed nunc lacinia a lobortis enim mollis. Ut tempus enim sit amet lorem feugiat sit amet eleifend velit pretium. **Nulla facilisi.** Phasellus ultricies lobortis gravida. Praesent

pharetra ligula vitae nunc lacinia quis accumsan eros tincidunt. Sed tellus massa, euismod ullamcorper vitae felis. Morbi viverra scelerisque suscipit. Quisque purus metus, ullamcorper eu scelerisque eu, mollis a ipsum.

8. Decrease the size of the browser window to see the effect of overflow content.

9. How can you prevent content from overflowing the second container? Make the necessary changes to the CSS code, save the file again, and view the results in the browser.

10. Close the file but leave the editing tool and Web browser open if you complete the next exercise in this session.

+ MORE INFORMATION

Visit the W3C "CSS Regions Module Level 3" Web page at http://dev.w3.org/csswg/css6-regions/ for the latest information on implementing CSS Regions. You can take a test drive of CSS Regions on the Microsoft Web site at http://bit.ly/veOZX2. (Note: This page may require Internet Explorer 10 for proper rendering.)

Using Columns and Hyphenation to Optimize the Readability of Text

CSS3 enables you to create multi-column layouts that work much like the columns feature in Microsoft Word. You can also enable hyphenation to properly break words at the end of lines, which avoids the problem of long words wrapping to the next line and leaving a gap on the previous line.

A few more features that are new to CSS3 are multi-column layouts and hyphenation. You can now create multiple columns—newspaper style—in HTML documents that scale based on the user's screen size. Hyphenation breaks words between syllables at the end of lines to create a more uniform right margin and eliminate gaps of whitespace within paragraphs.

CREATING COLUMNS

CSS3 properties for *multi-column layout* let you create columns by dividing text across multiple columns, specify the amount of space that appears between columns (the gap), make vertical lines (rules) appear between columns, and define where columns break.

The main CSS properties you use to create and manipulate multiple columns in an HTML document are:

- column-count: Sets the number of columns an element should be divided into; can also use the columns property with values to set column-count and column-width properties simultaneously
- column-gap: Specifies the gap between the columns, which is also known as the gutter or alley
- column-rule: Creates a vertical line in the gap between columns and sets the width, style (single or double line, solid, dashed, 3D, etc.) and color of the rule

CSS3 multi-column layout uses the concept of the "column box" to refer to the container that holds content and displays it in columns. The column box is between the content box and the content in the original CSS Box model. (Refer to Lesson 5 if you need a refresher on the box model.)

Table 6-1 lists all column properties that work in CSS3.

Table 6-1

Multi-column properties used in CSS3

Property	Values	Description
break-after	auto always avoid left right page column region avoid-page avoid-column avoid-region	Inserts a break after the generated column box
break-before	(same as break-after)	Inserts a break before the generated column box
break-inside	auto avoid avoid-page avoid-column avoid-region	Inserts a break within the generated column box
column-count	integer auto	Sets the number of columns an element will use
column-fill	auto balance	Specifies how to fill columns; balances content equally between columns, if possible, or fills columns sequentially

(continued)

Table 6-1

Continued

PROPERTY	VALUES	DESCRIPTION
column-gap	length normal	Specifies the gap between columns
column-rule	column-rule-width column-rule-style column-rule-color transparent	Is a shorthand property that sets the column-rule-width, column-rule-style, and column-rule-color properties at the same place in a style sheet
column-rule-color	color	Specifies the color of the rule between columns
column-rule-style	border-style	Specifies the style of the rule between columns, such as solid or double, dashed, and so on
column-rule-width	border-width	Specifies the width of the rule between columns
column-span	none all	Specifies whether an element should span no columns or all columns
column-width	length auto	Specifies the width of a column or columns
columns	column-width column-count	Sets the column-width and column-count properties simultaneously

CERTIFICATION READY
How do you create multiple columns in an HTML document using CSS?
3.3

Now let's look at how the CSS code works. This code uses the column-count property to create three columns using the text in the HTML markup that follows:

```
<head>
  <style>
    .tricolumn { column-count: 3; }
  </style>
</head>

<body>
<h2>Three Columns</h2>
<div class="tricolumn">
Lorem ipsum . . . orci.
</div>
</body>
```

Because CSS3 columns are still a work in progress, you may need to add vendor prefixes to column-related property names. In this case, we modified the code as follows for all four of the major browsers:

```
<style>
  .tricolumn {
    -ms-column-count: 3;
    -moz-column-count: 3;
    -o-column-count: 3;
    -webkit-column-count: 3;
  }
</style>
```

The results look like Figure 6-8 in the Mozilla Firefox Web browser.

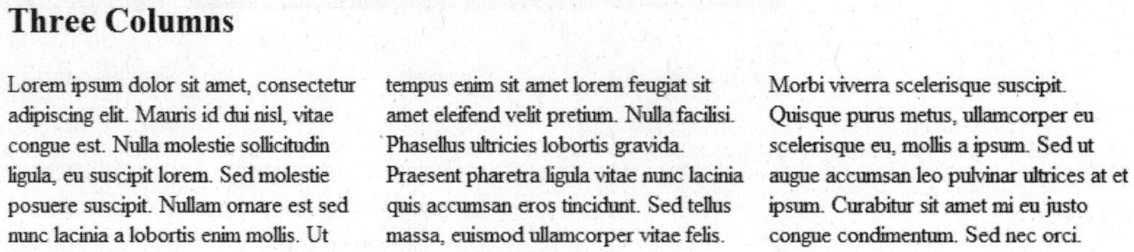

Figure 6-8

Three columns

Three Columns

Lorem ipsum dolor sit amet, consectetur adipiscing elit. Mauris id dui nisl, vitae congue est. Nulla molestie sollicitudin ligula, eu suscipit lorem. Sed molestie posuere suscipit. Nullam ornare est sed nunc lacinia a lobortis enim mollis. Ut

tempus enim sit amet lorem feugiat sit amet eleifend velit pretium. Nulla facilisi. Phasellus ultricies lobortis gravida. Praesent pharetra ligula vitae nunc lacinia quis accumsan eros tincidunt. Sed tellus massa, euismod ullamcorper vitae felis.

Morbi viverra scelerisque suscipit. Quisque purus metus, ullamcorper eu scelerisque eu, mollis a ipsum. Sed ut augue accumsan leo pulvinar ultrices at et ipsum. Curabitur sit amet mi eu justo congue condimentum. Sed nec orci.

You could accomplish multiple columns using the `columns` property, which is a shorthand way of setting the number of columns and the column width in one declaration. The following code uses the `auto` value for column width:

```
.tricolumn { columns: 3 auto; }
```

Another way to use the columns property is to assign a number value to `column-width` and leave `column-count` set to `auto`. This example sets `column-width` to `15em`, which means the multi-column element will have a column width of 15 ems (or 15 times the width of the font size of the content in the column):

```
columns: auto 15em;
```

Now let's add a column rule. This property sets the width, style, and color of the rule between all columns. The syntax for a dashed blue line that's 3 pixels wide is:

```
column-rule: 3px dashed blue;
```

To control the size of the gutter between columns, use the `column-gap` property. This property uses an integer value, as shown below, or the keyword `normal`.

```
column-gap: 3em;
```

The combined effect of three columns with a column rule and a 3em gap is shown in Figure 6-9 (with vendor prefixes applied). Resizing the browser window also resizes the columns and reflows the content between them, as shown in Figure 6-10.

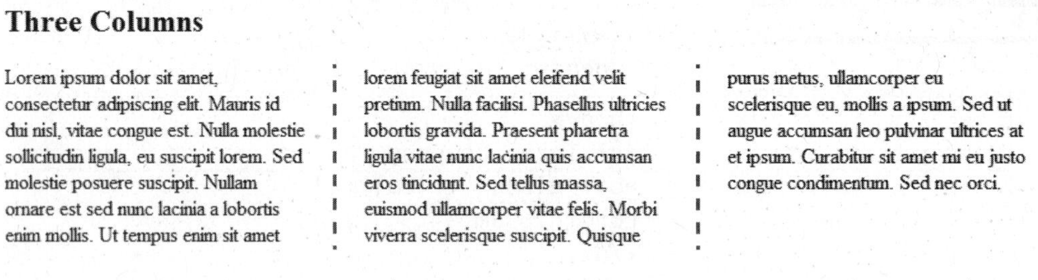

Figure 6-9

Three columns with a larger gap and a rule

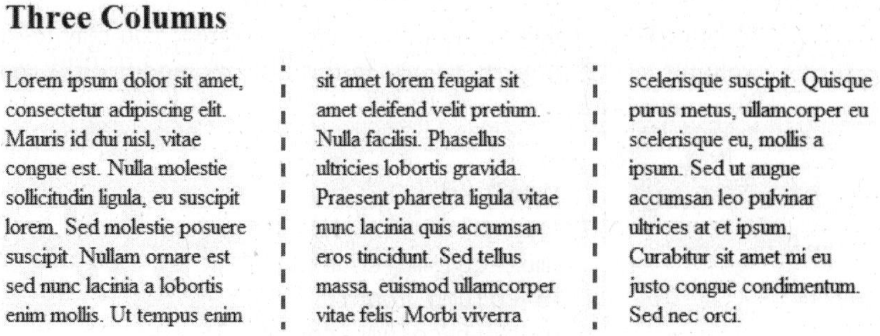

Three Columns

Lorem ipsum dolor sit amet, consectetur adipiscing elit. Mauris id dui nisl, vitae congue est. Nulla molestie sollicitudin ligula, eu suscipit lorem. Sed molestie posuere suscipit. Nullam ornare est sed nunc lacinia a lobortis enim mollis. Ut tempus enim sit amet

lorem feugiat sit amet eleifend velit pretium. Nulla facilisi. Phasellus ultricies lobortis gravida. Praesent pharetra ligula vitae nunc lacinia quis accumsan eros tincidunt. Sed tellus massa, euismod ullamcorper vitae felis. Morbi viverra scelerisque suscipit. Quisque

purus metus, ullamcorper eu scelerisque eu, mollis a ipsum. Sed ut augue accumsan leo pulvinar ultrices at et ipsum. Curabitur sit amet mi eu justo congue condimentum. Sed nec orci.

Figure 6-10

Resizing the browser window changes the columns

Three Columns

Lorem ipsum dolor sit amet, consectetur adipiscing elit. Mauris id dui nisl, vitae congue est. Nulla molestie sollicitudin ligula, eu suscipit lorem. Sed molestie posuere suscipit. Nullam ornare est sed nunc lacinia a lobortis enim mollis. Ut tempus enim

sit amet lorem feugiat sit amet eleifend velit pretium. Nulla facilisi. Phasellus ultricies lobortis gravida. Praesent pharetra ligula vitae nunc lacinia quis accumsan eros tincidunt. Sed tellus massa, euismod ullamcorper vitae felis. Morbi viverra

scelerisque suscipit. Quisque purus metus, ullamcorper eu scelerisque eu, mollis a ipsum. Sed ut augue accumsan leo pulvinar ultrices at et ipsum. Curabitur sit amet mi eu justo congue condimentum. Sed nec orci.

To specify whether an element such as a heading should span columns, use the `column-span` property. This property is set to a number of columns to span or uses the `all` or `none` keywords, which means an element spans all columns or does not span any columns, respectively.

```
column-span: all;
```

As you can see, the column-related properties provide flexible content display with minimal CSS declarations.

 CREATE A MULTI-COLUMN LAYOUT

GET READY. To create a multi-column layout, perform the following steps:

1. In an editing tool or app development tool, create a proper HTML document that includes the following content:

```
<!doctype html>
<html>
<head>
    <meta charset="utf-8" />
    <title>Three Columns</title>
 <style>
    .tricolumn {
    -moz-column-count: 3;
    }
  </style>
</head>

<body>
<h2>My Three Columns</h2>
<div class="tricolumn">
Lorem ipsum . . . orci.
</div>
</body>
</html>
```

The ellipsis (. . .) in the Lorem ipsum paragraph means some content has been omitted for presentation purposes. In your HTML document, include a paragraph of dummy text that's at least 10 lines long. Also notice the use of the Mozilla vendor prefix (-moz-). We could have included all vendor prefixes, but used only one prefix for simplicity.

2. Save the file as **L6-columns-exercise.html**.

3. Specify a column gap of 2em and specify a column rule that's 2px wide and solid green. The syntax for the column-gap and column-rule properties are shown as follows:

```
.tricolumn {
    -moz-column-count: 3;
    -moz-column-gap: 2em;
    -moz-column-rule: 2px solid green;
}
```

4. Save the file again and view it in the Firefox Web browser. The results should look similar to Figure 6-11.

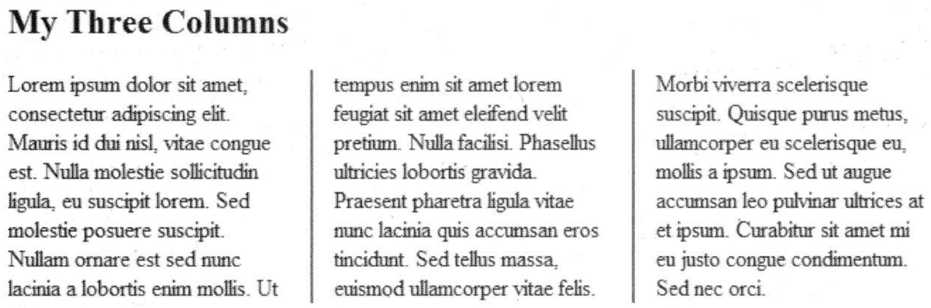

Figure 6-11

The results of the three-column exercise

My Three Columns

Lorem ipsum dolor sit amet, consectetur adipiscing elit. Mauris id dui nisl, vitae congue est. Nulla molestie sollicitudin ligula, eu suscipit lorem. Sed molestie posuere suscipit. Nullam ornare est sed nunc lacinia a lobortis enim mollis. Ut

tempus enim sit amet lorem feugiat sit amet eleifend velit pretium. Nulla facilisi. Phasellus ultricies lobortis gravida. Praesent pharetra ligula vitae nunc lacinia quis accumsan eros tincidunt. Sed tellus massa, euismod ullamcorper vitae felis.

Morbi viverra scelerisque suscipit. Quisque purus metus, ullamcorper eu scelerisque eu, mollis a ipsum. Sed ut augue accumsan leo pulvinar ultrices at et ipsum. Curabitur sit amet mi eu justo congue condimentum. Sed nec orci.

5. Resize the browser window to see the effect on the columns.

6. (Optional) Replace "My Three Columns" with a longer heading. Try spanning the heading over all three columns.

7. Close the file but leave the editing tool and Web browser open if you complete the next exercise in this session.

➕ MORE INFORMATION

To learn more about multi-column layouts, visit the "Multi-column regions" section of the "CSS Regions Module Level 3" Web page at http://bit.ly/IA03vV and the W3schools.com page on CSS3 multiple columns at http://bit.ly/KpY0Gz.

USING HYPHENATION

CERTIFICATION READY
How do you enable hyphenation in an HTML document using CSS?
3.3

Hyphenation is the process of connecting two words with a hyphen mark (-) or breaking words between syllables at the end of a line. Hyphenation is highly useful for multi-column layouts to eliminate whitespace within columns left by long words that automatically wrap to the next line, making text appear more professional. Generally, automatic hyphenation attempts to justify text at the right margin.

CSS3 introduces the `hyphens` property, which controls hyphenation. The property uses the values `none`, `manual`, and `auto`:

- `auto`: Enables automatic hyphenation of words based on line-break opportunities within words or by a "language-appropriate hyphenation resource"

- `manual`: Enables hyphenation of words based only on line-break opportunities within words

- `none`: Prevents hyphenation

The W3C points out that you must declare a language using the HTML `lang` or XML `xml:lang` attributes for correct automatic hyphenation to occur. That means if your entire HTML document is in the same language (English, for example) and you want to enable automatic hyphenation, add the attribute to your HTML element or `doctype` declaration, such as:

TAKE NOTE *
A list of language codes is displayed on the W3schools.com "HTML Language Code Reference" Web page at http://www.w3schools.com/tags/ref_language_codes.asp

```
<!doctype html>
<html lang="en-us">
```

or

```
<html xmlns="http://www.w3.org/1999/xhtml"
xml:lang="en" lang="en">
```

You need to include vendor prefixes with the hyphens property, such as `-ms-hyphens` for Internet Explorer 10, `-moz-hyphens` for Firefox, and so on.

Microsoft provides additional hyphenation properties that are specific to Microsoft environments, as follows:

- `-ms-hyphenate-limit-zone`: Specifies the width of the trailing whitespace (called the hyphenation zone, illustrated in Figure 6-12) that can be left in a line before hyphenation occurs; the property's value is a length in pixels or a percentage

- `-ms-hyphenate-limit-chars`: Specifies the minimum number of characters in a word that may be hyphenated; if the character count is lower than the minimum, the word is not hyphenated

Figure 6-12

The hyphenation zone

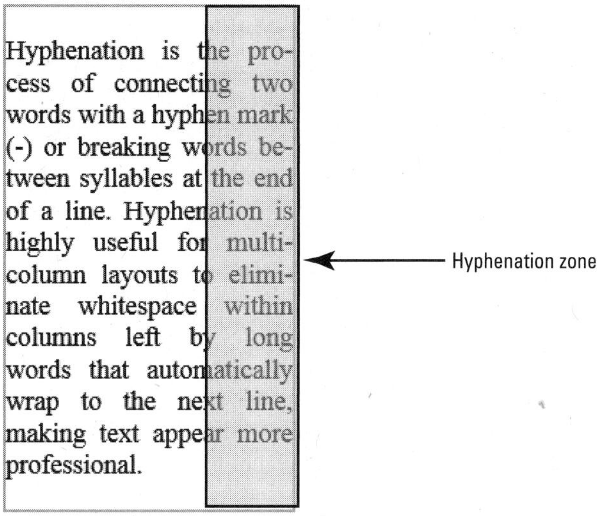

Hyphenation is the pro-
cess of connecting two
words with a hyphen mark
(-) or breaking words be-
tween syllables at the end
of a line. Hyphenation is
highly useful for multi-
column layouts to elimi-
nate whitespace within
columns left by long
words that automatically
wrap to the next line,
making text appear more
professional.

← Hyphenation zone

- `-ms-hyphenate-limit-lines`: Specifies the maximum number of consecutive hyphenated lines that may contain hyphenated words

The following markup with inline CSS uses the `-ms-hyphens` property, which is set to `auto`:

```
<!doctype html>
<html lang="en-us">
<body>
   <div style="width: 200px;
   border: 2px solid orange;">

   <p style="-ms-hyphens: auto;
    text-align: justify;
    font-size: 14pt;">
    Hyphenation is the process of connecting . . .
    more professional.</p>
   </div>
</body>
</html>
```

This markup appears in Internet Explorer 10 as shown in Figure 6-13.

Figure 6-13

The `-ms-hyphens` property rendered in Internet Explorer 10

Hyphenation is the pro-
cess of connecting two
words with a hyphen mark
(-) or breaking words be-
tween syllables at the end
of a line. Hyphenation is
highly useful for multi-
column layouts to elimi-
nate whitespace within
columns left by long
words that automatically
wrap to the next line,
making text appear more
professional.

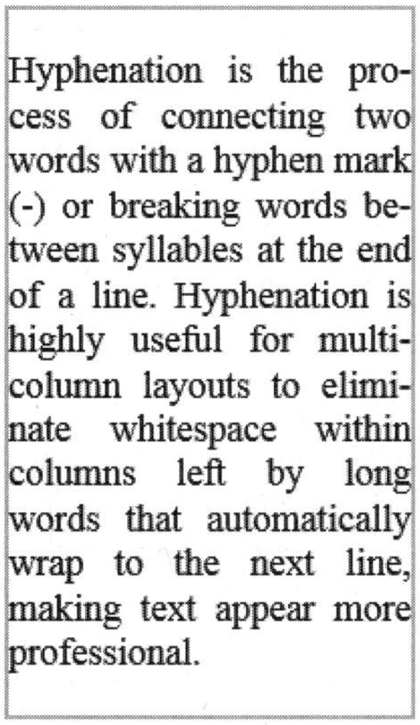

Although Microsoft has enabled several hyphenation properties in Internet Explorer 10 and Windows 8 applications, the W3C specification for hyphenation is still evolving. The W3C is working on the `hyphenate-character`, `hyphenate-limit-zone`, `hyphenate-limit-word`, `hyphenate-limit-lines`, and `hyphenate-limit-last` properties as of this writing.

 ENABLE AUTOMATIC HYPHENATION

GET READY. To enable automatic hyphenation, perform the following steps:

1. In an editing tool or app development tool, create an HTML document that includes the following content. Notice that we're using the Mozilla vendor prefix as an example in this exercise. Replace the paragraph text that begins with "Hyphenation is" with a four-line biography about yourself, your instructor, a classmate, or a celebrity:

```
<!doctype html>
<html lang="en-us">
<head>
    <meta charset="utf-8" />
    <title>Hyphenation Example</title>
</head>
<body>
  <div style="width: 200px;
  border: 2px solid orange;">

  <p style="-moz-hyphens: auto;
   text-align: justify;
   font-size: 14pt;">
   Hyphenation is . . . professional.</p>
</body>
</html>
```

2. Save the file as **L6-hyphen-exercise.html** and view it in the Firefox Web browser.

3. Close the file but leave the editing tool and Web browser open if you complete the next exercise in this session.

➕ **MORE INFORMATION**

For further details on hyphenation, browse the "Hyphenation" section on the W3C "CSS Text Level 3" Web page at http://dev.w3.org/csswg/css3-text/#hyphenation. Microsoft provides information on hyphenation properties specific to Internet Explorer at http://bit.ly/IQpgj4.

Using CSS Exclusions to Create Text Flow around a Floating Object

A **positioned float** is a CSS construct that enables you to position images, text, and boxes anywhere in an HTML document and then wrap text completely around these elements. Positioned floats are called **CSS Exclusions** in the latest W3C specification.

You might have noticed that floats were used in the exercise on regions earlier in the lesson. Both floats were assigned the `left` value, which made them appear side by side when rendered. The placement was relative to the rest of the document. In addition, if you don't specify a height or width for a float, the element automatically resizes to fit its contents.

CERTIFICATION READY
What is a positioned float or CSS Exclusion?
3.3

With CSS Exclusions, you can control the position of a float precisely, at a specified distance from the top, bottom, left, or right sides of a container. You can also create a float in any shape: rectangular, circular, triangular, and just about anything in between. The other parts of the document simply flow around the exclusion.

The CSS Exclusions example shown in Figure 6-14 uses a multi-column layout with an exclusion (referred to as positioned float on the Web site) in the middle. You can move the box anywhere in the example layout and see that the surrounding text automatically flows around the blue box.

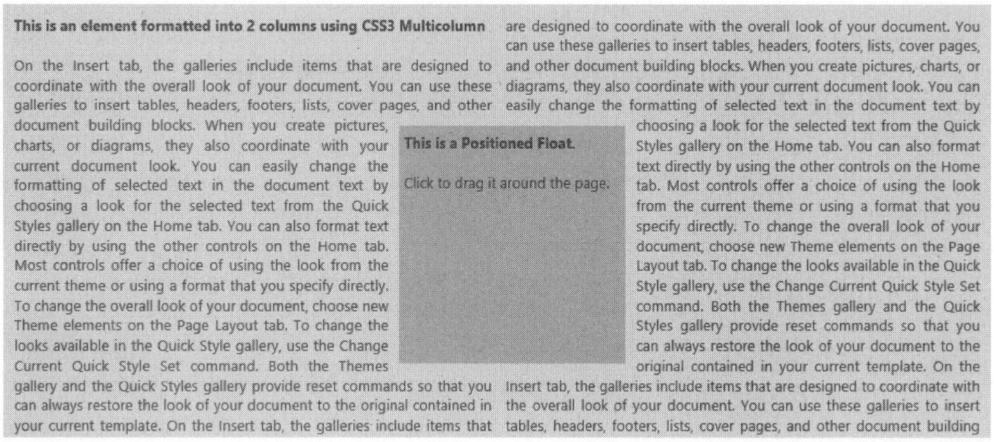

Figure 6-14
A positioned float in a multi-column layout in Internet Explorer 10

In another exclusions example, Figure 6-15 shows text surrounding a circle in the middle of a paragraph. This image includes a margin around the circle, but the text could bump up directly against the circle.

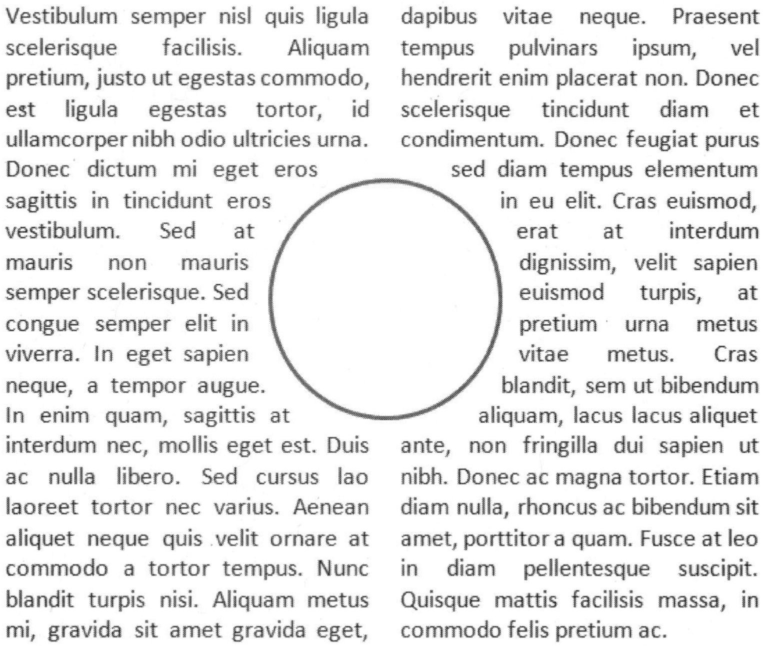

Figure 6-15
A custom container in the shape of a circle

Table 6-2 lists the W3C properties related to CSS Exclusions.

Table 6-2

CSS Exclusions properties

PROPERTY	VALUE	DESCRIPTION
shape-outside	auto shape url	Creates the general shape of an exclusion
shape-inside	outside-shape auto shape uri	Modifies a shape's contents
wrap	wrap-flow wrap-margin wrap-padding	Is a shorthand method of setting the wrap-flow, wrap-margin, and wrap-padding properties in one declaration
wrap-flow	auto both start end maximum clear	Specifies how exclusions affect inline content within block-level elements
wrap-margin	length	Provides an offset for content outside the element
wrap-padding	length	Provides a pad (an offset) for content inside an element
wrap-through	wrap none	Specifies how content should wrap around an exclusion element

To create a simple CSS exclusion, use the `wrap-flow: both` property to display content on all sides of the exclusion. Another option is to use `wrap-flow: clear`, which displays content above and below the exclusion but leaves the sides blank.

You declare an exclusion shape using the `shape-inside` and `shape-outside` properties, which define the content and the general shape of an exclusion, respectively.

Currently, CSS Exclusions do not work reliably in any of the major browsers. If you want to experiment with CSS Exclusions, try Internet Explorer 10. To use any CSS Exclusions properties for rendering in Internet Explorer 10, add the `-ms-` vendor prefix. Microsoft also uses the `-ms-wrap-side` and `-ms-flow-wrap` properties, which aren't part of the W3C specification.

 EXPLORE CSS EXCLUSIONS PROPERTIES

GET READY. To explore CSS Exclusions properties, perform the following steps:

1. Using a Web browser, go to the W3C "CSS Exclusions and Shapes Module Level 3" Web page at http://dev.w3.org/csswg/css3-exclusions/.
2. Browse the examples of CSS Exclusions.
3. In Internet Explorer 10, copy the code from an example that interests you, create a proper HTML document, and test the file in Internet Explorer 10.

4. Visit the Microsoft Positioned Floats test drive at http://bit.ly/lQulDB. Access the page using each of the major browsers. Select each setting one at a time to see the effects.

5. Close any open files and programs.

➕ MORE INFORMATION

To learn more about CSS Exclusions, visit the W3C "CSS Exclusions and Shapes Module Level 3" Web page at http://dev.w3.org/csswg/css3-exclusions/. The Microsoft "Exclusions" Web page at http://bit.ly/ImadRV provides information on CSS Exclusions and Microsoft-specific properties for Windows 8 and Internet Explorer 10 applications.

SKILL SUMMARY

IN THIS LESSON YOU LEARNED:

- Content flow has, historically, been a manual procedure in HTML documents. Today, CSS Regions, CSS Exclusions, and multi-column layouts help you flow content dynamically.
- CSS Regions lets you flow content between neighboring or distant areas in an HTML document.
- To create and work with CSS Regions, you need to identify a content source and create content containers. You accomplish both tasks using the flow-into and flow-from CSS properties.
- CSS3 enables you to create multiple columns—newspaper style—in HTML documents that scale based on the user's screen size.
- Hyphenation breaks words between syllables at the end of lines to create a more uniform right margin and eliminate gaps of whitespace within paragraphs.
- A positioned float is a CSS construct that enables you to position images, text, and boxes anywhere in an HTML document and then wrap text completely around these elements. Positioned floats are called CSS Exclusions in the latest W3C specification.

■ Knowledge Assessment

Fill in the Blank

Complete the following sentences by writing the correct word or words in the blanks provided.

1. _____ are defined areas of an HTML document where content can flow. They're used instead of multiple columns in more complex layouts.

2. CSS3 properties for _____ let you create columns by dividing text across multiple columns, specify the amount of space that appears between columns (the gap), make vertical lines (rules) appear between columns, and define where columns break.

3. A _____ may be one or more blocks of text in the same or a separate HTML document that holds the content you want to flow through a CSS Regions layout.

4. _____ are the part of CSS Regions into which content is flowed.

5. _____ is the process of connecting two words with a hyphen mark (-) or breaking words between syllables at the end of a line.

6. A _____ is a positioned float that enables you to position images, text, and boxes anywhere in an HTML document and then wrap text completely around these elements.

7. The _____ CSS property creates a content container for CSS Regions.

8. The _____ CSS property identifies the content source for CSS Regions.

9. A(n) _____ is a mini HTML document embedded in an HTML document.

10. The value of the `flow-into` property is called a _____.

Multiple Choice

Circle the letter that corresponds to the best answer.

1. You are creating a CSS Regions content source named "main." Which of the following is the correct syntax?
   a. `flow-from: main`
   b. `flow-into: main`
   c. `main: flow-into`
   d. `main: flow-from`

2. You are creating a CSS Regions content container to be associated with a content source named "main." Which of the following is the correct syntax?
   a. `flow-from: main`
   b. `flow-into: main`
   c. `main: flow-into`
   d. `main: flow-from`

3. What are the options for handling overflow text in the last container of a CSS region? (Choose all that apply.)
   a. Truncation
   b. Continue overflowing and be visible
   c. Continue overflowing but be hidden
   d. Duplication

4. How does Microsoft's implementation of CSS Regions differ from the W3C's specification?
   a. Microsoft uses the `flow-into` property.
   b. Microsoft uses the `flow-from` property.
   c. Microsoft does not use iframes.
   d. Microsoft uses iframes.

5. Which CSS3 property creates scalable columns?
   a. `column-count`
   b. `add-columns`
   c. `wrap-columns`
   d. none of the above

6. Which CSS3 property creates a line between columns in a multi-column layout?
   a. `break-inside`
   b. `column-fill`
   c. `column-gap`
   d. `column-rule`

7. Which of the following is *not* a legal value for the CSS3 hyphens property?
   a. `none`
   b. `lines`
   c. `manual`
   d. `auto`

8. Which of the following specifies the width of the trailing whitespace that can be left in a line before hyphenation occurs?
   a. -ms-hyphenate-limit-chars
   b. -ms-hyphenate-limit-lines
   c. -ms-hyphenate-limit-zone
   d. none of the above

9. Which of the following is the formerly used term for CSS Exclusions?
   a. left/right floats
   b. positioned floats
   c. shape changer
   d. the DOM

10. Which CSS3 property creates a CSS exclusion?
    a. wrap-flow
    b. flow-wrapper
    c. shape-wrapper
    d. wrapper-shape

True / False

Circle T if the statement is true or F if the statement is false.

T | F 1. A CSS Exclusion must be either rectangular or circular in shape.

T | F 2. You must declare a language using the HTML lang or XML xml:lang attributes for correct automatic hyphenation to occur.

T | F 3. You can center a heading across multiple columns using the column-span: all property.

T | F 4. You combine CSS Regions with CSS layout techniques, such as columns, flexboxes, and grid layouts.

T | F 5. In CSS Regions, the value for the flow-from property must match the value of the flow-into property.

■ Competency Assessment

Scenario 6-1: Flowing Content in a Newsletter

Changpu is fellow intern at Malted Milk Media. He was asked by his manager to create a newsletter layout using HTML5 and CSS3. The newsletter will be viewed by employees using PCs, tablets, and possibly smartphones. Changpu created a template with sections, articles, a header and footer, and asides. He wants some items to automatically move overflow content to different areas of the layout, but he's not sure how to do it. How do you advise him?

Scenario 6-2: Distinguishing between Content Source and Content Containers

Changpu decided to use CSS Regions to provide dynamic content flow in his newsletter, but he's confused about content sources and content containers. How do you explain the two features to Changpu?

Proficiency Assessment

Scenario 6-3: Understanding Hyphenation Requirements

Salih is a friend of yours from college. He is creating an HTML document that has content in Arabic for his language skills group, and he wants the document to be hyphenated. He used the hyphens property and is viewing the document in a supported Web browser, but the hyphenation isn't working. Is there something else Salih needs to do to the document?

Scenario 6-4: Understanding CSS Exclusions Essentials

Gladys just transferred to the Web and application development team from the Web site maintenance team. She is just beginning to research CSS Exclusions and saw you walking past her work area. She stops and asks you for a jumpstart on basic information on CSS Exclusions properties.

Managing the Graphical Interface by Using CSS

EXAM OBJECTIVE MATRIX

SKILLS/CONCEPTS	MTA EXAM OBJECTIVE	MTA EXAM OBJECTIVE NUMBER
Managing the Graphical Interface with CSS	Manage the graphical interface by using CSS.	3.4

KEY TERMS

animation

border-radius property

drop shadow

gradient

keyframe

linear gradient

opacity

perspective

radial gradient

rotate

scale

skew

SVG filter

transform

transition

translate

transparency

Web Open Font Format (WOFF)

Web safe

The Malted Milk Media development team is ready to freshen its own Web site with a more contemporary look and feel. They've asked you to review the major areas of the site and suggest graphical enhancements that are based on CSS3 and will help Malted Milk stand apart from the competition.

Managing the Graphical Interface with CSS

THE BOTTOM LINE

New properties in CSS3 provide an easy means to a more graphical and appealing user interface for Web sites and applications.

CSS3 enables you to create stunning graphical elements for Web sites and applications, which ratchet up the satisfaction of the user experience. You can create graphics effects such as rounded corners and drop shadows, and apply 2D and 3D transformations like rotations and

CERTIFICATION READY
In what ways can you manage the graphical user interface with CSS?
3.4

scaling. Transitions and animations, performed completely with HTML and CSS3, bring life to otherwise static images, boxes, and text.

In addition, many of the same CSS3 properties apply to canvas figures, and SVG comes with a comprehensive set of filters that produce similar effects as CSS3 properties.

Creating Graphics Effects

CSS3 provides the `border-radius` property to create rounded corners, the `box-shadow` property for drop-shadows, the `opacity` property for transparency effects, and `linear-gradient` and `radial-gradient` properties for background gradients.

CERTIFICATION READY
Which new graphics effects can you create with CSS3?
3.4

CSS3 enables you to easily apply several new graphics effects to HTML elements, making the user interface more appealing. Some of the new graphics effects include rounded corners, drop-shadows, transparency, and background gradients. You can even apply some of these properties, like shadows, to text.

CERTIFICATION READY
Which CSS property creates rounded corners around layout elements?
3.4

CREATING ROUNDED CORNERS

You use the CSS3 **border-radius property** to create rounded corners around layout elements, like headers, footers, sidebars, graphics boxes, and outlines around images. `border-radius` is a length, which is usually expressed in pixels or ems but can be a percentage. The length is the radius of the circle that defines the "roundedness" of each box corner. The lower the number, the less rounded the corner. Some browsers have problems rendering the percentage properly, so use a pixel or em length whenever possible.

To create a box with a rounded border, the CSS code and markup might look like this:

```
<!doctype html>
<html>
<head>
  <meta charset="utf-8" />
<title>Rounded Corners</title>
<style type="text/css">
div {
  padding: 40px 40px;
  background: dodgerblue;
  width: 400px;
  color: #fff;
  font-family: sans-serif;
  font-size: xx-large;
  border-radius: 25px;
  margin-left: auto;
  margin-right: auto;
  margin-top: 100px;
}
</style>
</head>

<body>
  <div>A box with rounded corners</div>
</body>
</html>
```

The rounded box renders in a Web browser as shown in Figure 7-1.

Figure 7-1

A box with four rounded corners

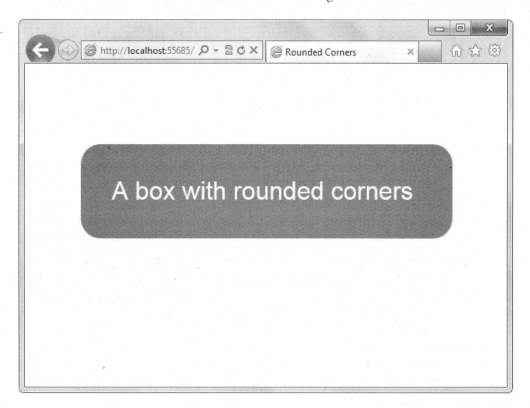

You can also round a single corner of a box using the following properties:

- `border-top-left-radius`
- `border-top-right-radius`
- `border-bottom-right-radius`
- `border-bottom-left-radius`

Figure 7-2 shows an example of each box.

Figure 7-2

Boxes with one rounded corner each

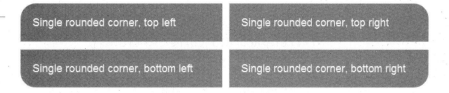

If you plan to use single rounded corners on several elements in an HTML document, you can save time by creating a separate class for each (top left, top right, bottom left, and bottom right). The syntax would look similar to the following:

```
.top-left-corner { border-top-left-radius:25px; }
```

TAKE NOTE *

The Microsoft "Hands-on: border-radius" Web page at http://ie.microsoft.com/testdrive/ Graphics/hands-on-css3/hands-on_border-radius.htm lets you see how changes made to the border-radius length affect a box's corners.

CREATING SHADOWS

CSS3 introduces the box-shadow property to create drop shadows around layout elements. A *drop shadow* is a visual effect in which an object is repeated behind and slightly below itself to create the illusion that the object floats over its background.

CERTIFICATION READY
Which CSS property creates drop shadows around layout elements?
3.4

The CSS syntax for creating a shadow is:

```
box-shadow: h-shadow v-shadow blur spread color inset;
```

The *h-shadow* and *v-shadow* attributes indicate the horizontal and vertical position of the shadow in relation to the box. Both of these attributes are required. The *h-shadow* value defines the horizontal offset of the shadow. A positive value offsets the shadow to the right of the element, and a negative value to the left. The *v-shadow* value defines the vertical offset of the shadow. A positive value offsets the shadow from the bottom of the element, and a negative value from the top.

The remaining attributes are optional. The `blur` attribute, in pixels, indicates the amount of blur applied to the shadow. The `spread` attribute indicates the size of the shadow, color specifies the color of the drop shadow, and `inset` moves the shadow from the outside to the inside of the box.

Figure 7-3 shows an example of the rounded-corners box with a drop shadow. The shadow was created from these values, which specify the horizontal and vertical shadow position, the amount of blur, and the color of the shadow:

```
box-shadow: 10px 10px 5px #808080;
```

Figure 7-3

A drop shadow applied to a box

A box with a drop shadow

CSS3 also provides the `text-shadow` property to apply shadowing to text. The attributes are the same as the `box-shadow` property, except that `spread` and `inset` are not included.

CREATE A BOX WITH ROUNDED CORNERS AND A SHADOW

GET READY. To create a box with rounded corners and a shadow, perform the following steps:

1. In an editing or app development tool, create an HTML document that includes the following content:

```
<!doctype html>
<html>
<head>
  <meta charset="utf-8" />
  <title>Rounded Corners</title>
<style type="text/css">
div {
    border: 3px solid #000;
    background-color: #000;
    padding: 1em;
    width: 300px;
    border-radius: 8px;
    margin-left: auto;
    margin-right: auto;
    margin-top: 100px;
    color: #fff;
    font-family: sans-serif;
    font-size: large;
    text-align: center;
}
</style>
</head>
```

```
<body>
  <div>A box example</div>
</body>
</html>
```

2. Save the file as **L7-box-exercise.html**. View the file in a Web browser, which should look similar to Figure 7-4.

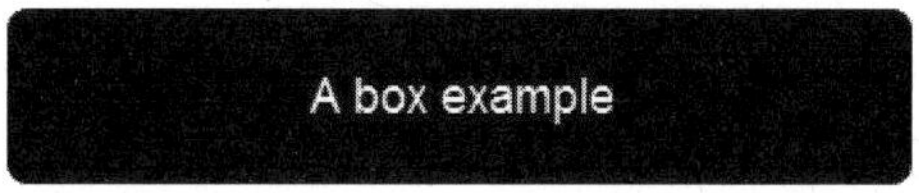

Figure 7-4
A box with rounded corners

3. To add a drop shadow, add the following line to the style element:

```
box-shadow: 5px 5px 5px #999;
```

4. Save the file and view the results in a Web browser. The box should resemble Figure 7-5.

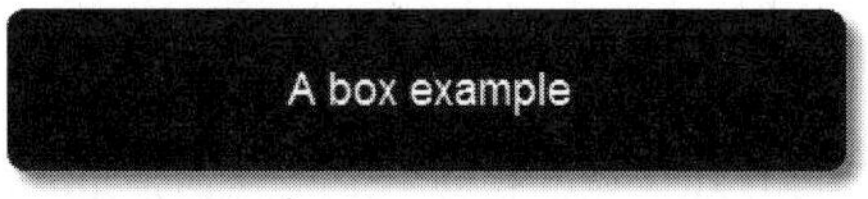

Figure 7-5
A box with rounded corners and a drop shadow

5. Leave the file, editing tool, and Web browser open if you complete the next exercise during this session.

APPLYING TRANSPARENCY

An opaque item does not let light pass through, whereas you can see through a transparent item. Even though the terms are opposite, by reducing the opacity of an item or increasing its transparency, you eventually reach the same point.

Figure 7-6 shows the effect of ***transparency*** (or reduced ***opacity***) on an image. The original image is on the left; the image with a 50% transparency applied is on the right.

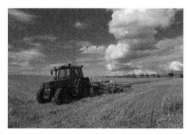

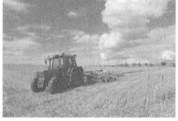

Original   With transparency

Illustrations: © AVTG/iStockphoto

Figure 7-6
Transparency applied to an image

CERTIFICATION READY
Which CSS property enables you to apply a transparency to an image or element?
3.4

The syntax for applying a transparency to an image or other element is:

```
opacity: value
```

The value is a floating-point value between 0.0 (100% transparent) and 1.0 (100% opaque). To apply a 45% transparency, for example, you would use the value 0.55 (1.0 – 0.45).

ADD TRANSPARENCY TO A BOX

GET READY. To add transparency to a box, perform the following steps:

1. Open **L7-box-exercise.html** in an editing or app development tool, if it isn't already open.

2. Add the following line to the style element:

   ```
   opacity: 0.6;
   ```

3. Save the file as **L7-tranparency-exercise.html** and view the results in a Web browser. The box should resemble Figure 7-7.

Figure 7-7

A rounded-corner box, with a drop shadow and 40% transparency

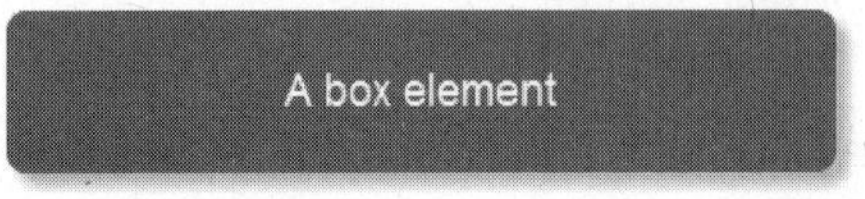

A box element

4. Leave the file, editing tool, and Web browser open if you complete the next exercise during this session.

APPLYING BACKGROUND GRADIENTS

A *gradient* is a smooth change of colors, either within the same hue, such as from dark green to light green, or starting with one color and ending with a different color, such as starting with blue and ending with yellow. Developers commonly use gradients for subtle shading within backgrounds, buttons, and more.

The different types, or methods, of CSS3 gradients are:

- `linear-gradient`: Creates a gradient from top to bottom or vice versa, or from corner to corner

- `radial-gradient`: Creates a gradient that radiates out from a central point

- `repeating-linear-gradient`: Creates a repeating linear gradient, which results in straight bands of gradient color

- `repeating-radial-gradient`: Creates a repeating radial gradient, which results in circular bands of gradient color

To apply a gradient to an HTML image, use the `background` property with one of the gradient methods listed above, along with the parameters specific to each method. The possible values for the methods are listed on the W3C "CSS Image Values and Replaced Content Module Level 3" Web page at http://dev.w3.org/csswg/css3-images/#repeating-gradients.

A *linear gradient* is a horizontal, vertical, or diagonal gradient. To create a linear gradient from black to white, use the following CSS code:

```
background: linear-gradient(black, white);
```

The default gradient goes from top to bottom. You can insert "top," "bottom," "right," or "left" as the first value to control the direction of the gradient. Figure 7-8 shows the black-to-white gradient that spans from top to bottom.

Figure 7-8

A linear gradient from black (top) to white (bottom)

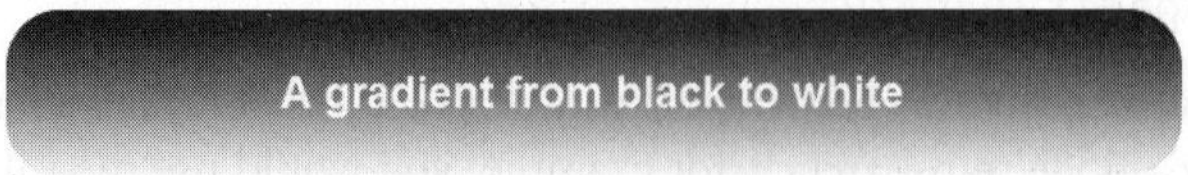

A gradient from black to white

A diagonal gradient is a type of linear gradient that extends from one corner of a container diagonally to another corner. The code for a diagonal gradient that starts in the lower-left corner and extends to the upper-right corner of a container is:

```
background: linear-gradient(45deg, white, black);
```

CSS3 gradients also support color interpolation in the alpha color space, which is part of the red blue green alpha (RGBA) color model, to produce smoother color transitions in gradients. (You've probably seen some gradients where you can readily see the transition from one shade to the next—they look like thin bands of color. Color interpolation in the alpha color space eliminates the "bandy" look.) You can specify multiple color stops, with an RGBA color and position for each one.

The following is an example of the use of rgba colors:

```
linear-gradient(to right, rgba(255,255,255,0)
```

Radial gradients start from a central point and radiate color out to the edges of a container. The values for radials differ slightly from linear gradients. The general syntax for radial gradients is:

```
radial-gradient(position,size and shape,color stops);
```

Let's look at an example of a radial gradient that begins with light blue (indicated by the hexidecimal code #99CCFF) at the center and changes to a darker blue (indicated by #3D5266) at the edges. The code might look like the following, which renders in a browser as shown in Figure 7-9.

```
radial-gradient(50% 50%, 70% 70%, #99CCFF, #3D5266);
```

Figure 7-9

A radial gradient

The first set of percentages (50% 50%) defines the horizontal and vertical center values. In this case, the gradient starts in the center of the element. The second set of percentages (70% 70%) specifies the size and shape of the gradient. Because a radial gradient resembles an ellipse, the percentages refer to radii. The hexadecimal codes in the example are the color stops; the first color stop is the starting point and the second color stop is the ending point.

TAKE NOTE* You might see the background-image property in some sources; it works the same as the shorthand background property.

APPLY A BACKGROUND GRADIENT TO A BOX

GET READY. To apply a background gradient to a box, perform the following steps:

1. Open **L7-tranparency-exercise.html** in an editing or app development tool, if it isn't already open.

2. Add the following lines to the style element:

```
background: linear-gradient(black,white);
background: -ms-linear-gradient(black,white);
background: -moz-linear-gradient(black,white);
background: -o-linear-gradient(black,white);
background: -webkit-linear-gradient(black,white);
```

TAKE NOTE *

Notice the use of vendor prefixes in this code. By including all of the major vendor prefixes, your HTML document is more likely to be rendered properly by the largest number of users. As a reminder from Lesson 5, however, including all four vendor prefixes in your code doesn't guarantee the CSS3 feature will work within all of the browsers. A browser that doesn't support a certain feature will not display the feature properly, even with a vendor prefix. Some browsers offer partial support for a feature, which can produce mixed results. During the transition to CSS3, you should test your code in all of the major browsers before using a certain feature in HTML/CSS documents that will be displayed to a wide audience.

4. Remove the border (not border radius), opacity, and box shadow lines from the CSS.

5. Save the file as **L7-gradient-exercise.html** and view the file in various Web browsers. Do all of the browsers display the gradient? The box should resemble Figure 7-10 in any browser that supports linear gradients.

Figure 7-10

A box with a background gradient applied

A box element

6. Close the file and the Web browsers but leave the editing tool open if you plan to complete the next exercise during this session.

+ MORE INFORMATION

The Microsoft "Explore new ideas in website design and layout" Web page at http://bit.ly/KtYr1W provides links to information on creating rounded corners, drop-shadows, and much more. The W3C "CSS Color Module Level 3" Web page at http://www.w3.org/TR/css3-color/ provides the specification for color properties and opacity. You can also visit the W3schools.com Web site and search for "CSS3" and the topic of your choice.

Understanding Typography and the Web Open Font Format

Web developers are beginning to use the Web Open Font Format (WOFF) as a way to enhance UIs with just about any font available or custom-created fonts. The flexibility to use any font is a big change from the pre-WOFF restrictions on font usage in HTML documents.

Typography is the art of arranging type, historically in printed matter, and fonts play a prominent role in typography. You use CSS font-related properties such as `font-family`, `font-size`, `font-style`, `font-variant`, and `font-weight` to style HTML documents. For years, Web and application developers have been limited to a set of standard fonts that are considered *Web safe*, which means they are typically located on a user's computer and therefore render consistently in the majority of browsers.

Web-safe fonts don't work in every situation. For example, many companies use particular fonts as part of their brand identity, which aren't often part of the Web-safe font set. Designers and developers strive to make sites look interesting, more appealing, and unique, which can't always be accomplished with Web-safe fonts.

X REF

Lesson 4 discusses the CSS-related aspects of typography, such as fonts, font families, monospace, and the @font-face rule.

To use a non-standard font in a heading, title, or block of text, developers have had to create the content in a page layout or graphics program, save it as an image, and then use the `<img>` tag in an HTML document. This method has several drawbacks:

- It's time-consuming.
- It interferes with accessibility page readers; images of text cannot be read aloud.
- It reduces the effectiveness of search engine optimization (SEO) because search engines look for text, not images of text.

CERTIFICATION READY
What is the purpose of the Web Open Font Format (WOFF)?
3.4

Developers have also used embedded fonts, which are font sets loaded on their servers. The designer inserts a link to the font set within an HTML document or CSS file, which helps the browser render the font properly. Although embedded fonts are still widely used, a new and better technique for handling non-standard fonts is WOFF.

The ***Web Open Font Format (WOFF)*** is a means of bringing better typography to the Web. WOFF allows Web developers to use custom fonts—pretty much any font—instead of being limited to the standard Web fonts. WOFF files are compressed True Type, OpenType, or Open Font Format fonts that contain additional metadata.

To use WOFF, you can host fonts on your server or use a Web font service. Free fonts are available from a variety of sources like fontsquirrel and the Open Font Library. Font services include FontFont and FontShop, among others. They require a paid subscription, which gives you full rights to use the font on your Web site as long as the subscription is current.

To use a WOFF font from a font vendor's site, for example, include the `@font-face` rule in the CSS file, similar to the following:

```
<style>
@font-face {
        font-family: "font-family-name";
        src: url("http://website/fonts/fontfile")
        }
</style>
```

Some WOFF fonts work better than others depending on the browser in which they're being viewed. For example, where one Web browser might render the font perfectly, another browser might display the font bitmapped or with inappropriate boldface. Before purchasing a WOFF font or font package, be sure to research the font on the Web to find out if other developers have had any problems using it. Some font vendors provide a way for you to preview fonts in all of the major browsers before purchase.

➕ MORE INFORMATION

The WOFF specification is on the W3C Web site at http://www.w3.org/TR/WOFF/. For an easier read about WOFF, visit the "Fonts on the Web" page at http://www.w3.org/Fonts/ and the "WOFF Frequently Asked Questions" page at http://www.w3.org/Fonts/WOFF-FAQ.html.

Applying 2D and 3D Transformations

The CSS3 transform property translates, scales, rotates, skews, and even spins 2D and 3D elements.

In HTML5/CSS3, a ***transform*** is an effect that lets you change the size, shape, and position of an element. Transformations are either 2D or 3D, and include translating (moving), scaling, rotating, skewing (stretching), and spinning elements.

You use the CSS transform property to specify different kinds of transformations made to HTML elements. The transform property uses several methods for 2D and 3D transformations, as listed in Table 7-1.

TAKE NOTE ✱
JavaScript or some other form of scripting would be required to actually see a 2D or 3D transformation taking place. Without scripting, you only view the end result of a transformation.

Table 7-1

Methods for the transform property

VALUE	DESCRIPTION
matrix (n,n,n,n,n,n)	Specifies a 2D transformation using a six-value matrix
matrix3d (n,n,n,n,n,n,n, n,n,n,n,n,n,n,n,n)	Specifies a 3D transformation using a 4x4 matrix of 16 values
perspective(n)	Specifies a perspective view for a 3D element that's been transformed
rotate (angle)	Rotates an element in 2D
rotate3d (x,y,z,angle)	Rotates an element in 3D
rotateX (angle)	Rotates an element in 3D along the x-axis
rotateY (angle)	Rotates an element in 3D along the y-axis
rotateZ (angle)	Rotates an element in 3D along the z-axis
scale (x,y)	Scales an element in 2D (width and height)
scale3d (x,y,z)	Scales an element in 3D (width, height, and an arbitrary vector in 3D space)
scaleX (x)	Scales an element in 3D along the x-axis
scaleY (y)	Scales an element in 3D along the y-axis
scaleZ (z)	Scales an element in 3D along the z-axis (a vector in 3D space)
skew (x-angle,y-angle)	Skews an element in 2D along the x-axis and the y-axis
skewX (angle)	Skews an element in 3D along the x-axis
skewY (angle)	Skews an element in 3D along the y-axis
translate (x,y)	Translates (moves) an element in 2D
translate3d (x,y,z)	Translates (moves) an element in 3D
translateX (x)	Translates an element in 3D using the x-axis
translateY (y)	Translates an element in 3D using the y-axis
translateZ (z)	Translates an element in 3D using the z-axis

Now that you understand the essence of 2D and 3D transformations, let's look at some specific examples.

CERTIFICATION READY
Which CSS property transforms elements?
3.4

CERTIFICATION READY
What does it mean to translate an element?
3.4

2D TRANSLATION

To *translate* an element means to move it, without rotating, skewing, or otherwise turning the image. To move an element, you use the `translate()` method in CSS and provide x- and y-axis values to position the element relative to its original or default position. The x-axis value specifies the left position of the element, and the y-axis value specifies the top position. For example, the following code moves the element 100 pixels from the left and 50 pixels from the top:

```
transform: translate(100px,50px);
```

An example of a translated element is shown in Figure 7-11.

2D SCALING

To *scale* an element is to increase or decrease its size. To grow or shrink an element dynamically, you use the `scale()` method in CSS and provide x-axis (width) and y-axis (height) values. For example, the following code increases the width of the element two times its original size, and increases the height four times its original size:

```
transform: scale(2,4);
```

An example of a scaled element is shown in Figure 7-12.

➡ **TRANSLATE AND SCALE A 2D SHAPE**

GET READY. To translate and scale a 2D shape, perform the following steps:

1. In an editing or app development tool, create an HTML document that includes the following content:

```
<!doctype html>
<html>
<head>
    <meta charset="utf-8" />
    <title></title>
<style type="text/css">
div
{
padding: 20px 20px;
background: tomato;
width: 150px;
height: 75px;
color: #fff;
font-family: sans-serif;
font-size: x-large;
}
</style>
</head>
```

```
<body>
<div>This element can move</div>
</body>
```

2. Save the file as **L7-translate-exercise.html** and view it in at least two different Web browsers. The box should appear in the upper-left corner of the browser windows.

3. Add the following lines to the style element:

```
transform: translate(200px,100px);
-ms-transform: translate(200px,100px);
-moz-transform: translate(200px,100px);
-o-transform: translate(200px,100px);
-webkit-transform: translate(200px,100px);
```

4. Save the file and view it in the same Web browsers. The box should have moved down and to the right.

5. To scale the box so that it's twice as wide and twice as tall as the original box, add `scale(2,2)` to the transform lines, as follows:

```
transform: translate(200px,100px) scale(2,2);
-ms-transform: translate(200px,100px) scale(2,2);
-moz-transform: translate(200px,100px) scale(2,2);
-o-transform: translate(200px,100px) scale(2,2);
-webkit-transform: translate(200px,100px) scale(2,2);
```

6. Change the div text to read **This element can scale**.

7. Save the file as **L7-scale-exercise.html** and view it in the Web browsers. The display should look similar to Figure 7-13.

Figure 7-13

The box has moved and is twice as large as the original box

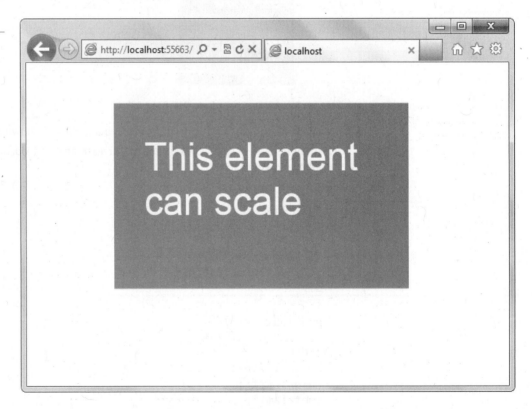

8. Close the file but leave the editing tool and Web browsers open if you plan to complete the next exercise during this session.

2D AND 3D ROTATION

To ***rotate*** an element turns it clockwise by a specified number of degrees. To rotate an element, you use the `rotate()` method in CSS and specify the degrees of rotation.

For example, the following code rotates an element by 30 degrees in the 2D plane:

```
transform: rotate(30deg);
```

An example of a 2D rotated element is shown in Figure 7-14.

Figure 7-14

The original and the 2D rotated image

CERTIFICATION READY
Which transform method rotates an element in 3D around the x-axis?
3.4

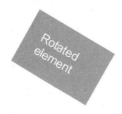

3D rotation uses the `rotateX()` and `rotateY()` methods. With `rotateX()`, the element rotates around its x-axis, and `rotateY()` rotates the element around its y-axis.

The following code rotates an element 180 degrees. If the element contains text, the text would appear upside down after the rotation, as shown in Figure 7-15. Remember, to see the 3D effect occurring requires JavaScript or some other form of scripting; what you see in Figure 7-15 is the end result of the rotation.

```
transform: rotateX(180deg);
```

Figure 7-15

The original and the 3D x-axis rotated image

Using the `rotateY(180deg)` method with an element that display text results in the text appearing backwards, as shown in Figure 7-16.

Figure 7-16

The original and the 3D y-axis rotated image

2D AND 3D SKEWING

To *skew* an element is to stretch it in one or more directions. To skew an element using CSS, you use the skew() method and provide x-axis and y-axis values, in degrees, to create an angular shape. For example, the following code turns an element 20 degrees around the x-axis and 30 degrees around the y-axis:

```
transform: skew(20deg,30deg);
```

An example of a skewed element is shown in Figure 7-17.

Figure 7-17

A skewed element

CERTIFICATION READY
Which transform method skews an element in 3D around the y-axis?
3.4

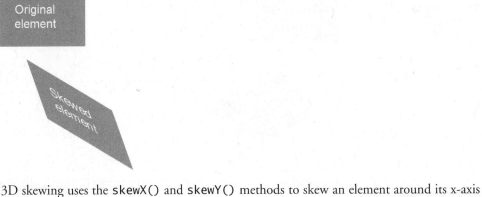

3D skewing uses the skewX() and skewY() methods to skew an element around its x-axis and y-axis, respectively. As an example, the following code skews an element 45 degrees, as shown in Figure 7-18.

```
transform: skewX(45deg);
```

Figure 7-18

A 3D skew around the x-axis

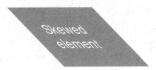

ROTATE AND SKEW A 2D SHAPE

GET READY. To rotate and skew a 2D shape, perform the following steps:

1. Open **L7-scale-exercise.html** in an editing or app development tool, if it isn't already open.
2. Modify the transform lines to replace scale with a 30-degree rotation, as follows:

```
transform: translate(200px,100px) rotate(30deg);
-ms-transform: translate(200px,100px) rotate(30deg);
-moz-transform: translate(200px,100px) rotate(30deg);
-o-transform: translate(200px,100px) rotate(30deg);
-webkit-transform: translate(200px,100px) rotate(30deg);
```

3. Change the div text to read **This element is rotated.**

4. Save the file as **L7-rotate-exercise.html** and view the file in the Web browsers. Are the box and text rotated as shown in Figure 7-19?

Figure 7-19

A box rotated at a 30-degree angle

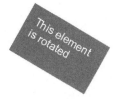

5. To skew the box by 45 degrees, replace rotate with skew in the transform lines, as follows:

```
transform: translate(200px,100px) skew(45deg);
-ms-transform: translate(200px,100px) skew(45deg);
-moz-transform: translate(200px,100px) skew(45deg);
-o-transform: translate(200px,100px) skew(45deg);
-webkit-transform: translate(200px,100px) skew(45deg);
```

6. Change the div text to read **This element is skewed.**
7. Save the file as **L7-skew-exercise.html** and view it in the Web browsers. The display should look similar to Figure 7-20.

Figure 7-20

A box skewed at a 45-degree angle

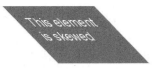

8. Close the file but leave the editing tool and Web browsers open if you plan to complete the next exercise during this session.

UNDERSTANDING 3D PERSPECTIVE, TRANSITIONS, AND ANIMATIONS

CERTIFICATION READY
What is the purpose of the CSS3 3D perspective property?
3.4

Perspective, in terms of drawings and illustrations, is the convergence of lines that give the illusion of depth. The CSS3 3D perspective property defines how a browser renders the depth of a 3D transformed element. The perspective property takes on a number value: lower values (in the range of 1 to 1000) create a more pronounced effect than higher values. Another important thing to remember is that perspective applies only to 3D transformed elements.

The general syntax for perspective is:

```
perspective: number;
```

An example of perspective with a 3D rotation applied is:

```
perspective: 600; margin: 100px 0 0 50px;
transform: rotate3d(0, 1, 1, 45deg);
```

The following is a complete markup example for perspective and is shown in Figure 7-21 using a webkit-supported browser.

```
<!doctype html>
<html>
<head>
<style type="text/css">
div
{
padding: 40px 40px;
background: #B8860B;
width: 150px;
```

```
color: #fff;
font-family: sans-serif;
font-size: xx-large;
}
div#div2
{
margin: 100px;
perspective: 600; margin: 100px 0 0 50px;
-ms-perspective: 600; margin: 100px 0 0 50px;
-moz-perspective: 600; margin: 100px 0 0 50px;
-o-perspective: 600; margin: 100px 0 0 50px;
-webkit-perspective: 600; margin: 100px 0 0 50px;

transform: rotate3d(0, 1, 1, 45deg);
-ms-transform: rotate3d(0, 1, 1, 45deg);
-moz-transform: rotate3d(0, 1, 1, 45deg);
-o-transform: rotate3d(0, 1, 1, 45deg);
-webkit-transform: rotate3d(0, 1, 1, 45deg);
}
</style>
</head>

<body>
    <div>Original element</div>
    <div id="div2">Transformed element</div>
</body>
</html>
```

Figure 7-21

Perspective applied with a 45-degree rotation

Now let's focus on transitions and animation. A **_transition_** is a change from one thing to another; in CSS, a transition is the change in an element from one style to another.

You can think of a gradient as a type of transition in that the background color of a container changes from one color to another. However, a gradient is itself a static thing—it's either present or not. In CSS3, the action of a transition is visible. The changes render onscreen in an animated fashion as if powered by a script, but no scripts are involved.

You use the transition property to create a CSS3 transition. At a minimum, you must specify the CSS property to be acted upon during the transition. This can be an element's position, size, color, background color, letter spacing, rotation, and so on. Most transitions also specify the length (duration) of the transition. If the duration value is not set, the default is 0. You specify CSS3 transitions using the properties described in Table 7-2.

Table 7-2

CSS3 transition properties

PROPERTY	DESCRIPTION
transition	Is the shorthand way to specify settings for transition-property, transition-delay, transition-duration, and transition-timing-function at once
transition-property	Specifies the CSS properties that are to be transitioned
transition-delay	Specifies the amount of time that passes after the value changes and before the transition starts; in seconds or milliseconds
transition-duration	Specifies the length of the transition in seconds or milliseconds; starts after the transition-delay property
transition-timing-function	Specifies the speed curve of the transition effect; allows a transition to change speed over its duration Default value = ease, which starts relatively fast and slows down toward the end

The following is an example of a simple transition that displays text in a box. When a user hovers the mouse pointer over the box, the text changes. Figure 7-22 shows the before and after boxes.

```
<style type="text/css">
#wrapper { transition-property: opacity;
           transition-duration: 3s;
           transition-delay: 1s;
           transition-timing-function: linear; }
#wrapper #before, #wrapper:hover #after {
  opacity: 1; }
#wrapper:hover #before, #wrapper #after {
  opacity: 0; }
</style>
</head>

<body>
<div id="wrapper">
  <div id="before">Now you see me</div>
  <div id="after">Now you don't</div>
</div>
</body>
```

Figure 7-22

This simple transition hides text and displays new text when hovering the mouse pointer

CREATE A TRANSITION USING CSS

GET READY. To create a transition using CSS, perform the following steps:

1. In an editing or app development tool, create an HTML document that includes the following content:

```html
<!doctype html>
<html>
<head>
    <meta charset="utf-8" />
    <title>Transition and Opacity Example</title>
<style type="text/css">
#wrapper {
padding: 40px 40px;
background: dodgerblue;
width: 200px;
font-family: sans-serif;
font-size: xx-large;
margin-left: auto;
margin-right: auto;
margin-top: 100px;
color: #fff;
}

#wrapper #front, #wrapper:hover #back {
opacity:1;
-ms-opacity: 1;
-moz-opacity: 1;
-o-opacity: 1;
-webkit-opacity: 1;

transition-property: opacity;
-ms-transition-property: opacity;
-moz-transition-property: opacity;
-o-transition-property: opacity;
-webkit-transition-property: opacity;

transition-duration: 1s;
-ms-transition-duration: 1s;
-moz-transition-duration: 1s;
-o-transition-duration: 1s;
-webkit-transition-duration: 1s;

transition-timing-function: linear;
-ms-transition-timing-function: linear;
-moz-transition-timing-function: linear;
-o-transition-timing-function: linear;
-webkit-transition-timing-function: linear;
}

#wrapper:hover #front, #wrapper #back {
opacity: 0;
-ms-opacity: 0;
-moz-opacity: 0;
```

```
-o-opacity: 0;
-webkit-opacity: 0;
}
</style>
</head>

<body>
<div id="wrapper">
  <div id="front">Knock knock</div>
  <div id="back">Who's there?</div>
</div>

</body>
</html>
```

2. Save the file as **L7-transition-exercise.html**. Open the file in each of the major Web browsers. Hover your mouse pointer over the box in each browser. The display should look similar to Figure 7-23.

Figure 7-23

A simple transition

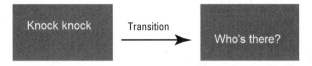

3. To add a delay, enter the following after the transition-duration property lines:

```
transition-delay: 1s;
-ms-transition-delay: 1s;
-moz-transition-delay: 1s;
-o-transition-delay: 1s;
-webkit-transition-delay: 1s;
```

4. Save the file as **L7-transition-delay-exercise.html**. Open the file in each Web browser and hover your mouse pointer over the box. Do you notice the delay?
5. Close the file but leave the editing tool and Web browser open if you plan to complete the next exercise during this session.

An ***animation*** is the display of a sequence of static images at a fast enough speed to create the illusion of movement. Like transitions, animations affect CSS properties and transformations, and you can also specify timings. One difference is that animations use ***keyframes***, a construct that enables you to change values anywhere within the animation. You can also pause, resume, and reverse animations.

CERTIFICATION READY
What is a keyframe?
3.4

To create an animation, you begin by specifying a CSS style within the `@keyframes` rule. For example, a rule for a fadeout might look like the following:

```
@keyframes fadeout {
from { opacity: 1; }
to { opacity: 0; }
}
```

Then you specify the animation's properties. Many of the properties used in animations are similar to transitions. The animation properties are described in Table 7-3.

Table 7-3

CSS3 animation properties

Property	Default Value	Description
@keyframes		Creates the animation
animation		Is a shorthand way to specify all animation properties at once, other than the animation-play-state property
animation-name		Specifies the @keyframes animation name
animation-duration	0	Specifies the length of an animation; in seconds or milliseconds
animation-timing-function	ease	Specifies how the animation progresses during one cycle
animation-delay	0	Specifies when the animation starts
animation-iteration-count	1	Specifies the number of cycles of an animation
animation-fill-mode	none	Specifies the values applied by the animation outside the time it executes
animation-direction	normal	Specifies whether the animation plays in reverse on alternate cycles
animation-play-state	running	Specifies the state of the animation; values are running or paused

The following is a snippet of code that configures animation properties for a fadeout:

```
div { animation-duration: 3s;
      animation-delay: 0s;
      animation-timing-function: ease; }
div:hover { animation-name: fadeout; }
```

This fadeout starts immediately when the user hovers the mouse pointer over a div element, lasts for three seconds, and uses and ease timing function.

X REF

Lesson 9 shows you how to create animation using JavaScript.

 CREATE AN ANIMATION USING CSS

GET READY. To create an animation using CSS, perform the following steps:

1. In an editing or app development tool, create an HTML document that includes the following content:

```
<style type="text/css">
div { width: 200px;
      height: 200px;
      background: limegreen;
      animation: a1 3s; }

@keyframes a1 { from {background: limegreen;}
                to {background: dodgerblue;} }
</style>
</head>
```

```
<body>
<div></div>
</body>
```

2. Save the file as **L7-animation-exercise.html**. Open the file in each of the major Web browsers. The animation consists of a rectangular box that cycles from green to blue and back to green. Did the animation occur in all of the Web browsers? Make a note of which Web browsers support animation.

3. Replace the animation line in the CSS div section with the following:

```
animation-name: a1;
animation-duration: 4s;
animation-delay: 2s;
```

4. Save the file as **L7-animation-mod-exercise.html**. Open the file in the Web browsers in which the animation occurred originally. Do you notice the delay?

5. Close the file but leave the editing tool and Web browser open if you plan to complete the next exercise during this session.

Applying SVG Filter Effects

> SVG filters are a way to style SVG graphics. The long list of filters range from the feBlend filter, which combines images, to feOffset, which moves an image relative to its current position, to several filters that affect the way lighting is calculated in a figure.

Lesson 2 introduced you to SVG, or Scalable Vector Graphics, a language for describing 2D graphics in Extensible Markup Language (XML). You saw a few examples of how to create simple vector images using SVG, and learned that they render well whether viewed on large or small screens.

CERTIFICATION READY
What is the purpose of an SVG filter?
3.4

This section takes a look at filter effects you can apply to SVG graphics. An **SVG filter** is a set of operations that use CSS to style or otherwise modify an SVG graphic. The enhanced graphic is displayed in a browser while the original graphic is left alone. The filters available in SVG are:

- feBlend
- feColorMatrix
- feComponentTransfer
- feComposite
- feConvolveMatrix
- feDiffuseLighting
- feDisplacementMap
- feFlood
- feGaussianBlur
- feImage
- feMerge
- feMorphology
- feOffset

- feTile
- feTurbulence
- feDistantLight
- fePointLight
- feSpecularLighting
- feSpotLight

Many of the filter names are fairly intuitive. For example, the feBlend filter combines images, feColorMatrix filters for color transformations, feOffset moves an image relative to its current position, and the last four in the list filter for lighting.

You use the filter element to define SVG filters; you must include the id attribute to name the filter. For example, the following code is an example feGaussianBlur filter, the results of which are shown in Figure 7-24:

Figure 7-24

A Gaussian blur filter applied to an SVG graphic

```
<body>
<svg>
  <defs>
    <filter id="a1" x="0" y="0">
      <feGaussianBlur in="SourceGraphic"
        stdDeviation="20" />
    </filter>
  </defs>
  <rect width="150" height="150" stroke="plum"
    stroke-width="3" fill="plum" filter="url(#a1)" />
</svg>
</body>
```

The id attribute within the filter element specifies the filter name. The feGaussianBlur element specifies the blur effect. Within this element are in="SourceGraphic", which indicates the entire element will be blurred, and the stdDeviation attribute, which specifies the amount of the blur. The rectangle being created is linked to the filter through the filter="url(#a1)" attribute in the rect element.

In another example, the following feOffset filter creates a drop shadow under a rectangle. A shadow fits the "action" of the offset filter because a shadow is merely a box that has been moved down and to the right of the source image. The dx and dy attributes specify the amount to move the image along the x-axis and y-axis, respectively. The rendered image is shown in Figure 7-25.

Figure 7-25

An offset filter applied to an SVG graphic

```
<body>
<svg>
  <defs>
    <filter id="i1" x="0" y="0">
    <feOffset dx="5" dy="5" />
    </filter>
  </defs>
  <rect width="150" height="150" fill="grey"
   filter="url(#i1)" />
  <rect width="150" height="150" fill="plum" />
</svg>
</body>
```

APPLY AN OFFSET AND GAUSSIAN BLUR TO AN SVG DRAWING

GET READY. To apply an offset and Gaussian blur to an SVG drawing, perform the following steps:

1. In an editing or app development tool, create an HTML document with the following content:

```
<!doctype html>
<html>
<head>
    <meta charset="utf-8" />
    <title>SVG Offset and Gaussian Blur Example</title>
</head>
</style>

<body>
<svg>
  <defs>
    <filter id="i1" x="0" y="0">
    <feOffset dx="5" dy="5" />
    </filter>
  </defs>
  <rect width="150" height="150" fill="grey"
   filter="url(#i1)" />
  <rect width="150" height="150" fill="springgreen"
   />
</svg>
</body>
</html>
```

2. Save the file as **L7-SVGoffset-exercise.html**. Open the file in all of the major Web browsers. The results should look similar to Figure 7-26. Did the image render with an offset in all of the Web browsers? Make a note of which Web browsers support the offset.

Figure 7-26

An SVG graphic with a drop shadow

3. Add the following line in the filter element to apply the Gaussian blur filter:

   `<feGaussianBlur stdDeviation="5" />`

4. Save the file as **L7-SVGgblur-exercise.html** and view it in the Web browsers that support the SVG offset feature. The results should look like Figure 7-27.

Figure 7-27

An SVG graphic with a drop shadow and Gaussian blur applied to the offset

5. Close the file but leave the editing tool and Web browser open if you plan to complete the next exercise during this session.

Using Canvas to Enhance the GUI

You can use CSS properties to add color and gradients, apply transformations and animations, and make other enhancements to canvas object.

In addition to SVG, you learned about the canvas element in Lesson 2. You can use canvas to draw pixel-based shapes. Although the canvas element accepts only two attributes—height and width—you can use most CSS properties to style the canvas element, adding color, gradients, pattern fills, transformation, animation, and much more. This section walks you through some of the stylistic effects you can apply to canvas drawings to enhance the graphical use interface (GUI).

CERTIFICATION READY
How can you use canvas to enhance the graphical user interface?
3.4

The following code creates a basic canvas box:

```
<script>
    function f1() {
        var canvas =
        document.getElementById("smlRectangle");
        context = canvas.getContext("2d");
        context.fillStyle = "blue";
        context.fillRect(10, 20, 200, 100);
    }
</script>

<body onload = "f1();">
<canvas id="smlRectangle" height='300' width='500'>
</canvas>
</body>
```

This sample already uses the `fillStyle` attribute for the `getContext("2d")` object. Let's change the color to apply a gradient with coral as the start color and khaki as the end color. Replace the `fillStyle` line with the following, which render as shown in Figure 7-28:

```
var grd=context.createLinearGradient(0,0,150,0);
grd.addColorStop(0.3,"coral");
grd.addColorStop(0.7,"khaki");
context.fillStyle=grd;
```

Figure 7-28

A canvas object with a gradient applied

To rotate the canvas, you use the formula `degrees*Math.PI/180`. You must also add the rotation before the rectangle is generated. So, to rotate our canvas 20 degrees, add the following line before the `context-fillRect` line:

```
context.rotate(20*Math. PI/180);
```

The result is shown in Figure 7-29. You can also translate (move), scale, and skew the object similar to transforming HTML elements.

Figure 7-29

A canvas object rotated 20 degrees

Finally, let's see how to generate text by using canvas (see Figure 7-30). You use the `fillText` and font methods:

```
<body>
<canvas id="myText" width="400" height="250" style="border:3px
solid #0000FF;">
</canvas>
```

```
<script type="text/javascript">
    var canvas = document.getElementById("myText");
    context = canvas.getContext("2d");
    context.font = "30px Arial";
    context.fillText("Canvas-generated text", 40, 120);
</script>
</body>
```

Figure 7-30

Canvas-generated text surrounded by a border

Canvas-generated text

Whereas the `fillText` method creates solid-filled text in any color (black by default), you can replace `fillText` with `strokeText` to create bordered letters (letters without fill).

 ENHANCE A CANVAS OBJECT

GET READY. To enhance a canvas object, perform the following steps:

1. In an editing or app development tool, create an HTML document that includes the following content:

```
<!doctype html>
<html>
<head>
    <meta charset="utf-8" />
    <title>Canvas Exercise</title>
<script>
    function f1() {
        var canvas =
        document.getElementById("smlRectangle");
        context = canvas.getContext("2d");
        context.fillStyle = "coral";
        context.fillRect(10, 20, 200, 100);
    }
    </script>
    </head>
<body onload = "f1();">
<canvas id="smlRectangle" height='300' width='500'>
</canvas>
</body>
</html>
```

2. Save the file as **L7-canvas-exercise.html**. Open the file in a Web browser to verify that you see a coral-colored rectangle.

3. Replace the solid color with a gradient that starts with light blue and ends with dark blue. To do so, replace the current `fillStyle` line with the following:

```
var grd = context.createLinearGradient(0, 0, 150, 0);
        grd.addColorStop(0.3, "lightblue");
        grd.addColorStop(0.7, "darkblue");
        context.fillStyle = grd;
```

4. Scale the rectangle so that it's five times as wide and five times as tall as the original rectangle. To do so, add the following after the new `fillStyle` line:

```
context.scale(5,5);
```

5. Save the file again and view it in a Web browser. The results should look similar to Figure 7-31.

Figure 7-31

A canvas rectangle with a gradient and scaled to be five times larger than the original

6. Close all files and applications.

SKILL SUMMARY

IN THIS LESSON YOU LEARNED:

- Some of the new graphics effects you can easily achieve with CSS3 are rounded corners, drop shadows, transparency, and background gradients.
- The border-radius property creates rounded corners, the box-shadow property creates drop shadows, the opacity property creates transparency effects, and the background property with one of the four gradient attributes creates linear and radial gradients.
- The Web Open Font Format (WOFF) is a means of bringing better typography to the Web. WOFF allows Web developers to use nearly any font instead of being limited to the standard Web fonts.
- WOFF files are compressed True Type, OpenType, or Open Font Format fonts that contain additional metadata.
- The CSS3 transform property translates, scales, rotates, skews, and even spins 2D and 3D elements.
- Perspective, in terms of drawings and illustrations, is the convergence of lines that give the illusion of depth

- A transition is a change from one thing to another; in CSS, a transition is the change in an element from one style to another.
- An animation is the display of a sequence of static images at a fast enough speed to create the illusion of movement.
- An SVG filter is a set of operations that use CSS to style or otherwise modify an SVG graphic. The enhanced graphic is displayed in a browser while the original graphic is left alone.
- Although the canvas element accepts only two attributes—height and width—you can use most CSS properties to style the canvas element, adding color, gradients, pattern fills, transformation, animation, and much more.

■ Knowledge Assessment

Fill in the Blank

Complete the following sentences by writing the correct word or words in the blanks provided.

1. A _____ is a smooth change of colors, either within the same hue or starting with one color and ending with another.

2. To _____ an element is to increase or decrease its size.

3. A _____ is a visual effect in which an object is repeated behind and moved slightly below itself to create the illusion that the object floats over its background.

4. A _____ is a change from one thing to another; in CSS, it is the change in an element from one style to another.

5. The _____ enables Web developers to use custom fonts—pretty much any font—instead of being limited to the standard Web fonts.

6. The CSS3 _____ property enables you to create rounded corners around layout elements, such as headers, footers, sidebars, graphics boxes, and outlines around images.

7. _____ is reduced opacity.

8. To _____ an element means to move it, without rotating, skewing, or otherwise turning the image.

9. In HTML5/CSS3, a _____ is an effect that lets you change the size, shape, and position of an element.

10. An SVG _____ is a set of operations that use CSS to style or otherwise modify an SVG graphic.

Multiple Choice

Circle the letter that corresponds to the best answer.

1. Which of the following creates a gradient from top to bottom, left to right, or from corner to corner, without reiterating colors?
   a. linear-gradient
   b. radial-gradient
   c. repeating-linear-gradient
   d. repeating-radial-gradient

2. Which of the following is *not* true of the `border-radius` property?
   a. It creates rounded corners around layout elements.
   b. It can be expressed in pixels.
   c. It can be expressed as a percentage.
   d. It can animate an object.

3. To apply a 60% transparency to an image or element, which property do you use?
   a. `opacity: 40`
   b. `opacity: 0.4`
   c. `transparency: 40`
   d. `transparency: 0.4`

4. Which of the following are disadvantages of Web-safe fonts? (Choose all that apply.)
   a. They must be loaded on a Web server.
   b. They are limited in number and variety.
   c. They make brand identity difficult to achieve on the Web.
   d. They are expensive.

5. Keyframes are associated with which of the following?
   a. Rounded corners
   b. Transitions
   c. Animations
   d. None of the above

6. When creating a transition, which of the following must be specified?
   a. A start delay
   b. The CSS property to be acted upon during the transition
   c. The transition timing function
   d. The keyframe

7. What is a primary advantage to using color interpolation in the alpha color space?
   a. It produces smoother color transitions in gradients.
   b. It enables you to add color to SVG drawings.
   c. Both a and b
   d. Neither a nor b

8. Which of the following do you use to add color to canvas text?
   a. `fillStyle`
   b. `strokeStyle`
   c. `textColor`
   d. `strokeColor`

9. What are the two play states of an animation?
   a. started
   b. running
   c. paused
   d. resumed

10. In the following code sample, what controls the amount of blur?

```
<defs>
    <filter id="a1" x="0" y="0">
        <feGaussianBlur in="SourceGraphic"
          stdDeviation="20" />
    </filter>
</defs>
```

   a. `feGaussianBlur`
   b. `SourceGraphic`
   c. `stdDeviation`
   d. none of the above

True / False

Circle T if the statement is true or F if the statement is false.

T | F   **1.** An opaque item does not let light pass through, whereas you can see through a transparent item.

T | F   **2.** In CSS, to rotate an element turns it counterclockwise by a specified number of degrees.

T | F   **3.** An animation is the display of a sequence of static images at a fast enough speed to create the illusion of movement.

T | F   **4.** Radial gradients start from a central point and radiate color out to the edges of a container.

T | F   **5.** Perspective, in terms of drawings and illustrations, is the convergence of lines that give the illusion of depth.

Competency Assessment

Scenario 7-1: Troubleshooting CSS3 Code

Ali is a vintage car enthusiast who restores old cars and sells them for a profit. He posts photos and descriptions on his Web site, which he maintains himself. Ali is transitioning to HTML5 and CSS3 as much as possible. He has been trying to apply the translate and scale transformations to a 2D image on his site but neither transformation is working. This is the code he's using:

```
<style>
img { transform: translate(100px,50px);
      transform: scale(2,4); }
</style>
```

What advice do you give to Ali?

Scenario 7-2: Displaying Before and After Images

Ali's wife Linda thinks his vintage car Web site could use some enhancements to attract more visitors. One of her suggestions is to show before and after photos of the cars that Ali has restored. They ask you what options they have using CSS3 to make it easy on users to see the photos. What do you tell them?

Proficiency Assessment

Scenario 7-3: Creating Buttons with Enhancements

Edward is creating a set of buttons for a Web application and wants the buttons to have rounded corners and a small drop shadow that's slightly blurred. He asks you which CSS3 properties to use. What do you tell him?

Scenario 7-4: Understanding 3D Perspective

Meghan is a university student who is studying for a fine arts degree. She's learning about digital graphics in one of her courses, and a fellow student said he's interested in the CSS3 3D perspective. She hadn't heard of it before, so she asks you to briefly explain it to her. What do you tell her?

Understanding JavaScript and Coding Essentials

EXAM OBJECTIVE MATRIX

SKILLS/CONCEPTS	MTA EXAM OBJECTIVE	MTA EXAM OBJECTIVE NUMBER
Managing and Maintaining JavaScript	Manage and maintain JavaScript.	4.1
Updating the UI by Using JavaScript	Update the UI by using JavaScript.	4.2

KEY TERMS

callback

computer program

dynamic application

event handler

events

function

identifiers

interactivity

JavaScript library

jQuery

library

methods

subroutines

validation

variable

Malted Milk Media has a working, successful mobile application. It's clumsy, though; users must push more keys and wait longer than what's generally acceptable. The development team has decided that JavaScript will go a long way toward making the app more responsive and annoyance-free.

■ Managing and Maintaining JavaScript

THE BOTTOM LINE

HTML5 and CSS3 make a great foundation for your Web site or mobile application. To do anything more than presentation of structured content, though—to respond with individualized data about a specific end user, or transact on-line commerce, or derive results based on data already entered, for instance—takes real programming. JavaScript is a capable programming language with great abilities to express the interactions you want your end users to have with your app.

Think of a service-related mobile application that displays the time of the next service visit to a customer. It offers a hyperlink to telephone a dispatcher in case it's necessary to reschedule. That's a silly thing to do, though, outside business hours when no one will be there to answer. How can the hyperlink change, depending on the time of day?

Any job of this sort—the kind that, for a human worker, requires a decision, or a calculation, or research—is the province of programming. For us, a **computer program** is a recipe we direct the computer to execute that results in a particular display or action. Whereas many Web pages are built to be static in that they look the same for all readers, under all circumstances, JavaScript programming makes applications dynamic and interactive; they adjust and respond to particular end users and the actions of those end users. **Interactivity** enables an end user to take an action in an application, usually by clicking a button or pressing a key. A **dynamic application** adjusts and responds to such actions by end users. JavaScript also expands the opportunities to animate displays, that is, to have parts of the display move and update while an end user watches.

> **CERTIFICATION READY**
> How does JavaScript make an application dynamic and interactive?
> 4.1

With JavaScript programs, several different elements have to cooperate to get the result you're after. JavaScript differs from CSS and HTML in a few key aspects, and you'll learn new concepts to make the best use of JavaScript. HTML and CSS, for example, are largely focused on getting things to *look* a particular way. In JavaScript, more of the attention is on how things *act*. To test a JavaScript program, you often need to look at the display at several moments through time, and perhaps to interact with it.

Even more than with HTML and CSS, your JavaScript work will depend on a development environment you understand and that makes you comfortable. A useful development environment can be as simple as a copy of Notepad and Internet Explorer, or as complex as an Integrated Development Environment (IDE) with built-in editor, debugger, application generator, and so on. While the exercises in this lesson assume the simplest possible tools, they are easy to adapt to fancier facilities.

 TAKE NOTE *

The terms program and script are near synonyms. Some people say "script" to emphasize that a source is small, or not in C or Java, or for even more vaguely defined reasons. Don't worry about the differences. For the purpose of this lesson, the terms program, script, source file, and code are nearly the same.

This lesson focuses on creating JavaScript programs and using functions. You'll learn how to create simple programs from scratch, and use code from JavaScript libraries, jQuery, and other third-party libraries. You'll also learn how to locate and access elements, listen and respond to events, show and hide elements, update the content of elements, and add elements on the fly.

CREATE A SIMPLE JAVASCRIPT PROGRAM

GET READY. To create a simple JavaScript program, perform the following steps:

1. Using an editing or app development tool, create a file with the following content:

```
<!doctype html>
<html>
<head>
<title>My first JavaScript program</title>
</head>
<body>
<h1>My first JavaScript program</h1>
<p>This is text.
<button type = 'button' onclick = "alert('You clicked the
button');">I'm a button; click me</button>
</body>
</html>
```

2. Save the file as **L8-js1.html**.

3. To run the JavaScript program, open **L8-js1.html** in a Web browser. The results should look similar to Figure 8-1.

Figure 8-1

Your first JavaScript program

If the JavaScript program doesn't display, you need to enable JavaScript in your Web browser's preference settings. In Internet Explorer 9, for example, select **Tools > Internet options**. In the Internet Options dialog box, click the **Security** tab. Click the **Custom level** or **Default level** button, whichever is available. In the Security Settings dialog box, scroll down to the **Scripting** section (see Figure 8-2). Click the **Enable** radio button under Active scripting, and then click **OK** twice to close the dialog boxes. Try opening the **L8-js1.html** file again in your Web browser to run the JavaScript program.

Figure 8-2

Checking JavaScript settings in Internet Explorer

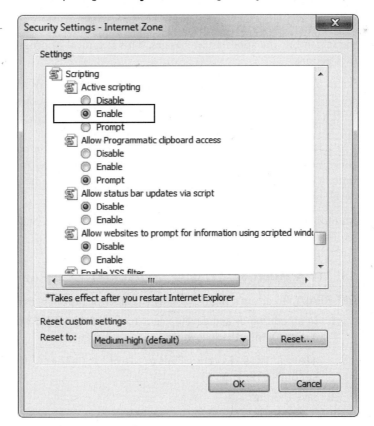

4. Click the button you created in JavaScript that's shown on the screen. An alert box displays, as shown in Figure 8-3. This indicates your JavaScript program is working properly.

 XREF

In previous lessons, you learned the basics of editing HTML markup and CSS code and viewing the resulting display. Use the same skills to work with JavaScript.

5. Click **OK** to close the alert box.
6. Leave the HTML file, editing tool, and Web browser open if you plan to complete the next exercise during this session.

This is your first JavaScript program. Not only does it have a particular appearance on the screen but the appearance changes. This is typical of programs: they respond to user actions.

It's an unusual program, though, in that the JavaScript part of it is nearly invisible. Do you see the JavaScript program? It's the single fragment within quotes, as follows:

```
alert('You clicked the button');
```

The `alert()` itself is too intrusive to appear in production code released for use by consumers, and thus almost never appears in reference documentation. At the same time, it's the simplest way to start with JavaScript and can be exceedingly useful during development or debugging.

An ordinary JavaScript program is a sequence of statements. Statements are separated by semi-colons, as you'll see in the next exercise.

CREATE A MULTI-STATEMENT JAVASCRIPT PROGRAM

GET READY. To create a multi-statement JavaScript program, perform the following steps:

1. In an editing or app development tool, update **L8-js1.html** by replacing the `alert()` with the following:

```
alert('This is the first alert'); alert('This is the
second alert');
```

2. Save the file.

3. Run the updated JavaScript program by opening the HTML file in a Web browser.

4. When the first alert box displays, close it by clicking **OK**. The JavaScript program proceeds to its next statement, that is, the second alert. The second alert is shown in Figure 8-4.

Figure 8-4

The second alert box becomes visible only after the first one has been dismissed

5. Close the second alert box by clicking **OK**.

6. Close the HTML file, but leave the editing tool and Web browser open if you plan to complete the next exercise during this session.

+ MORE INFORMATION

For more details about JavaScript, visit the W3schools.com JavaScript Web page at http://www.w3schools.com/js/default.asp. For information about Microsoft and JavaScript, search for **msdn javascript** using your favorite search engine.

Creating and Using Functions

A function is a segment of a program defined and performed in isolation from other parts. The action of a function is the sequence of the actions of the statements inside of it.

In principle, an entire JavaScript program could be written with one statement following another in the exact sequence they should execute. Programmers have found, however, that it is useful to introduce symbols, or names, for special parts of a program.

The first such part is a function. In programming, a ***function*** is a segment of a program defined and performed in isolation from other parts. Think for a moment of a cooking recipe. There is no need in each written recipe to explain all the steps involved in extraction of an egg white from an egg; a conventional recipe simply writes, "add one egg white" and assumes that the reader knows to look elsewhere for a detailed "implementation," or directions on how best to choose an egg, crack open the egg, separate its parts, and so on.

In the kitchen, it might even be the responsibility of an assistant to prepare egg whites without direct involvement of the person following the recipe. Programming operates analogously; it is common in programming to use functions written by other people, sometimes without close inspection of exactly how they operate.

Writing a programming function serves two principal purposes:

- A task done in multiple situations can be defined only once and used in multiple cases with confidence its behavior will be the same. This kind of "abbreviation" is more concise and less error-prone than repetition of an entire sequence of steps in each context where the sequence might be needed.
- For the convenience of the human who writes, maintains, or reads the program, it is useful and informative to identify meaningful segments of operation with function names. Just as books have chapters, with names that report their actions or themes, computer programs have functions.

It's important to understand that the action of a function is the sequence of the actions of the statements inside of it. When you run a program that contains a function, the program simply runs statements within the function.

Also important is to distinguish *definition* and *execution* of a function. The expression of a function—the "`function example1() {...}`" part—doesn't perform any of the code within the function. What you see in the source code is only the definition of a function. Only when the function is *invoked* or *executed* or *launched*—these are synonyms, for our purpose—does something useful happen.

 USE A JAVASCRIPT FUNCTION

GET READY. To learn how to use a JavaScript function, perform the following steps:

1. In an editing or app development tool, create **L8-js2.html** with the following content:

```
<!doctype html>
<html>
<head>
<title>First use of a function</title>
<script type = "text/javascript">
function example1() {
    alert("This is the first alert.");
    alert("This is the second alert.");
}
</script>
</head>
<body>
<h1>First use of a function</h1>
<p>This is text.
<button type = 'button' onclick = "example1();">I'm a button;
click me</button>
</p>
</body>
</html>
```

2. Open **L8-js2.html** in a browser. The program displays, as shown in Figure 8-5. Notice the text and button; at this point, there's no evidence of JavaScript.

Figure 8-5

This program looks just like L8-js1.html

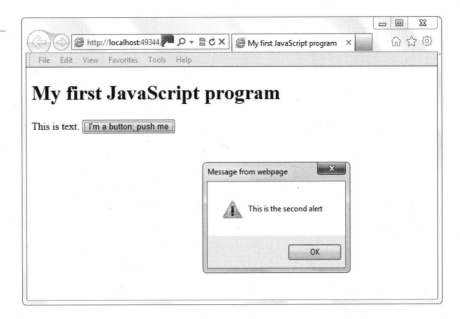

3. Click the button. Compare the action of this page with the behavior of the L8-js1.html file that contains two alerts. Do you see how they act the same although they are written somewhat differently? The alert box looks the same whether called from within a function definition or not.

4. Close the HTML file, but leave the editing tool and Web browser open if you plan to complete the next exercise during this session.

This example introduces at least two other new concepts, beside use of a function. First, it exhibits JavaScript embedded in `<script>` tags within HTML. There are several ways to "connect" a JavaScript program to the HTML to which it applies. This use of `<script>` within `<head>` is common, especially for medium-sized JavaScript projects.

Also, the name "example1" of the function deserves attention. This name is under our control. When we write href as part of a hyperlink, or `alert()` to pop up an alert, we rely on keywords defined in the standards for HTML and JavaScript, respectively. The function name example1, though, is in no such standards. It is our choice. We simply must be consistent; if we write `"my_example"` instead of "example1" in the definition of the function, then we must also use `"my_example"`.

While the function name is under our control, there are a few restrictions on our choice: the name must be made up of letters, digits, underscores, and dollar signs, and the first character of the **name** must be a letter, underscore, or dollar sign. `"example$1"` is a possible JavaScript function name, but `"not.with.periods"`, `"1wrong"`, and `"first name/last name"` are not.

JavaScript programs have one other kind of symbolic abbreviation, or name, that's common. It is a called a *variable*. While a function names a sequence of actions, a variable stands for a piece of data. You use the `var` syntax to define a new variable in JavaScript.

TAKE NOTE*

The rules for JavaScript *identifiers*—basically, the names of variables and functions—are actually somewhat more complicated than written above. Identifiers cannot be the same as words already used in the language; "if", for example, has a special meaning in JavaScript statements, and is not available as a variable name. However, the characters permitted in a name might be from alphabets other than the English one, under certain circumstances. A full definition of JavaScript's naming rules is beyond the scope of this lesson.

USE A VARIABLE IN A JAVASCRIPT PROGRAM

GET READY. To use a variable in a JavaScript program, perform the following steps:

1. In an editing or app development tool, create **L8-js3.html** with the following content:

```
<!doctype html>
<html>
<head>
<title>First use of a variable</title>
<script type = "text/javascript">
function example1() {
    var version_name = "serial number X358-AA-3T601-22"
    alert("This is the first alert of " + version_name);
    alert("This is the second alert of " + version_name);
}
</script>
</head>
<body>
<h1>First use of a variable</h1>
<p>This is text.
<button type = 'button' onclick = "example1();">I'm a button;
click me</button>
</body>
</html>
```

2. Open **L8-js3.html** in a browser and click the button. The first alert displays on-screen, as shown in Figure 8-6.

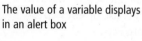

Figure 8-6

The value of a variable displays in an alert box

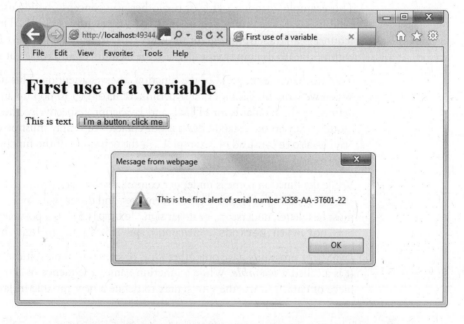

3. Click **OK** to dismiss the first alert and proceed to the second alert. Do you see how a variable might be useful? A serial number or other important quantity might display in several different places in a program. You don't have to copy the value in each location; instead, JavaScript lets you use the *name* of the variable that holds the value.

4. Click **OK** to close the second alert box.

5. Close the HTML file, but leave the editing tool and Web browser open if you plan to complete the next exercise during this session.

Using jQuery and Other Third-Party Libraries

> The most effective programmers know how to make good use of what others write. A programming library contains snippets of code, subroutines, classes, and other resources you can re-use to create software. There are many JavaScript libraries available, and jQuery is one of the most popular.

Other programmers have already thought about many of the tasks you'll face, whether your job involves confirmation that credit card numbers are invalid, display of medical images, or construction of a chat facility for a team spread across four continents. You can take advantage of what others have already written by use of JavaScript libraries. A *library* is collection of resources, like pre-written function code and subroutines, that developers use to create programs. (JavaScript programmers sometimes identify functions that return no value as *subroutines*.) A *JavaScript library* is pre-written JavaScript code.

Most workplaces will already have established before your arrival policy on which libraries to use, and how to invoke them. The Web is full of advice about libraries and their applicability, and supports a rich marketplace of available ones. Many, but not all, are available without fee. Some have more-or-less formal "support" policies, that is, a commitment to respond when faults are reported. Some are intended for only a small number of programmers—a library which facilitates development of applications which control industrial-scale bakeries, for instance—while others are aimed at everyone who codes in JavaScript.

jQuery is the leading JavaScript library of this sort. Over half of the 10,000 most-visited Web sites in the world use jQuery. jQuery is available for use with no fee and minimal restriction; you'll need to consult an attorney, of course, for details on how its licenses apply in your situation. Also note that Microsoft and other industry leaders make copies of jQuery available for anyone to download and use.

CERTIFICATION READY
What is jQuery?
4.1

USE JQUERY

GET READY. To use jQuery, perform the following steps:

1. In an editing or app development tool, create **L8-js4.html** with the following content:

```
<!doctype html>
<html>
<head>
<title>First use of jQuery</title>
<script type = "text/javascript"
        src =
"http://ajax.aspnetcdn.com/ajax/jquery/jquery-1.5.js"></script>
<script type = "text/javascript">
    // Once the HTML document loads, execute
    // the function within ready().
$(document).ready(function() {
        // Each paragraph receives a "click" action:
        // hide that particular paragraph.
    $("p").click(function() {
        $(this).hide();
    });
});

</script>
</head>
```

```
<body>
<p>This is the first paragraph. Click on me to make me
disappear.
<p>This is the second paragraph.
<p>This is the third paragraph.
</body>
</html>
```

2. Open **L8-js4.html** in a browser. The page displays, as shown in Figure 8-7. Notice that three sentences display.

Figure 8-7

A simple HTML display, before any JavaScript has been executed

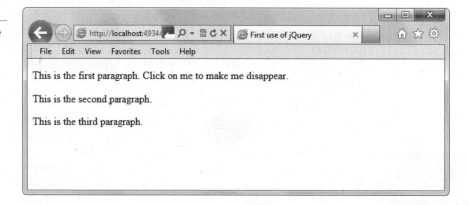

3. Click anywhere within the first paragraph. The paragraph disappears, as shown in Figure 8-8.

Figure 8-8

JavaScript has acted to hide a paragraph

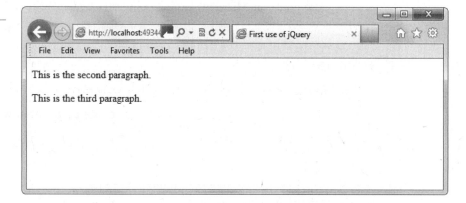

4. Click anywhere in the second paragraph to make it disappear.

5. Close the HTML file, but leave the editing tool and Web browser open if you plan to complete the next exercise during this session.

Do you see how this is a model for useful behavior in one of your Web or mobile or game console applications? You might want the information displayed to your end users to change depending on circumstances. While it's possible to write "pure" JavaScript, without jQuery, that behaves as L8-js4.html does, it takes considerably more coding. jQuery makes many common operations shorter, easier to understand, and easier to express correctly.

You might be called to use many third-party libraries beside jQuery. Most often, you'll be given explicit instructions about which library to use. When a choice is available to you, expect to be able to find abundant information on the World Wide Web with a search for the name of the library. Aside from jQuery, other popular libraries include Dojo, MooTools, and YUI. When using a third-party library, you typically need to include an element such as the following:

```
<script type = "text/javascript"
           src = "web or local address of the JavaScript library
source"></script>
```

Why is it necessary to include this tag? When you want to use `wonderful_function()` from a third-party library in one of the pages you are writing, the only way that the browser knows what you mean by `wonderful_function()` is through reference to its appearance in the library. The `<script ...>` provides that reference.

You also need to read the documentation for the library you intend to use, and perhaps make licensing arrangements.

■ Updating the UI by Using JavaScript

 THE BOTTOM LINE   JavaScript is essential for nearly all the effects of modern, responsive HTML-based applications.

You know the basic concepts of HTML: navigation by way of hyperlinks and the Back button, data retrieved on submission of forms, and all the visual styling of traditional HTML markup. Trusty Lawn Care wants an application that does more; it needs to display live updates about crew schedules, respond swiftly and in detail about account information, customize advice depending on the individual and the weather, and much more. Only JavaScript makes all this dynamism and interactivity possible.

For an example of what JavaScript makes possible, build a small in-browser calculator.

→ CREATE AN IN-BROWSER CALCULATOR USING JAVASCRIPT

GET READY. To create an in-browser calculator using JavaScript, perform the following steps:

1. In an editing or app development tool, create **L8-js5.html** with the following content:

```
<!doctype html>
<html>
<head>
<title>In-browser calculator</title>
</head>
</body>

<h1>In-browser calculator</h1>
<form name="calculator">
<table border=4>
<tr>
<td>
<input type="text" name="Input" Size="20">
<br>
</td>
</tr>
<tr>
<td>
<input type="button" name="one"   value=" 1  "
   OnClick="calculator.Input.value
```

```
+= '1'">
<input type="button" name="two"   value="  2   "
    OnCLick="calculator.Input.value
+= '2'">
<input type="button" name="three" value="  3   "
    OnCLick="calculator.Input.value
+= '3'">
<input type="button" name="plus"  value="  +   "
    OnClick="calculator.Input.value
+= ' + '">
<br>
<input type="button" name="four"  value="  4   "
    OnClick="calculator.Input.value
+= '4'">
<input type="button" name="five"  value="  5   "
    OnCLick="calculator.Input.value
+= '5'">
<input type="button" name="six"   value="  6   "
    OnClick="calculator.Input.value
+= '6'">
<input type="button" name="minus" value="  -   "
    OnClick="calculator.Input.value
+= ' - '">
<br>
<input type="button" name="seven" value="  7   "
    OnClick="calculator.Input.value
+= '7'">
<input type="button" name="eight" value="  8   "
    OnCLick="calculator.Input.value
+= '8'">
<input type="button" name="nine"  value="  9   "
    OnClick="calculator.Input.value
+= '9'">
<input type="button" name="times" value="  x   "
    OnClick="calculator.Input.value
+= ' * '">
<br>
<input type="button" name="clear" value="  c   "
    OnClick="calculator.Input.value
= ''">
<input type="button" name="zero"  value="  0   "
    OnClick="calculator.Input.value
+= '0'">
<input type="button" name="DoIt"  value="  =   "
    OnClick="calculator.Input.value
= eval(calculator.Input.value)">
<input type="button" name="div"   value="  /   "
    OnClick="calculator.Input.value
+= ' / '">
</td>
</tr>
</table>
</form>

</body>
</html>
```

2. Open **L8-js5.html** in a browser. The calculator displays as shown in Figure 8-9.

Figure 8-9

A calculator created using JavaScript

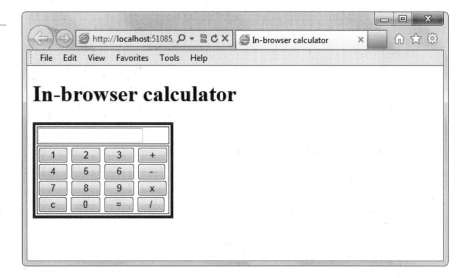

3. Try out your calculator. Click the buttons **7 × 14 + 2 =** and observe the result. Did the calculator display 100, as shown in Figure 8-10?

Figure 8-10

When you click or tap the equal sign in your JavaScript calculator, it immediately computes a result, just as with a conventional hand-held calculator

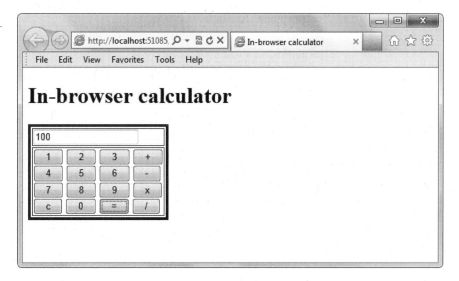

4. Close the HTML file, but leave the editing tool and Web browser open if you plan to complete the next exercise during this session.

This small example illustrates that a JavaScript program can do *within the browser* essentially anything any other application does, and sometimes in only a few lines of source code. JavaScript capabilities include data entry, response to keyboard strokes and mouse movements, display of results, complex calculations, and more, as the following exercises illustrate. Mobile applications built on an HTML5 basis of course have all the same capabilities.

Locating and Accessing Elements

If you see something in your browser, JavaScript can "get at it" and put it under programmatic control. You can use the getElementById() method to access display elements.

CERTIFICATION READY
Which JavaScript method returns a reference to the first element with a specific ID or NAME attribute?
4.2

Often in your programming career, you'll be able to give an English-language description of what you want—something like, "then we need to check that what the end user has entered is"—but won't know how to translate the idea into JavaScript. Many times, the challenge will be to identify and isolate what happens with a particular element you see on the screen. "Element" here might be a button, input field, figure, piece of text, or so on.

One important way to access display elements is with the `getElementById()` method. This method returns a reference to the first object with the specified `id` or `NAME` attribute.

> **TAKE NOTE** * "Object" is computer-speak for "thing" or "element"—the most general category of items under consideration. Technically, JavaScript is an "object-based" language, that is, one which emphasizes that such programmatic instances as "first paragraph" have both properties and methods which provide information about the paragraph and opportunities to act on the paragraph.

USE THE GETELEMENTBYID() METHOD FOR USER INPUT

GET READY. To learn how to use the `getElementByID()` method to gather user input, perform the following steps:

1. In an editing or app development tool, create **L8-js6.html** with the following content:

```html
<!doctype html>
<html>
<head>
<title>Validation of a user entry</title>

<script type = "text/javascript">
function validate() {
    var value = document.getElementById("input1").value;
    if (isNaN(value)) {
        modifier = "not ";
    } else {
        modifier = "";
    }
    var report = "You entered '" + value + "'; this is " +
modifier + "a valid number.";
alert(report);
}
</script>
</head>
<body>

<h1>Validation of a user entry</h1>
<form name="calculator">
<input type = "text" id = "input1"></input>
<button type = "button" onclick = "validate();">Click me to see
what I think of your entry</button>
</form>

</body>
</html>
```

2. Open **L8-js6.html** in a browser.

3. Type a short word in the input area and then click the button. The results are shown in Figure 8-11. Click **OK** to add your changes and close the dialog box.

Figure 8-11

A model for validation of user input by JavaScript

4. Type a number in the input area and click the button. How did the pop-up message change from the previous step? Click **OK** to add your changes and close the dialog box.

5. Close the HTML file, but leave the editing tool and Web browser open if you plan to complete the next exercise during this session.

Validation is an important responsibility for JavaScript: has the user entered a figure which fits a budget constraint? Is it a legal credit card number? Is an email address permissible and not in conflict with an existing one? The L8-js6.html file is a small model for the general theme of validation. We often need to confirm that a user's entry is, in fact, numeric, in the sense that 0 and 3.141 are proper numbers, but abc and 3.141. are not. While it would make sense for JavaScript to have an is_a_number() function, for historical reasons it builds in only isNaN.

Why do we call getElementById a "method"? Doesn't JavaScript build in a library of *functions* to perform useful tasks?

Yes and no. Although JavaScript builds in a library of useful functions for many common operations, some JavaScript capabilities are tied strongly to particular objects HTML defines. These capabilities are called ***methods***. They differ from functions only in that they're always associated and used with a particular object. isNaN() is an example of a JavaScript function, which tests for "not a number." If isNaN() returns a value of 0 (false), the value is a number. document.getElementById() is an example of a JavaScript method; you can effectively only use getElementById with the special document object.

Listening and Responding to Events

An "event" is a crucial concept in interactive programming. Much JavaScript programming has to do with responses when something happens. The Load event is commonly used and triggers when its owner is complete.

Many application requirements involve ***events***, which are actions that trigger other actions to occur. Descriptions in terms of "when" or "if" are typically coded in JavaScript in terms of events. This can surprise programmers coming from other languages, where the emphasis is on sequence:

1. Do the first thing.
2. Then do the second thing.

3. Then do the third thing.

4. Complete the sequence.

Event-based programming, in contrast, looks more like a dialogue: a user takes some action, then the JavaScript program responds, and so on.

All the JavaScript example programs presented to this point have involved events. To assign a value to the onClick *event handler* for the Click event has this effect: "when the end user clicks on the element in question, then execute the script given by the onClick value." In this case, the click action is the event, and the script is the response, or *callback*.

JavaScript references tabulate all recognized events. Among those often programmed, beyond clicking on an element, are as follows:

- submission of a form
- keystrokes
- other mouse maneuvers including double-clicks and moving the mouse
- selection of an item from a listbox
- the time when an image has finished loading

The onLoad event handler is more important than many beginners recognize. OnLoad "belongs" to HTML items; it triggers when its owner is complete. The onLoad for an <img> image occurs when the image is fully rendered and visible; the onLoad for a <table> fires once all the cells in that table have been drawn.

USE THE ONLOAD EVENT HANDLER

GET READY. To use the onLoad event handler, perform the following steps:

1. In a text editor or app development tool, create **L8-js7.html** with the following content:

```
<!doctype html>
<html>
<head>
<title>The onLoad event handler</title>

<script type = "text/javascript">
function validate() {
    var value = document.getElementById("input1").value;
    if (isNaN(value)) {
        modifier = "not ";
    } else {
        modifier = "";
    }
    var report = "You entered '" + value + "'; this is " +
modifier + "a valid number.";
    alert(report);
}

function init() {
    alert("At this point, it is guaranteed that all HTML
elements have loaded.")
;
}
</script>
</head>
<body onload = "init();">
```

```
<h1>The onLoad event handler</h1>
<form name="calculator">
<input type = "text" id = "input1"></input>
<button type = "button" onclick = "validate();">Click me to see
what I think of your entry</button>
</form>

</body>
</html>
```

2. Open **L8-js7.html** in a browser. A form displays, as shown in Figure 8-12. The alert that's visible signals the <body> has finished loading; that's the meaning of onload = "init();".

3. Click **OK** to close the dialog box.

4. Enter a value in the input field and click the button. Observe this program's judgment of the value, an example of which is shown in Figure 8-13.

5. Experiment with other values.

6. Close the HTML file, but leave the editing tool and Web browser open if you plan to complete the next exercise during this session.

One common symptom of flawed JavaScript programs is that they are erratic—they give different results at different times. In some cases, this is because the program is written in such a way that it depends on the existence of a particular screen element but doesn't assure that the element exists. Launching the program at different times can result in slightly different loading order, and thus results that look unpredictable. One tactic for such problems is to begin calculations only after onLoad has "fired," as in L8-js7.html.

Showing and Hiding Elements

> You can show and hide elements using the HTML display attribute to make your displays "intelligent," showing the end user pertinent information and hiding it when it's no longer needed.

A particular display might show different kinds of information depending on the circumstances: an after-hours telephone number outside of the business day, a warning about usage only during a month with excessive traffic, or notices about the activity of other users only when those other users are logged in. One convenient way to organize such variations is to lay out the display with all possible messages, then show only the pertinent ones. HTML elements have a display attribute useful for this approach.

The next exercise has you create a small application that shows and hides a paragraph based on the value an end user enters. The program displays a message if the user enters the value 80 or higher.

CERTIFICATION READY
Which HTML attribute can you use to show elements using JavaScript?
4.2

HIDE PARTS OF THE DISPLAY BASED ON USER ACTION

GET READY. To create an application that shows and hides a paragraph based on the value an end user enters, perform the following steps:

1. In a text editor or app development tool, create **L8-js8.html** with the following contents:

```html
<!doctype html>
<html>
<head>
<title>Show/hide responsively</title>

<script type = "text/javascript">
function check_range() {
    var value = document.getElementById("price1").value;
    var paragraph_list = document.getElementsByTagName("p");
    var first_paragraph = paragraph_list[0];
    if (value >= 80) {
        display = "block";
    } else {
        display = "none";
    }
    first_paragraph.style.display = display;
}
</script>
</head>
<body>
```

```
<h1>Show/hide responsively</h1>
<form>
Enter a price: <input type = "number" id = "price1"
min = "1" max = "100"
        oninput = "check_range();"
  ></input>
</form>
<p style = "display:none;">Warning: you are within
20% of your limit.</p>

</body>
</html>
```

2. Open **L8-js8.html** in a browser. The results are shown in Figure 8-14.

Figure 8-14

The program interface

3. Using the keyboard, enter each of these "prices" by pressing the Enter key after each one: **1**, **50**, **79**, **80**, **90**, and **60**. A warning displays after you enter 80 and 90, as shown in Figure 8-15.

Figure 8-15

Your JavaScript program warns you when the value you enter approaches a particular range

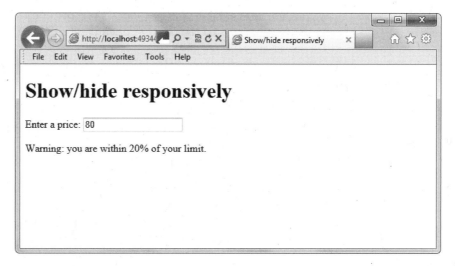

4. Close the HTML file, but leave the editing tool and Web browser open if you plan to complete the next exercise during this session.

A common mistake beginners make is to forget one of "show" and "hide." L8-js8.html begins with the warning paragraph hidden, then uses JavaScript to show it under certain circumstances.

Remember when you test show/hide functionality that your JavaScript hides again, through assignment of the display attribute, once the conditions for "show" have passed. Otherwise, once it is shown it will never turn off again.

Updating the Content of Elements

> Does a part of a display depend on another part? Use JavaScript and the innerHTML property to keep the two synchronized instantly.

The last exercise responded to entry of a price by showing or hiding a warning paragraph. JavaScript has the ability to do far more complex calculations than just a show/hide. It can compute a distance, a recommendation, or, as L8-js9.html shows, a total price.

JavaScript uses the innerHTML property to change the current content of HTML elements (referred to as "inner content") or insert new content.

UPDATE CONTENT VISIBLE ON THE SCREEN

GET READY. To create an application that updates content visible on the screen, perform the following steps:

1. In an editing or app development tool, create **L8-js9.html** with the following content:

```
<!doctype html>
<html>
<head>
<title>Compute element</title>

<script type = "text/javascript">
    // check_range assigns the display style
    // of the first paragraph as a function of
    // the displayed price–whether it's 80 and
    // above, or 79 and below.
function check_range() {
    var value = document.getElementById("price1").value;
    var paragraph_list = document.getElementsByTagName("p");
    var first_paragraph = paragraph_list[0];
    if (value >= 80) {
        display = "block";
    } else {
        display = "none";
    }
    first_paragraph.style.display = display;
}
  // compute_total() has the responsibility
  // to update the display with the total of
  // the price and its tax.
function compute_total() {
    var value = document.getElementById("price1").value;
    if (isNaN(value)) {
        total = "INDETERMINATE";
    } else {
            // Assume an 8% tax.
        total = 1.08 * value;
        total = total.toFixed(2);
    }
```

```
        var total_slot = document.getElementById("total");
        total_slot.innerHTML = total;
}
</script>
</head>
<body><h1>Compute element</h1>
<form>
Enter a price: <input type = "number" id = "price1" min = "1"
max = "100"
        oninput = "check_range(); compute_total();"
  ></input> The total price, including tax,
                is <span id = "total">INDETERMINATE</span>.
</form>
<p style = "display:none;">Warning: you are within 20% of your
limit.</p>
</body>
</html>
```

2. Open **L8-js9.html** in a Web browser.

3. Using the keyboard, type the number **1** in the text box. A message displays, shown in Figure 8-16, showing the price plus 8 percent tax on a $1 item. Notice how quickly and smoothly the display updated.

Figure 8-16

JavaScript can compute immediately a total that includes sales tax based on a user entry

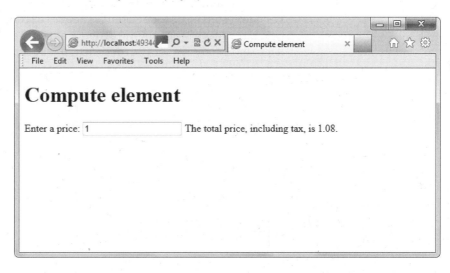

4. Press **Enter**.

5. Type **50** into the text box and notice how the displayed message changes.

6. Repeat steps 3 and 4 using the values **79**, **80**, **90**, and **60** each time.

7. Close the HTML file, but leave the editing tool and Web browser open if you plan to complete the next exercise during this session.

Adding Elements

You can use the `createElement` command and the `appendChild` method in JavaScript to add elements after the HTML is complete.

JavaScript makes even more radical amendments to a display possible. When necessary, it is possible to create new elements and fit them into an existing display. This is accomplished with the `createElement` command and the `appendChild` method.

CERTIFICATION READY
What does the
createElement
command do?
4.2

ADD AN ELEMENT TO THE DISPLAY

GET READY. To create an application that adds elements to the display, perform the following steps:

1. In an editing or app development tool, create **L8-js10.html** with the following content:

```html
<!doctype html>
<html>
<head>
<title>Create a new element</title>
<script type = "text/javascript">
function add_paragraph() {
    var original = document.getElementById("original");
    var new_paragraph = document.createElement("p");
    var current_time = new Date()
    var this_text = "This new paragraph appeared at " +
current_time + ".";
        // Even after the browser has rendered
        // all HTML, it's possible to add *new*
        // HTML elements.  createTextNode()-
        // appendChild()-insertBefore() is one
        // typical pattern for adding new textual
        // content.
        var new_content = document.createTextNode(this_text);
        new_paragraph.appendChild(new_content);
        document.body.insertBefore(new_paragraph, original);
}
</script>
</head>
<body>

<h1>Create a new element</h1>
<p id = "original">This is the text that appears when the
display first loads.</p>
<button type = "button" onclick =
"add_paragraph();">Click on me to
        add new content</button>
<p style = "display:none;">Warning: you are within 20% of your
limit.</p>

</body>
</html>
```

2. Open **L8-js10.html** in a Web browser. The program displays, as shown in Figure 8-17.

Figure 8-17

The initial program interface

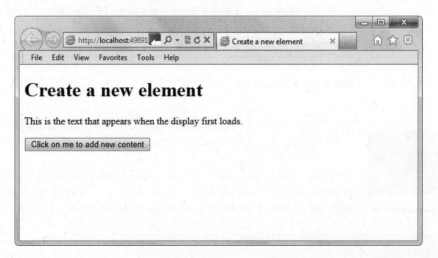

3. Click the button. The screen changes, as shown in Figure 8-18.

Figure 8-18

A display made up of simple HTML elements along with others created by JavaScript in response to user action

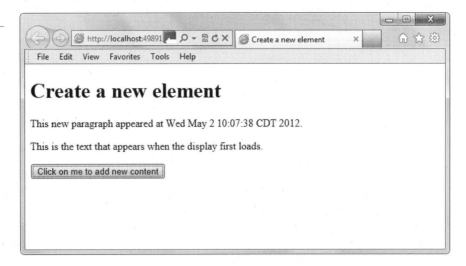

4. Click the button a few more times to see the results.

5. Close the HTML file, but leave the editing tool and Web browser open if you plan to complete the next exercise during this session.

It's a bit more delicate an operation to create an element than to update an existing one; you need to use JavaScript to create relations that HTML otherwise performs automatically on your behalf.

SKILL SUMMARY

IN THIS LESSON YOU LEARNED:

- HTML5 and CSS3 make a great foundation for your Web site or mobile application. To do anything more than presentation of structured content, though—to respond with individualized data about a specific end user, or transact on-line commerce, or derive results based on data already entered, for instance—takes real programming. JavaScript is a capable programming language with great abilities to express the interactions you want your end users to have with your app.
- A function is a segment of a program defined and performed in isolation from other parts. The action of a function is the sequence of the actions of the statements inside of it.
- The most effective programmers know how to make good use of what others write. A programming library contains snippets of code, subroutines, classes, and other resources you can re-use to create software. There are many JavaScript libraries available, and jQuery is one of the most popular.
- JavaScript is essential for nearly all the effects of modern, responsive HTML-based applications.
- If you see something in your browser, JavaScript can "get at it" and put it under programmatic control. You can use the getElementById() method to access display elements.
- An "event" is a crucial concept in interactive programming. Much JavaScript programming has to do with responses when something happens. The onLoad event is commonly used and triggers when its owner is complete.
- You can show and hide elements using the HTML display attribute to make your displays "intelligent," showing the end user pertinent information and hiding it when it's no longer needed.
- You can use the createElement command and the appendChild method in JavaScript to add elements after the HTML is complete.

■ Knowledge Assessment

Fill in the Blank

Complete the following sentences by writing the correct word or words in the blanks provided.

1. A _____ is a recipe we direct the computer to execute to result in a particular display or action.

2. You use the var syntax to define a new _____ in JavaScript.

3. Many application requirements involve _____, which are actions, such as a mouse click, that trigger other actions to occur.

4. You notice that a part of your JavaScript program represents a sequence of actions that is logically separate from other parts of program. It likely will be useful to define a _____ to perform that specific sequence.

5. The _____ event associated with <body> constitutes a guarantee that all HTML has been displayed.

6. A common coding pattern is to attach an id to a specific HTML element, then access that element through JavaScript with _____.

7. JavaScript _____ are the names of variables and functions.

8. A _____ is collection of resources, like pre-written code and subroutines, that developers use to create programs.

9. A _____ is pre-written JavaScript code.

10. More than half of leading Web sites use the _____ JavaScript library.

Multiple Choice

Circle the letter that corresponds to the best answer.

1. JavaScript programming makes applications which of the following? (Choose all that apply.)
   a. static
   b. dynamic
   c. syntactically correct
   d. interactive

2. Which of the following are JavaScript libraries? (Choose all that apply.)
   a. Dojo
   b. MooTools
   c. YUI
   d. jQuery

3. Which of the following names a valid JavaScript variable?
   a. `my.variable`
   b. `1st-variable`
   c. `ord['a']`
   d. `[TBC]var1_$`

4. When can JavaScript not be used?
   a. With HTML 4.01 and previous
   b. When the user has set a browser preference to disable JavaScript
   c. When the user hasn't installed JavaScript on his or her desktop
   d. none of the above

5. JavaScript uses which property to change the current content of HTML elements?
   a. `changeHTML`
   b. `modInnerHTML`
   c. `innerHTML`
   d. `HTMLinner`

6. A particular Web page has a single <form>. How does JavaScript best reach this?
   a. `document. getElementsByTagName("form")[0]`
   b. `document. getElementsByTagName("form")[1]`
   c. `document. getElementsByTagName("form")`
   d. `[document. getElementsByTagName("form")]`

7. The user has checked a box in a form indicating that he has not traveled recently in a country with an elevated incidence of hepatitis. How would you use JavaScript to hide an advisory paragraph?
   a. `warning.style.display = "none"`
   b. `warning.style.display = 0`
   c. `hide(warning)`
   d. `warning.style.hide()`

8. An individual statement in JavaScript ends in a _____.
   a. hash mark
   b. closing parenthesis
   c. period
   d. semicolon

9. Which of the following does JavaScript use to add new elements to a program display? (Choose all that apply.)
   a. `createElement`
   b. `appendChild`
   c. `getElement`
   d. `addChild`

10. Which of the following can you use to show and hide elements in a JavaScript program?
    a. `display` attribute
    b. `show-hide` attribute
    c. `show` command
    d. `innerHTML`

True / False

Circle T if the statement is true or F if the statement is false.

T | F **1.** The names of functions are listed in the JavaScript standard.

T | F **2.** In HTML source, JavaScript typically appears inside a `<script>` element.

T | F **3.** It is possible to write JavaScript code in such a way that it executes before all images are loaded.

T | F **4.** If function `f2()` uses function `f1()`, and the definitions for both functions appear in the same `<script>`, then the definition for `f1()` must appear first.

T | F **5.** The `getElementByElement()` method returns a reference to the first object with the specified `id` or `NAME` attribute.

■ Competency Assessment

Scenario 8-1: Validating Input

You've been asked to code a JavaScript function that judges whether a user entry might be a valid U.S. Social Security number or not. How would you go about this? What would you deliver back to your team?

Scenario 8-2: Understanding Function Names

Raymond is creating a program that includes several functions. He has listed his function names and their descriptions in a table for easy reference while he develops his application. Some of his applications aren't working and he asks you for advice. You notice that the functions in question begin with hash marks or slashes. What do you tell Raymond about naming functions?

■ Proficiency Assessment

Scenario 8-3: Picking a JavaScript Library

CiCi wants to begin using JavaScript libraries to speed the production time of her programs, but she's not sure where to start. There are so many libraries available that it's hard to choose. What do you tell her?

Scenario 8-4: Distinguishing between Methods and Functions

Andre is new to JavaScript programming and is struggling to understand the difference between methods and functions. What do you tell him?

Creating Animations, Working with Graphics, and Accessing Data

EXAM OBJECTIVE MATRIX

SKILLS/CONCEPTS	MTA EXAM OBJECTIVE	MTA EXAM OBJECTIVE NUMBER
Coding Animations by Using JavaScript	Code animations by using JavaScript.	4.3
Working with Images, Shapes, and Other Graphics	Code animations by using JavaScript.	4.3
Sending and Receiving Data	Access data access by using JavaScript.	4.4
Loading and Saving Files	Access data access by using JavaScript.	4.4
Using JavaScript to Validate User Form Input	Access data access by using JavaScript.	4.4
Understanding and Using Cookies	Access data access by using JavaScript.	4.4
Understanding and Using LocalStorage	Access data access by using JavaScript.	4.4

KEY TERMS

animation

AppCache

canvas element

cookies

data type

encapsulate

JSON

LocalStorage

parsing

recursion

XMLHttpRequest API

The Malted Milk Media development team has two new client projects to complete this week. Attaboy Pet Services wants its logo animated when users first open the company's homepage, and Attaboy wants the logo created by the canvas element. The Trusty Lawn Care mobile application project is at the point of needing code added to exchange data with a server. The development team wants you to join both efforts to learn more about these aspects of using JavaScript.

■ Coding Animations by Using JavaScript

 THE BOTTOM LINE — HTML and CSS have a number of facilities for fast animation of common effects. However, JavaScript is far more flexible and can produce remarkable results.

CERTIFICATION READY
What is an animation?
4.3

Animation is the display of a sequence of static images at a fast enough speed to create the illusion of movement. Regarding the user interface, animation has to do with changing a display to make it dynamic—not just a one-time change but a seamless one. JavaScript is flexible enough to produce spectacular animation effects, in the right hands.

Recursion is a key part of animation. *Recursion* is a programming technique in which a function calls itself. A common technique in JavaScript animation is to use `setTimeout` recursively, that is, to have it invoke another execution of the same function from which the `setTimeout()` was called. This is generally the most effective way to introduce a "timing element" into JavaScript.

TAKE NOTE* Outside of programming, recursion isn't always considered good behavior. If you're writing a dictionary or glossary term, for example, it's a best practice to define a term without using the same words that appear in the term. Let's say you're defining the word "politics." A definition such as "the field of political behavior" might be frowned upon by many editors because of the use of "political." For computing, recursion turns out to be not only permissible but powerful.

Creating Animations

Remember that JavaScript is a powerful general-purpose programming language. If you can imagine a particular animation, there's probably a way to create it in JavaScript.

CERTIFICATION READY
Which JavaScript function can you use to create an animation?
4.3

Animation, like other JavaScript effects, is under computational control. That means that sufficiently clever coding can make animation do what you choose.

The `move_paragraph()` function in the source code of the following exercise is considered recursive because `move_paragraph` itself appears in the last statement that defines the function. This exercise creates a continuously updated animation in the style of a "ticker."

 CREATE A SIMPLE ANIMATION

GET READY. To create a simple application, perform the following steps:

1. Create **L9-js1.html** with the following content:

```
<!doctype html>
<html>
<head>
<title>Animate with JavaScript</title>

<script type = "text/javascript">
  // Create a "ticker-tape" effect by sliding
  // the paragraph of text one pixel to the
  // right, over and over, until the right-hand
  // limit of 300 pixels is reached.  At that
  // point, restart the animation all the way
  // to the left.
```

```
function move_paragraph() {
    next = current + "px";
    current += 1;
    if (current > 300) {
        current = 0;
    }
    paragraph.style.left = next;
        // Pause for 18 milliseconds before
        // the next move.
    var rate = 18;
    setTimeout(move_paragraph, rate);
}
function init() {
    paragraph = document.getElementById("original");
    paragraph.style.position = "absolute";
    current = 0;
    move_paragraph();
}
</script>
</head>
<body onload = "init();">

<h1>Animate with JavaScript</h1>
<p id = "original">Do you see me scrolling across the
    screen?</p>

</body>
</html>
```

2. Open **L9-js1.html** in your Web browser. Does the paragraph move across your screen, as shown in Figure 9-1?

3. Close the file but leave the editing tool and Web browser open.

Figure 9-1

Two snapshots of a "ticker" display at different points in time

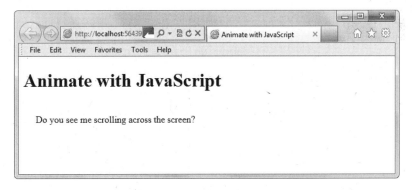

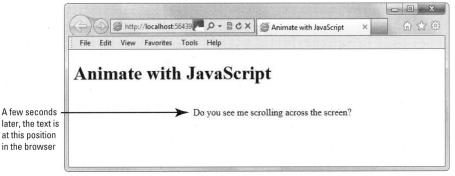

A few seconds later, the text is at this position in the browser

CREATE AN INTERACTIVE ANIMATION

GET READY. To create an animation responsive to the action of a user, perform the following steps:

1. Create **L9-js2.html** with the following content:

```html
<!doctype html>
<html>
<head>
<title>Animate with JavaScript</title>

<script type = "text/javascript">
    // This page acts much the same as L9-js1.html
    // did, with the exception that the frequency
    // of moving the paragraph depends on the numeric
    // value the end-user has entered in the input
    // field.
function move_paragraph() {
    next = current + "px";
    current += 1;
    if (current > 300) {
        current = 0;
    }
    paragraph.style.left = next;
    var rate = document.getElementById("rate").value;
    setTimeout(move_paragraph, rate);
}
function init() {
    paragraph = document.getElementById("original");
    paragraph.style.position = "absolute";
    current = 0;
    move_paragraph();
}
</script>
</head>
<body onload = "init();">

<h1>Animate with JavaScript</h1>
    <!-- The number <input> tag is new with HTML5.
    It provides a convenient way to enforce that
    the end-user inputs a valid numeral within a
    specified range. -->
<form>
<input id = "rate" type = "number" value = "18" min =
    "5" max = "100"></input>
</form>
<p id = "original">Do you see me scrolling across the screen?</p>

</body>
</html>
```

2. Open **L9-js2.html** in a Web browser. The interface displays, as shown in Figure 9-2.

Figure 9-2

Nearly everything on the screen is under JavaScript's control, including the speed of animation

3. Replace the rate value (which is 18, initially) with a number that's higher or lower, and note the effect on the animation. Do you see the speed of the animation accelerate and decelerate as you adjust the input?

4. Close the file but leave the editing tool and Web browser open if you complete the next exercise during this session.

➕ MORE INFORMATION

For basic information and best practices on designing animation for the user interface, visit the Microsoft "Animations and Transitions" Web page at http://bit.ly/ziqs0G. The Animation Library at http://bit.ly/IgGj0f provides a suite of animations developed by Microsoft that can be used to create Metro Style apps.

■ Working with Images, Shapes, and Other Graphics

THE BOTTOM LINE

You can use JavaScript to display an image when a button is clicked or some other event occurs. The `createElement` method works well for this use.

CERTIFICATION READY
How can you display an image file using JavaScript?
4.3

JavaScript can display different types of graphics, from JPG and PNG files to shapes like boxes and circles. One method is to use the `createElement()` method. This method creates a reusable function to display an image:

```
function show_image(src, width, height, alt) {
    var img = document.createElement("img");
    img.src = src;
    img.width = width;
    img.height = height;
    img.alt = alt;

    // Adds it to the <body> tag
    document.body.appendChild(img);
}
```

To display the image, include this code:

```
<button onclick="show_image
('path/filename', 276,110, 'Logo');">
 Display logo</button>
```

Displaying an image when a button is clicked is a fairly simple task. Actually creating graphics on the fly requires the canvas element or SVG. This lesson covers graphics creating using canvas.

Manipulating the Canvas with JavaScript

With HTML5, JavaScript can readily control not only texts, forms, and static images, but it also can draw complex graphics.

HTML5's *canvas element* is a drawing area under programmatic control. The only graphical elements common in earlier HTML were static, such as PNG and JPG. Dynamic and especially interactive effects were difficult. Canvas changes all that.

As you learned in Lesson 2, the canvas element creates a container for graphics, and uses JavaScript to draw the graphics dynamically. With JavaScript, you can also animate objects by making them move, change scale, and so on.

To draw a canvas object, the primary constructs you use are the `getElementById()` function to find the canvas element, and `canvas.getContext` (sometimes abbreviated to `c.getContext`) to create the canvas object. You can then use a variety of methods to draw shapes, include images, and so on.

Entire applications, including impressive games and simulators, have been built with the HTML5 canvas.

USE CANVAS TO CREATE A CLOCKFACE WITH MOVING HANDS

GET READY. To demonstrate use of HTML5's canvas, perform the following steps:

1. Create **L9-js3.html** with following content:

```html
<!doctype html>
<html>
<head>
<title>Analogue clockface illustrates JavaScript's
    control of canvas</title>

<script type = "text/javascript">
function draw_leg(fraction) {
    dctx.lineTo(center_x + length * Math.sin(2 *
    Math.PI * fraction),
                center_y - length * Math.cos(2 *
    Math.PI * fraction));
}

function init() {
    var canvas =
    document.getElementById("clockface");
      // The following variables are created as
      // globals, so they can conveniently be
      // accessed by other functions.
    dctx = canvas.getContext('2d');
    dctx.fillStyle = "black";
    center_x = 100;
    center_y = 100;
    length = 100;
    show_hands();
}

// A single hand is drawn as an isosceles triangle
    // from the center to the edge of the clockface.
```

```
function show_hand(fraction, width) {
    dctx.beginPath();
    dctx.moveTo(center_x, center_y);
    draw_leg(fraction - width);
    draw_leg(fraction + width);
    dctx.fill();
}

function show_hands() {
        // Erase anything already present in the area
        // that represents the clock face.
    dctx.clearRect(0, 0, 200, 200);
        // What is the time *now*?
    var now = new Date();
    seconds = now.getSeconds();
    minutes = now.getMinutes() + seconds / 60;
    hours = now.getHours() + minutes / 60;
        // The second hand is "skinniest" of the three.
    show_hand(seconds / 60, 0.002);
    show_hand(minutes / 60, 0.005);
        // The hour hand is twice as wide as the minute
        // hand.
    show_hand(hours / 12, 0.01);
    var rate = 1000;
    setTimeout(show_hands, rate);
}
</script>
</head>
<body onload = "init();">

<h1>Analogue clockface illustrates JavaScript's
    control of canvas</h1>
<canvas id = "clockface" width = "200" height =
    "200"></canvas>

</body>
</html>
```

2. Open **L9-js3.html** in a Web browser. The display appears, as shown in Figure 9-3.

Figure 9-3

A snapshot of JavaScript-coded clock hands representing the time 11:47:28

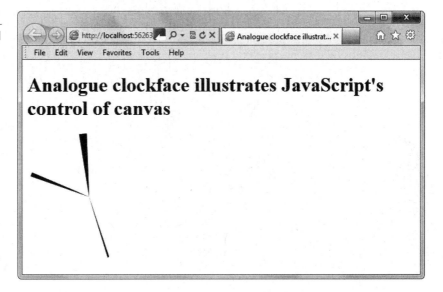

3. Close the file and the Web browser, but leave the editing tool open if you complete the next exercise during this session.

In another example, the following exercise creates an abstract drawing made by placing blocks on an HTML5 canvas. The exercise illustrates that it takes relatively few lines of JavaScript to produce quite complicated effects.

 CREATE ANIMATED BOXES USING CANVAS

GET READY. To create animated shapes using the canvas element, perform the following steps:

1. Create **L9-js4.html** with the following content:

```
<!doctype html>
<html>
<head>
<title>Blocks</title>

<script type = "text/javascript">
// This page is "for play"-it just places blocks of
// color on the screen with a bit of randomization,
// to achieve mildly interesting visual effects.
// Recursion is used in a couple of distinct ways
// below:  place_blocks() calls draw_spiral(), and
// draw_spiral() calls either place_blocks() or
// draw_spiral(), depending on how much of a spiral
// has been most recently drawn.
function init() {
    var canvas =
    document.getElementById("drawing_area");
    dctx = canvas.getContext('2d');
    place_blocks();
}

function draw_spiral() {
        // Once a block moves outside the drawing
        // area, stop the current spiral, and create
        // a new one.
    if (x > 500 || y > 500 || x < 0 || y < 0) {
        place_blocks();
    }
    ratio = 1.6;
    newx = x;
    newy = y;
    dx = size;
    dy = size;
        // Each block is turned 90 degrees away
        // from the last one.
    switch (direction) {
        case "up":
                dy = -size;
                newy += dy;
                direction = "left";
                break;
```

```
                case "left":
                    dx = -size;
                    dy = -size;
                    newx += dx;
                    direction = "down";
                    break;
                case "down":
                    dx = -size;
                    newy += dy;
                    direction = "right";
                    break;
                case "right":
                    newx += dx;
                    direction = "up";
                    break;
            }
            dctx.fillRect(x, y, dx, dy);
              // Each successively-drawn block is larger
              // than the last.
            size *= ratio;
            x = newx;
            y = newy;
            setTimeout(draw_spiral, delay);
        }
        function place_blocks() {
            dctx.fillStyle =
            '#'+Math.floor(Math.random()*16777215).toString(16
            );
            x = 100 + 300 * Math.random();
            y = 100 + 300 * Math.random();
            delay = 100 + 2000 * Math.random();
            size = 3 + 7 * Math.random();
            direction = "up";
            draw_spiral();
        }
        </script>
        </head>
        <body onload = "init();">

        <h1>Blocks</h1>
        <canvas id = "drawing_area" width = "500" height =
            "500"></canvas>

        </body>
        </html>
```

2. Open **L9-js4.html** in a Web browser. The screen fills with colored blocks, as shown in Figure 9-4.

3. Close the file but leave the editing tool and Web browser open if you complete the next exercise during this session.

Figure 9-4

A snapshot of an abstract drawing made by placing blocks on an HTML5 canvas

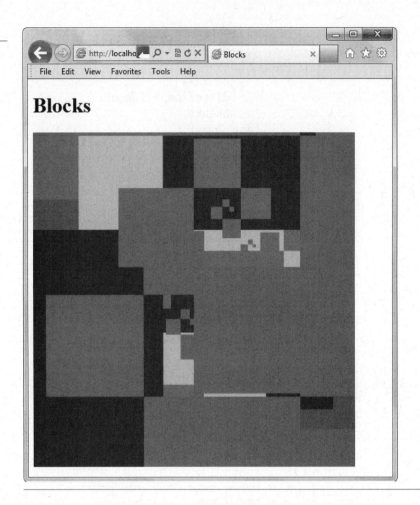

■ Sending and Receiving Data

THE BOTTOM LINE

If an application accessible from your computer exposes data to you as an end user, there's probably a way for JavaScript to reach the data. One of the most important roles of JavaScript is to communicate in real-time with remote data sources.

Part of the power of modern computer applications is their ability to coordinate information from many sources into a useful display: JavaScript can bring together server-side databases of customer history, memory local to the desktop or handheld in use with current shopping selections, the contents of the current page, and remote updates of pricing or weather details for comparison and calculation.

Creating JavaScript programs that send and receive data is challenging, not because the concepts are hard but because the JavaScript application has a different structure than any of the others. Nearly all the JavaScript examples in Lessons 8 were constructed as small, self-contained HTML pages. Each individual page can be loaded in a browser and fully exercised in the browser in isolation.

However, a JavaScript program that sends and receives data must have more parts: there must be a receiver or sender somewhere with which your JavaScript program can exchange data. Most often, HTML pages or mobile applications communicate with a networked server at some central application.

JavaScript data transactions often are presented as conceptually difficult and available only to those who have mastered AJAX, XML, JSON, and a complicated stew of other acronyms. This is not true. You already understand functions: functions are special little boxes that you supply zero or more arguments, then the box does something and perhaps returns a result to you. JavaScript network communication is much the same: pass zero or more pieces of data, and receive a result back. The great difficulty lies in first setting up your own "laboratory" with the parts necessary to make this dialogue work. Once you have that first channel working smoothly, you'll find that you quickly learn the security, control-flow, and encoding rules peculiar to JavaScript data communications.

One of the most essential techniques for data transfer involves the **_XMLHttpRequest API_** (sometimes abbreviated as XHR). XMLHttpRequest enables you to use JavaScript to pass data in the form of text strings between a client and a server. The general syntax might look like the following:

```
function load(url, data, callback) {
    var xhr = new XMLHttpRequest();
    xhr.open("GET", url, true);
    xhr.onload = function() {
        callback(xhr.responseText);
    }
    xhr.send(data);
}
```

The XMLHttpRequest object creates a call to the server. The open method specifies the HTTP method for contacting the server and provides the server's Web address. The callback function gets a response from the server. Finally, xhr.send(data) sends the data.

A few subsequent exercises, as you'll soon see, require a Web server; the Application Cache, for instance, only exists for sites accessed through a network connection. With the right approach, however, nearly any Web server makes a good practice companion. Your instructor will set up access to a Web server so you can try out Application Cache with little difficulty. To send and receive *data* explicitly in JavaScript is different; to make it work requires a dynamic Web server and server-side programming. Be sure you keep these distinctions clear:

- Most JavaScript functionality: can be demonstrated with a browser from the local desktop filesystem.
- ApplicationCache and a few other HTML5 facilities in JavaScript: require a Web server. Any Web server will do.
- XmlHttpRequest and comparable JavaScript data transmission facilities, including some introduced by HTML5: require a *dynamic* Web server.

In the absence of a dynamic Web server, the following exercise shows a very simple example of data access. When you do choose to work with Web servers, you'll have quite a selection of alternatives that are relatively easy for a newcomer to Web service. wamp for windows, mamp for mac, and lamp for linux are among the simplest starting points.

CERTIFICATION READY
Which API enables you to exchange data strings between a client and server?
4.4

ACCESS DATA

GET READY. As a minimal example of JavaScript's ability to access data, perform the following steps:

1. Create **L9-js5.html** with the following content:

```
<!doctype html>
<html>
<head>
<title>JavaScript accesses data</title>
```

```
<script type = "text/javascript">
function init() {
    var paragraph_object =
    document.getElementById('paragraph');
    message = "Notice that the title of this page is
    '" + document.title + "'.";
    paragraph_object.innerHTML = message;
}

</script>
</head>
<body onload = "init();">

<h1>JavaScript accesses data</h1>
<p id = "paragraph"></p>

</body>
</html>
```

CERTIFICATION READY
How is the
getElementById()
function used to access
data?
4.4

2. Open **L9-js5.html** in a Web browser. The display appears, as shown in Figure 9-5.

Figure 9-5

A simple HTML page with a paragraph computed by JavaScript

3. Notice that JavaScript can access HTML content.
4. Close the file but leave the editing tool and Web browser open if you complete the next exercise during this session.

What's the point of this example? If a programmer needs the title of a Web page, why wouldn't she just copy and paste it from the HTML?

One frequent answer: JavaScript of this sort is intended for a site-wide library. There might be a style or *policy* that is supposed to apply to *all* pages. In such a case, it's far more convenient and trouble-free to **encapsulate** the policy in a JavaScript library that knows how to retrieve the title for itself, rather than having to copy-and-paste the title of all pages for the entire site. Each page then includes an identical copy of the JavaScript library.

TAKE NOTE★

"Policy" is a word programmers use to mean, roughly, "style of action." A visual style might be something we humans express as "every page should appear with this particular subtle background image"; an example of a policy is "every page should make its text visible nearly instantaneously, and should still be readable even if resized horizontally." JavaScript helper functions and site-wide standards for coding can help realize policies of this sort.

TAKE NOTE *

"Encapsulate" is a bit of jargon programmers often say. In the JavaScript application that drew an analogue clockface on a canvas, the `show_hand()` function "encapsulates" all the trigonometry involved in drawing a single hand, whether for the hours, minutes, or seconds. The programmer uses `show_hand()` without concern for the details of what's "inside" (the capsule). For most people, it's far easier to "draw a box" or capsule around a piece of functionality, give the capsule a name, and think about the capsule as a whole, rather than looking at all its parts each time it's used.

Transmitting Complex Objects and Parsing

As a general-purpose language, JavaScript can communicate structured information much richer than the simple values used in most of this lesson.

CERTIFICATION READY
What is parsing?
4.4

In real-world programming, JavaScript can handle highly complicated operations. One might, for instance, receive an involved report on gasoline prices at a long list of retail outlets and need the ability to isolate just one of those figures. *Parsing* is a term used to describe analysis of complex information into constituent parts.

 PARSE COMPLEX DATA

GET READY. To demonstrate JavaScript's ability to parse complex data, perform the following steps:

1. Create **L9-js6.html** with the following contents:

```html
<!doctype html>
<html>
<head>
<title>Parsing complex data</title>

<script type = "text/javascript">

  // The next statement needs to appear
  // on a single line.
sample_data = "Mobil-17: 3.49; Kroger-03: 3.36;
   Exxon-01: 3.59; Kroger-04: 3.49;
   Valero-A: 3.41; Chevron-01: 3.52";
of_interest = "Kroger-04";

  // sample_data is an example of a typical piece of
  // structured data:  a string with parts separated
  // by semi-colons, where each of the parts has two
  // subparts separated by a colon.  Many other formats
  // are possible.  To parse this particular format,
  // init() splits on two distinct separators.
function init() {
     var paragraph_object =
     document.getElementById("paragraph");
     var data_list = sample_data.split(';');
     for (j = 0; j < data_list.length; j++) {
          parts = data_list[j].split(':');
          var site = parts[0].trim()
          if (site == of_interest) {
```

```
                                var message = "Given the sample data '" +
                         sample_data + "', this program parsed out the
                         price $" + parts[1].trim() + " for the " + site +
                         " site.";
                                paragraph_object.innerHTML = message;
                            }
                        }
                    }

    </script>
    </head>
    <body onload = "init();">

    <h1>Parsing complex data</h1>
    <p id = "paragraph">Welcome.</p>

    </body>
    </html>
```

2. Open **L9-js6.html** in a Web browser. The display should look like Figure 9-6.

Figure 9-6

JavaScript can extract data
embedded in a complex format

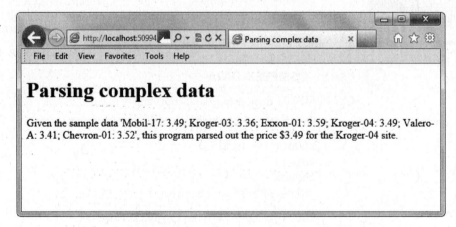

3. Close the file but leave the editing tool and Web browser open if you complete the next exercise during this session.

JavaScript and freely available JavaScript libraries supply a wealth of parsing facilities. Extraction of data from a human-readable external Web page is only one instance among many of how JavaScript can parse data.

For example, you can also use a subset of JavaScript called **JSON** (JavaScript Object Notation) to exchange JavaScript objects with a server. Using the JSON.parse and JSON.stringify APIs, the code might look like the following:

```
function loadJSON(url, data, callback) {
    var xhr = new XMLHttpRequest();
    xhr.open("GET", url, true);
    xhr.onload = function() {
        callback( JSON.parse(xhr.responseText) );
    }
    xhr.send( JSON.stringify(data) );
}

loadJSON("my.json", { id : 1 }, function(response) {
    setTitle(response.title);
});
```

This code is almost identical to the XMLHttpRequest code sample earlier in the lesson. The XMLHttpRequest object creates a call to the server, and the open method specifies the HTTP method for contacting the server and provides the server's Web address. The callback function uses JSON parse to get a response from the server. When the server responds, the JSON.parse API is called, which creates the JavaScript object. The object is sent back to the server. The data, however, is "stringified" first.

■ Loading and Saving Files

THE BOTTOM LINE
JavaScript can access files on your local computer and, with HTML5, can validate the file type before loading. JavaScript makes loading files a more interactive and error-free process.

CERTIFICATION READY
How can I restrict the type of file to load?
4.4

Many Web or mobile applications include a function to upload a file. This has long been a weakness of HTML, in that there is no effective way to specify, for example, "only allow uploads of images, as opposed to documents, and only if the images occupy less than 1.1 megabytes." Without this capability, it too often happens that users accidentally attempt to upload something other than what they intended or the application supports, and network delays make correction of the error a time-consuming process.

HTML5's ability to access local files means that an image intended for upload can be advertised as a thumbnail and validated *before* the upload. JavaScript's immediate actions help make uploading a more interactive and error-free process.

ACCESS A LOCAL FILE

GET READY. To demonstrate JavaScript's ability to access a local file, perform the following steps:

1. Create **L9-js7.html** with the following content:

```
<!doctype html>
<html>
<head>
<title>JavaScript accesses local files</title>

<script type = "text/javascript">
function acknowledge(file_handle) {
    var size = file_handle.size;
    var fname = file_handle.name;
    var message = "You have chosen the file '" +
fname + "'.  This appears to be a recognizable
image, totaling " + size + " bytes in size.";
    alert(message);

}

function complain(fname) {
    var message = "The file named '" + fname + "'
does not appear to have an acceptable extension.";
    alert(message);

}
```

```
function handle_file_selection(item) {
    var f = item.files[0];
    var fname = f.name;
    var last_index = fname.lastIndexOf('.');
    if (last_index == -1) {
        complain(fname);
        return;
    }
    var ext = fname.substr(last_index + 1);
    if (ext.toLowerCase() in {'gif': '',
                              'jpg': '',
                              'png': '',
                              'tif': ''
                             }) {
        acknowledge(f);
    } else {
        complain(fname);
    }
}

</script>
</head>
<body>

<h1>JavaScript accesses local files</h1>
<input type = 'file'
       onchange = 'handle_file_selection(this);' />

</body>
</html>
```

2. Open **L9-js7.html** in a Web browser.

3. Click **Browse** and then navigate to and select a file on your local computer that's not an image. Click **Open**. The display should look like Figure 9-7. The message box informs you that you selected the wrong file type. Click **OK** to close the message box.

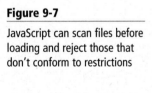

Figure 9-7

JavaScript can scan files before loading and reject those that don't conform to restrictions

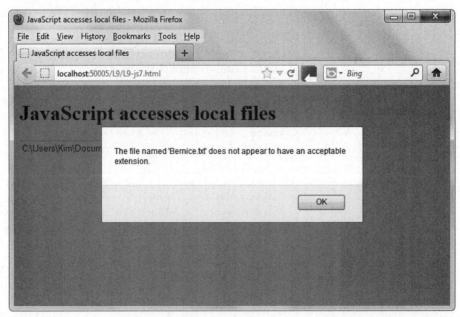

4. Repeat step 3 and this time open a file that is an image. The resulting message box should look similar to Figure 9-8, informing you that you selected an acceptable type of file. Click **OK** to close the message box.

Figure 9-8

This file meets the requirements for file loading

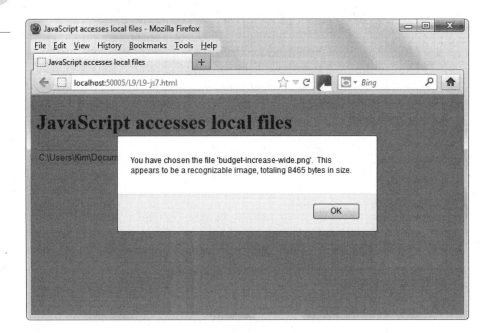

5. Close the file but leave the editing tool and Web browser open if you complete the next exercise during this session.

Notice this program doesn't actually upload the selected file. The point of this exercise is to show how JavaScript can access and manage the file and its contents even before uploading.

Using the Application Cache (AppCache)

Users want to be able to browse your site even when offline. The Application Cache (AppCache) API makes this possible. AppCache differs from browser cache in that browser cache contains all Web pages visited, whereas AppCache saves only the files listed in the cache manifest.

AppCache saves a copy of your Web site files locally, in a structured form. The files include HTML, CSS, and JavaScript, along with other resources the site needs to run. After a visitor has visited the site once, subsequent visits will load resources quickly from the local copy rather than waiting on a network connection.

Recall from Lesson 1 that AppCache uses a text file called a cache manifest to specify the files a Web browser should cache offline. Even if a user refreshes the browser while offline, the page will load and work correctly.

AppCache is not the same as a browser's cache. Whereas a browser's cache saves all Web pages visited, AppCache saves only the files listed in the cache manifest. You can apply AppCache to a single Web page or an entire site.

For AppCache to work, the Web server must be configured with the correct MIME type, which is text/cache-manifest. In addition, the preferred file extension for manifest files is .appcache.

 USE APPCACHE

GET READY. To demonstrate AppCache, perform the following steps:

1. Obtain privileges to use a Web server from your instructor. The server must have the MIME type configured to text/cache-manifest. AppCache is only effective for network accesses; it does not act when a Web resource is local.

2. Create **L9-appcache.html** with the following content:

```
<!doctype html>
<html manifest = "test.appcache">
<head>
<title>Minimal AppCache example</title>

</head>
<body>
<h1>Minimal AppCache example</h1>
<p>This page should reload after disconnecting from
   the Internet and refreshing the Web page.
</body>
</html>
```

3. Close **L9-appcache.html** and then upload the file to the Web server. The instructor will give you the Web address of the file.

4. In a Web browser, navigate to the Web address. The **L9-appcache.html** file opens.

5. Observe the display as shown in Figure 9-9. Does the page reload as expected?

Figure 9-9

Web page pulled from AppCache

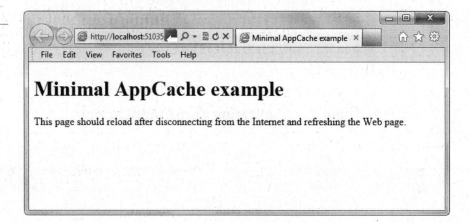

6. Disconnect your local computer from the Internet.

7. Confirm that you cannot access Web pages—the MSDN homepage, for example.

8. Refresh the image of **L9-appcache.html** in your browser.

9. Note that it displays quickly, even though L9-appcache.html is now unavailable.

10. Close the HTML file but leave the editing tool and Web browser open if you complete the next exercise during this session.

➕ MORE INFORMATION

For a great tutorial on AppCache, visit the "A Beginner's Guide to Using the Application Cache" Web page at http://www.html5rocks.com/en/tutorials/appcache/beginner/.

Understanding and Using Data Types

In JavaScript, data comes in a few different flavors. The most common are strings and numbers. Other data types include array, Boolean, null, object, and undefined.

CERTIFICATION READY
Which data types are available in JavaScript?
4.4

Values in JavaScript appear in special appearances or "dressings", called ***data types***. Most often encountered are strings and numbers. "ABCD" and "1234" are both examples of strings; the latter just happens to include only digits. The numeral "3" is a number, but "3 dollars" is a string.

Other data types are more specialized, such as array, Boolean, null, object, and undefined. Their use is relatively rare, and outside the scope of this lesson.

The main significance of data types at this level is that their definition leads to a few surprises. In JavaScript, the following example has the value 123:

```
"'1' + 2 + 3"
```

But the following has the value 6 or '33', depending on the JavaScript interpreter used:

```
"1 + 2 + '3'"
```

There are rules that define all this behavior, and each of the data types has its uses. For the purpose of this lesson, be aware of the distinction between, for example, a number and the characters that represent that number. If you accidentally run into a computation where JavaScript's handling of types surprises you, study MSDN reference material on data types. In the meantime, program JavaScript simply and carefully.

■ Using JavaScript to Validate User Form Input

↓ THE BOTTOM LINE
As end users enter data in a form, JavaScript can instantly validate entries and suggest alternatives.

You learned about HTML form input and validation in Lesson 3. With JavaScript, your forms can do much more for you and your end users.

Suppose, for example, that an end user needs to enter a serial number of the form XXX-XXX-XX-X, where each X is a digit. In the early days of Web application, end users typed this in as best they could, then "submitted" a complete form. The server checked for any errors, and reported them back as best it could.

CERTIFICATION READY
How is JavaScript used to perform client-side entry validation?
4.4

With JavaScript, client-side entry validation in the form of feedback and correction is instantaneous.

⊙ MANAGE A FORM WITH JAVASCRIPT

GET READY. To demonstrate JavaScript's ability to manage a form, perform the following steps:

1. Create **L9-js8.html** with contents:

```
<!doctype html>
<html>
<head>
<title>Form management</title>
```

```
<script type = "text/javascript">
                        // The action of the correct()
    function is to
                        // test the characters the user has
    entered
                        // against the pattern 'XXX-XXX-XX-
    X'.  If the
                        // user's entry does not match this
    pattern,
                        // remove the last character. This
    gives the
                        // user the impression that she or
    he can only
                        // enter valid characters.
function correct() {
    var input_object =
    document.getElementById("serial");
    var value = input_object.value;
    var current_length = value.length;
    if (current_length) {
        var last_character =
    value.substring(current_length - 1);
        switch (current_length) {
            case 4:
            case 8:
            case 11:
                if (last_character != '-') {
                    value = value.substring(0,
    current_length - 1);
                }
                break;
            default:
                if (!/\d/.test(last_character)) {
                    value = value.substring(0,
    current_length - 1);
                }
        }
        if (current_length > 12) {
            value = value.substring(0, current_length
    - 1);
        }
        current_length = value.length;
        switch (current_length) {
            case 3:
            case 7:
            case 10:
                value += "-";
        }
        input_object.value = value;
    }
}

</script>
</head>
<body>
```

```
<h1>Form management</h1>
<form>
Enter here a serial number in the pattern XXX-XXX-XX-
    X, where each X is a digit: <input id = "serial"
    type = 'text' size = '12'
                                        onkeyup =
    "correct();">.
</form>

</body>
</html>
```

2. Open **L9-js8.html** in a Web browser. The display appears, as shown in Figure 9-10.

Figure 9-10

Client-side entry validation is a good responsibility for JavaScript

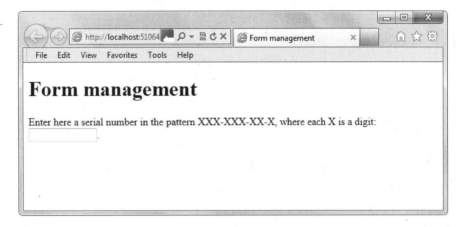

3. Begin typing characters. Notice that the entry field accepts only characters that match the XXX-XXX-XX-X pattern, ignoring any that don't match.

4. Close the file but leave the editing tool and Web browser open if you complete the next exercise during this session.

A real-world application would require more validation: it's not enough that an entry *look* like a serial number, but the application also should confirm that it *is* a serial number. While an end user might still enter a value incorrectly, simple JavaScript validation of form inputs goes a long way toward helping ensure success. Also, even with this validation, a sufficiently determined end user can use the mouse to enter certain values that don't match the serial-number pattern. A more sophisticated validator might trap mouse movements and deletions.

■ Understanding and Using Cookies

THE BOTTOM LINE

Cookies have traditionally held information that allows for personalization, customization, and convenience. JavaScript can create and retrieve cookies.

CERTIFICATION READY
What is a cookie?
4.4

Cookies are small text files that Web sites save to a computer's hard disk that contain information about the user and his or her browsing preferences. The content of cookies change as a user revisits a site and selects different items or changes preferences. From the perspective of JavaScript, a cookie is a variable, and you use JavaScript to both create and retrieve cookies.

Suppose you're in charge of a computer game coded in HTML and JavaScript. It works well enough, but requires a user to choose a "level" each time he begins a new game. Wouldn't it be better to have the game assume that the user wants to start one level beyond his last game, with an option to adjust? Not only is that better, but JavaScript's cookie capabilities make it easy to program.

➔ USE COOKIES

GET READY. To demonstrate JavaScript's ability to retain information on the desktop computer even with the browser shut down, perform the following steps:

1. Create **L9-js9.html** with the following content:

```html
<!doctype html>
<html>
<head>
<title>Use of cookies</title>

<script type = "text/javascript">

function getCookie(c_name) {
    var i,x,y,ARRcookies=document.cookie.split(";");
    for (i=0;i<ARRcookies.length;i++)
    {
x=ARRcookies[i].substr(0,ARRcookies[i].indexOf("="));
y=ARRcookies[i].substr(ARRcookies[i].indexOf("=")+1);
    x=x.replace(/^\s+|\s+$/g,"");
      if (x==c_name)
        {
        return unescape(y);
        }
      }
}

function init() {
    var message;
    level_object  = document.getElementById("level");
    var welcome = document.getElementById("welcome");
    var level = getCookie("level");
    if (level == null || level == '') {
        message = "It appears this is your first time
to play. You will start at level 1.";
        level = 1;
    } else {
        message = "When you last played, you reached
level " + level +".  You will start there now.";
    }
    welcome.innerHTML = message;
    level_object.value = level;
}

function save_level() {
    setCookie("level", level_object.value, 10);
}

function setCookie(c_name,value,exdays) {
    var exdate=new Date();
    exdate.setDate(exdate.getDate() + exdays);
    var c_value=escape(value) + ((exdays==null) ? ""
    : "; expires="+exdate.toUTC
String());
    document.cookie=c_name + "=" + c_value;
}
```

```
</script>
</head>
<body onload = "init();">

<h1>Use of cookies</h1>
<p id = "welcome">Welcome.</p>
<form>
You can update your level at any time.  It is
    currently set at
<input id = "level" type = "number" min = "1" max =
    "100"
        oninput = "save_level();" />.
</form>

</body>
</html>
```

2. Obtain privileges to use a Web server from your instructor. Cookies can only be enabled for Web pages accessed through the network, not locally.

3. Upload **L9-js9.html** to the Web server using a file transfer program, as described by your instructor. Your instructor also needs to give you the Web address for the file.

4. In a Web browser, use the Web address to navigate to and open **L9-js9.html**.

5. Notice the level at which you start, as shown in Figure 9-11.

Figure 9-11

Cookies have often been used to keep small pieces of data on the client machine

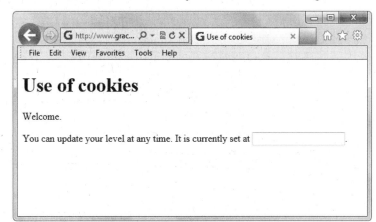

6. Pretend you've played for a while and reached a different level. Enter that level in the input area.

7. Close the application's window.

8. Open **L9-js9.html** again. Do you see how the application "remembered" your position from one browser session to another?

9. Using your browser's preferences settings, remove the cookie created in this exercise or, if more convenient, remove all cookies.

10. Open **L9-js9.html** again. Note that your level has reverted to the default of 1.

11. Close the file but leave the editing tool and Web browser open if you complete the next exercise during this session.

■ Understanding and Using Local Storage

THE BOTTOM LINE

Cookies are limited in the information they store, and therefore in the effects programming with them can achieve. Plus, cookies pose a threat to data privacy. HTML5 provides local storage to make personalization easier to program and more capable.

Cookies have limits. They have a bad reputation in some circles for contributing to spread of personal information without permission, and they are clumsy for storage of all but the simplest data. HTML5's *LocalStorage* has better security *and* makes programming easier than it is with cookies.

 SAVE TO LOCAL STORAGE

GET READY. To demonstrate JavaScript's ability to save information *without* cookies, perform the following steps:

1. Create **L9-js10.html** with the following content:

```html
<!doctype html>
<html>
<head>
<title>Use of local storage</title>

<script type = "text/javascript">
// This page demonstrates a simple model for
// saving a player's "level" in local storage.
function init() {
    var message;
    level_object  = document.getElementById("level");
    var welcome = document.getElementById("welcome");
        // "localStorage" is a keyword for an HTML5-
        // capable browser.  "localStorage.level" is
        // a variable name chosen for use by this
        // particular page.
    var level = localStorage.level;
    if (level == null || level == '') {
        message = "It appears this is your first time
    to play. You will start at level 1.";
        level = 1;
    } else {
        message = "When you last played, you reached
    level " + level +".  You will start there now.";
    }
    welcome.innerHTML = message;
    level_object.value = level;
}

function save_level() {
    localStorage.level = level_object.value;
}

</script>
</head>
<body onload = "init();">

<h1>Use of local storage</h1>
<p id = "welcome">Welcome.</p>
<form>
You can update your level at any time.  It is
    currently set at
<input id = "level" type = "number" min = "1" max =
    "100"
        oninput = "save_level();" />.
</form>

</body>
</html>
```

2. Obtain privileges to use a Web server from your instructor. Local storage can only be enabled for Web pages accessed through the network, not locally.

3. Upload **L9-js10.html** to the Web server using a file transfer program, as described by your instructor. Your instructor also needs to give you the Web address for the file.

4. In a Web browser, use the Web address to navigate to and open **L9-js10.html**.

5. Notice the level at which you start, as shown in Figure 9-12.

Figure 9-12

The program's initial interface

6. Pretend you've played for a while and reached a different level. Enter that level in the input area.

7. Close the application's window.

8. Open **L9-js10.html** again. Do you see how the application "remembered" your position from one browser session to another?

9. Close the file and any open programs or windows.

Notice how much more succinct programming of local storage is than the corresponding operations with cookies.

SKILL SUMMARY

IN THIS LESSON YOU LEARNED:

- HTML and CSS have a number of facilities for fast animation of common effects. However, JavaScript is far more flexible and can produce remarkable results.
- JavaScript is a powerful general-purpose programming language. If you can imagine a particular animation, there's probably a way to create it in JavaScript.
- You can use JavaScript to display an image when a button is clicked or some other event occurs. The `createElement` method works well for this use.
- If an application accessible from your computer exposes data to you as an end user, there's probably a way for JavaScript to reach the data. One of the most important roles of JavaScript is to communicate in real-time with remote data sources.
- As a general-purpose language, JavaScript can communicate structured information much richer than the simple values used in most of this lesson.
- JavaScript can access files on your local computer and, with HTML5, can validate the file type before loading. JavaScript makes loading files a more interactive and error-free process.

(Continued)

- Users want to be able to browse your site even when offline. The Application Cache (AppCache) API makes this possible. AppCache differs from browser cache in that browser cache contains all Web pages visited, whereas AppCache saves only the files listed in the cache manifest.
- In JavaScript, data comes in a few different flavors. The most common are strings and numbers. Other data types include array, Boolean, null, object, and undefined.
- As end users enter data in a form, JavaScript can instantly validate entries and suggest alternatives.
- Cookies have traditionally held information that allows for personalization, customization, and convenience. JavaScript can create and retrieve cookies.
- Cookies are limited in the information they store, and therefore in the effects programming with them can achieve. Plus, cookies pose a threat to data privacy. HTML5 provides local storage to make personalization easier to program and more capable.

■ Knowledge Assessment

Fill in the Blank

Complete the following sentences by writing the correct word or words in the blanks provided.

1. _____ is the display of a sequence of static images at a fast enough speed to create the illusion of movement.

2. You need to draw a complex diagram as part of an HTML5 display. One way is with the _____ element.

3. Before HTML5, the most common way to keep information on the client side of a Web application—that is, on the user's computer—was with _____.

4. _____ enables you to use JavaScript to pass data in the form of text strings, but not objects, between a client and a server.

5. _____ is a programming technique in which a function calls itself.

6. _____ is the label generally used for analysis of complex information into constituent parts.

7. The _____ API saves a copy of your Web site files locally, in a structured form.

8. Values in JavaScript appear in special different appearances, called _____, which are most often strings and numbers.

9. _____ is a subset of JavaScript that enables you to exchange JavaScript objects with a server.

10. _____ is an alternative to cookies.

Multiple Choice

Circle the letter that corresponds to the best answer.

1. Which of the following is the most common way to code JavaScript with a delayed effect?
   a. sleep()
   b. delay()
   c. wait()
   d. setTimeout()

2. JavaScript can display different types of graphics, from JPG and PNG files to shapes like boxes and circles. One method you can use to display graphics using Javascript is:
   a. `createElement`
   b. `move_paragraph`
   c. `JSON`
   d. `display`

3. What are the two primary constructs used to draw a canvas object?
   a. `getElementById()`
   b. `getCanvasContext`
   c. `getElementByCanvas()`
   d. `canvas.getContext`

4. Sending and receiving data in JavaScript requires a dynamic Web server and:
   a. client-side validation
   b. server-side programming
   c. CSS
   d. none of the above

5. The canvas element builds in which set of methods?
   a. `drawRect()`, `outlineRect()`, `eraseRect()`
   b. `fillRect()`, `strokeRect()`, `clearRect()`
   c. `beginPath()`, `fillPath()`, `endPath()`
   d. `beginPath()`, `fillPath()`, `closePath()`

6. Which JSON API converts a JavaScript object to string data for exchange with a server?
   a. `JSON.parsify`
   b. `XMLHttpRequest`
   c. `JSON.stringify`
   d. `getObjectString`

7. How does `AppCache` differ from browser cache?
   a. `AppCache` saves copies of Web pages.
   b. You first have to visit a Web page for it to be included in the cache.
   c. `AppCache` saves only those files listed in the cache manifest.
   d. `AppCache` and browser cache are the same thing.

8. Which of the following is *not* a data type used by JavaScript?
   a. composite
   b. string
   c. number
   d. Boolean

9. Which of the following poses a threat to data privacy?
   a. `AppCache`
   b. `LocalStorage`
   c. cookies
   d. animation

10. Which API enables you to work on remote files offline?
    a. `XMLHttpRequest`
    b. `AppCache`
    c. `JSON.parse`
    d. `JSON.stringify`

True / False

Circle T if the statement is true or F if the statement is false.

T F **1.** JavaScript doesn't allow recursion.

T F **2.** You use XMLHttpRequest to create animations.

T F **3.** It is possible to write JavaScript code in such a way that it executes before all images are loaded.

T F **4.** You can use LocalStorage to store a user's personal data.

T F **5.** A common technique in JavaScript animation is to use setTimeout recursively.

■ Competency Assessment

Scenario 9-1: Understanding Animation Basics

Roan works as an administrative assistant at a nonprofit organization that is producing an encyclopedia on wild plants. The outreach volunteer asked Roan if he could animate the graphic on the homepage so that it appears as though the seed grows to a full-grown swatch of prairie grass in 5 or 6 seconds. Roan knows nothing about animation and asks you for a quick summary.

Scenario 9-2: Creating a Warehouse Floor Plan App

Trudy is a warehouse manager. She wants a Web application that sketches an outline of the floor plan of the interior of a warehouse. She's supposed to submit a request to the development team soon but doesn't know the appropriate technology to include in her description. Trudy wants your opinion. What do you tell her?

■ Proficiency Assessment

Scenario 9-3: Enhancing the Warehouse Application

Trudy has decided to expand her request to the development team, and now wants to include an entry form that accepts stock-keeping unit (SKU) codes. The warehouse server has photographs of merchandise, indexed by SKU, as well as information on where in the warehouse items of that description are currently located. Trudy wants the program to place a photograph of the item on the aisle and shelf where it is currently located. Briefly, how can this be done? She needs to add the description to her request.

Scenario 9-4: Reviewing Documents Offline

An existing online application collects and scores reviewers' comments about different budget items in a highly structured process: each item links to proposal details, personnel involved, and so on. The application is successful. The reviewers complain, though, that it can only be used when online; they can't, for example, fill out the score sheets while on an airplane flight and without an Internet connection. They propose to download all the linked materials and fill out spreadsheets of their comments. What is your response?

JavaScript Coding for the Touch Interface, Device and Operating System Resources, and More

EXAM OBJECTIVE MATRIX

SKILLS/CONCEPTS	MTA EXAM OBJECTIVE	MTA EXAM OBJECTIVENUMBER
Responding to the Touch Interface	Respond to the touch interface.	4.5
Coding Additional HTML5 APIs	Code additional HTML5 APIs.	4.6
Accessing Device and Operating System Resources	Access device and operating system resources.	4.7

KEY TERMS

accelerometer

Blob

capacitive touch screen

civic data

device-independent

File API

geodetic data

Geolocation API

gesture event

local storage

platform-independent

polling

resistive touch screen

session storage

touch event

touch object

touchlist

Web Hypertext Application Technology Working Group (WHATWG)

Web Worker API

WebSocket API

The Malted Milk Media development team has asked you to help them complete the Trusty Lawn Care mobile application project. The app needs to include a touch interface, so your responsibility is to learn how to capture and respond to gestures. You should also become well-versed in geolocation, and hardware capabilities like GPS and accelerometer.

Responding to the Touch Interface

↓
THE BOTTOM LINE

A touch-enabled device interprets finger movements on a touch screen, called gestures, and converts them to instructions for an application. Many gestures have mouse equivalents.

Touch screens have become the most popular form of smartphone interface, and there are a fair number of desktop touch screen monitors in use. A touch-enabled device has a specially developed screen that senses touch data (called points), which begin in the form of pressure or electrical signals. There are two primary types of touch screens:

- A *resistive touch screen* is made up of several layers, the topmost of which flexes when pressed and pushes into the layer underneath. Sensors detect the pressure, which is how the system knows which part of the screen has been pressed. The touch screens used in hospitals and restaurants are often resistive.

- *Capacitive touch screens* use electrodes to sense objects touching the screen. Because the object must have conductive properties, a finger works but something like a stylus does not. Most touch-screen smartphones and computer monitors are capacitive.

CERTIFICATION READY
How do touch screens respond to user input?
4.5

A touch screen processor gathers the touch data and interprets them as gestures. Depending on the hardware involved, the data is sent from the processor directly to the user application, or from the processor to the operating system to the application, where the application uses the data to perform tasks.

CERTIFICATION READY
Which gestures provide input on touch screens?
4.5

A gesture is a technique using one or more fingers, or a pointing device like a stylus, over a control or object on the screen to provide input to a touch-enabled application. Tapping selects an object or presses a button, swiping a finger scrolls a set of photos or a list of contacts on the screen, and a pinchopen action increases the size of the screen display (zooms in). Microsoft defines gestures as shown in Table 10-1.

Table 10-1

Overview of touch gestures

GESTURE	MOUSE EQUIVALENT	DESCRIPTION
Tap	Left-click	Tap a finger on the screen
Double tap	Left double-click	Quickly tap a finger twice on the screen
Two-finger tap	N/A	Tap two fingers on the screen simultaneously
Press and tap	Right-click	Press and hold one finger while tapping another
Press and hold	Right-click	Press and hold a finger on the screen, then release
Selection/drag	Mouse drag (selection)	Drag a finger to the left or right
Panning with inertia	Scrolling	Press and hold a finger on the screen and then drag the finger
Flick	Move back or forward Pan up or pan down	Press a finger on the screen, move it in any direction, and then lift the finger to scroll
Rotate	N/A	Move two fingers over an object on the screen in a circular motion
Zoom	CTRL + mouse wheel forward or backward	Pinch an object inwards or outwards

You use the addEventListener method to attach an event handler to an HTML element, which can be a div, link, or anything you want. Using addEventListener lets you do something useful when an event is triggered. The following is general syntax for addEventListener:

```
object.addEventListener(event, eventListenerFunction);
```

For example, in the following code for a canvas drawing program, the startup function is called when the Web page loads. The program listens for a user touching the screen (the touchstart event), moving a finger (touchmove), and so on:

```
function startup() {
    var el = document.getElementsByTagName("cdraw")[0];
    el.addEventListener("touchstart", handleStart, false);
    el.addEventListener("touchmove", handleMove, false);
    el.addEventListener("touchend", handleEnd, false);
    el.addEventListener("touchcancel", handleCancel, false);
}
```

Let's look more closely at the handleStart function. It's declared in the following code, the same way other functions are declared in JavaScript except that the listener function must have one argument to represent the event. You can use any identifier as the event argument, but developers often use the letter "e" or an identifier that starts with the letter "e."

```
function handleStart(evt) {
    evt.preventDefault();
    var el = document.getElementsByTagName("cdraw")[0];
    var context = el.getContext("2d");
    var touches = evt.changedTouches;
for (var i=0; i<touches.length; i++) {
        ongoingTouches.push(touches[i]);
        var color = colorForTouch(touches[i]);
        context.fillStyle = color;
        context.fillRect(touches[i].pageX,
touches[i].pageY, 4, 4);
    }
}
```

The evt.preventDefault method stops the browser from continuing to process the touch event, which prevents it from scrolling in this instance. After getting the context (el.getContext), the list of changed touch points is pulled from the event's changedTouches property. Then, the program deals with the touch objects in the touchlist. PageX and pageY give the X and Y coordinates of the finger.

Gesture events are triggered for multi-finger gestures. The main gesture events are:

- gesturestart: Every new two-finger gesture triggers a gesturestart event.
- gesturechange: When both fingers move around the screen, a gesturechange event occurs.
- gestureend: Lifting both fingers from the screen triggers a gestureend event.

Gesture events are types of touch events, so they receive event objects that contain touch properties. In addition, gesture events may include these properties:

- scale: Indicates the amount of two-finger pinch zooming that occurred. The decimal value of the property starts at 1.0; the value is less than 1.0 when the fingers move toward each other, and the value is more than 1.0 when the fingers move apart.

Now that you understand the different types of touch gestures, let's see how they're captured and used in applications.

Capturing and Responding to Gestures

The primary touch events are touchstart, touchmove, touchend, and touchcancel. The primary gesture events are gesturestart, gesturechange, and gestureend.

The action an application takes in response to a gesture is called a **touch event**. You can use JavaScript to create touch events in touch-enabled apps. Developers can draw from a large set of input application programming interfaces (APIs) that work with touch screen data.

The primary JavaScript touch events are:

- **touchstart:** Every new finger touch triggers a touchstart event.
- **touchmove:** When a finger moves around the surface of the screen, a touchmove event occurs, which tracks the finger movement.
- **touchend:** Lifting the finger from the screen triggers a touchend event.
- **touchcancel:** The touchcancel event is triggered when the device launches another application.

TAKE NOTE*

The touchcancel event helps the browser keep track of active touch objects in the touchlist. It can also reset variables used during touchstart and touchmove events. However, developers seldom use the touchcancel event, so you won't see it very often in scripts.

CERTIFICATION READY
What are the four primary JavaScript touch events?
4.5

In JavaScript, the **touch object** detects input from touch-enabled devices. You reference touch objects in the **touchlist**, which includes all of the points of contact with a touch screen. A single tap has one entry in the touchlist, whereas a three-finger gesture would have a total of three entries. Touch objects are read-only and have the following properties:

- identifier: A unique identifier for the touch
- target: The HTML element that the touch affected
- clientx: Horizontal position, relative to browser window
- clienty: Vertical position, relative to browser window
- pagex: Horizontal position, relative to HTML document
- pagey: Vertical position, relative to HTML document
- screenx: Horizontal position, relative to the screen
- screeny: Vertical position, relative to the screen

Each touch event includes three different touchlists:

- touches: A list of all touch points currently in contact with the screen
- targetTouches: A list of touch points currently in contact with the screen and whose touchstart event occurred within the same node (inside the same target element as the current target element)
- changedTouches: A list of touch points that caused the current event to be fired; for example, in a touchend event, this is the finger that was removed

- rotation: Indicates the amount of two-finger rotation that occurred. The value of the rotation is in degrees; positive values are clockwise, and negative values are counterclockwise.

You can combine gesture events with CSS visual effects to enable scaling and rotation. For example, the following code implements the gesturechange event handler with scaling and rotation:

```
document.addEventListener('gesturechange',
function(event) {
    event.preventDefault();
    console.log("Scale: " + event.scale + ",
Rotation: " + event.rotation);
}, false);
```

An implied listener function is being created in this example. The event handler passes the event object as an implied argument called "event" to get specific information about the event.

Screens that can display in portrait or landscape trigger an orientationchanged event when the user changes the orientation of the screen. You can use orientationchanged to test for the rotation of the device. Each event has a numeric value representing the scale and rotation values.

DETECT TOUCH SCREEN CAPABILITY

GET READY. To check whether a user's device is touch-enabled, perform the following steps:

1. In an editing or app development tool, create a file named **L10-touch.html** with the following content:

```
<!doctype html>

<html>
  <head>
    <title>Detect Touch Screen</title>
    <meta charset="utf-8" />

    <style type="text/css">
      #canvas{background-color: dodgerblue;}
    </style>

    <script type="text/javascript">

        document.addEventListener("DOMContentLoaded",
init, false);

        function init() {
            var canvas =
document.getElementById("canvas");

            if ("ontouchstart" in
document.documentElement) {
            canvas.addEventListener("touchstart",
detect, false);
            }
```

```
        else {
            canvas.addEventListener("mousedown",
    detect, false);
        }
    }

    function detect() {
        if ("ontouchstart" in
    document.documentElement) {
            alert("Touch screen device
    detected!");
        }
        else {
            alert("No touch screen device
    detected.");
        }
    }

</script>

</head>

<body>
 <canvas id="canvas" width="100"
 height="100"></canvas>
 <br />
 <p>Click the box to start touch screen detection.</p>
</body>
</html>
```

This code draws a canvas box on the screen, followed by a text line that states Click the box to start touch screen detection. The initial function assigns the canvas element, and then the event listener listens for a touch event or a mouse click. If the user has a touch screen and touches the box, the program displays a Touch screen device detected message. If a mouse click is detected, the No touch screen detected message displays.

2. Open **L10-touch.html** in a Web browser. Your display should look like Figure 10-1.

Figure 10-1

The touch screen detection program interface

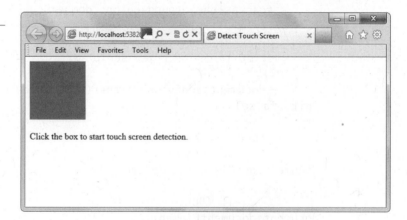

3. Click the blue box. If you're working on a computer with an ordinary monitor, the alert box shown in Figure 10-2 appears. Otherwise, an alert box appears that displays the text Touch screen device detected!

Figure 10-2

The alert box indicates that a touch screen is not present

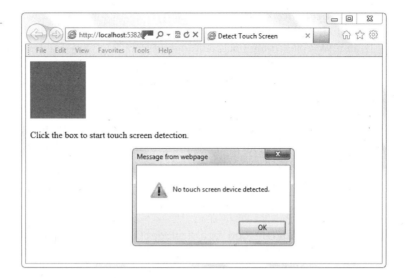

4. Click **OK** to close the alert box.

5. Close the file and Web browser but leave the editing tool open if you plan to complete the next exercise during this session.

➕ **MORE INFORMATION**

The W3C Touch Events version 2 specification is at Touch Events version 1 at http://www.w3.org/TR/touch-events/.

▪ Coding Additional HTML5 APIs

THE BOTTOM LINE

The Web Hypertext Application Technology Working Group (WHATWG) maintains a living HTML specification that includes APIs that were not originally part of the HTML5 specification. These include Geolocation, Web Workers, WebSockets, and File API.

As you've learned throughout this book, there are many HTML5 APIs available that provide new and enhanced functionality while easing development of HTML documents. What hasn't been specifically pointed out is that there are actually two versions of the HTML5 specification: one published by the W3C and another by WHATWG.

CERTIFICATION READY
What is WHATWG?
4.6

The *Web Hypertext Application Technology Working Group (WHATWG)* was formed by Apple, the Mozilla Foundation, and Opera Software to define and document the HTML5 specification. The WHATWG Web site at http://developers.whatwg.org/ is a good resource for learning more about new HTML5 elements and how to use them.

The living HTML specification maintained by WHATWG contains additional APIs to those described in the original W3C HTML5 specification. The applicable APIs covered in the following sections are Geolocation, Web Workers, WebSockets, and File API.

Coding to Capture GeoLocation

The Geolocation API gets a user's geographical coordinates (latitude and longitude). The API can also show a map with a marker showing the user's location based on the coordinates.

The *Geolocation API* defines an interface that provides a device's location, usually using latitude and longitude coordinates. The API exposes the latitude and longitude to JavaScript in a Web page using the geolocation object.

The two primary geolocation functions are as follows:

CERTIFICATION READY
Which JavaScript function gets a device's current geographic position?
4.6

- getCurrentPosition: Gets the device's current geographic position using the getCurrentPosition method.
- watchPosition: Watches the device's position as it changes over time using the watchPosition method, and generates an event if a change occurs. Calling clearWatch stops the watch.

The following is a simple example of a call to getCurrentPosition. The showmap callback function receives the latitude and longitude coordinates:

```
navigator.geolocation.getCurrentPosition(showmap);
function showmap(position) {
    var latitude = position.coords.latitude;
    var longitude = position.coords.longitude;
    // Code to display a map
}
```

You can present location data to users in two ways: geodetic and civic. *Geodetic data* provides raw location data, such as longitude and latitude, or meters. *Civic data* is location data that's more easily understood by humans, such as a map or an address like 637 Park Street.

The Geolocation API returns geodetic data from the functions, which you can present in its raw form or combine with an online mapping service like Bing Maps to display a map with a pointer to the user's location.

Be aware that privacy is a major concern for many users. Therefore, the Geolocation API allows users to hide their location, and many implementations prompt the user for permission to return the user's location coordinates.

Geolocation is geared mainly for smartphones and other mobile devices, and doesn't work consistently for desktop computers. When a device has no means of locating itself, the API generates a position unavailable error.

CREATE A GEOLOCATION APPLICATION

GET READY. To create a geolocation application that displays the user's current latitude and longitude, perform the following steps:

1. In an editing or app development tool, create a file named **L10-geolocation.html** with the following content:

```
<!doctype html>
<html>
<head>
    <title>Geolocation Example</title>
    <meta charset="utf-8" />
    <script>
        var messageDiv =
    document.getElementById('message');
```

```
            function initLocation() {

                var geolocation = navigator.geolocation;

                if (geolocation) {
                    try {
            navigator.geolocation.getCurrentPosition(
                                    successCallback,
                                    errorCallback
                        );

                    } catch (err) {
                        messageDiv.innerHTML = 'Error';
                    }
                } else {
                        messageDiv.innerHTML = 'Your browser
        does not support geolocation.';
                }

            }

            function successCallback(location) {
                    message.innerHTML = "<p>Latitude: " +
        location.coords.latitude + "</p>";
                    message.innerHTML += "<p>Longitude: " +
        location.coords.longitude + "</p>";
            }

            function errorCallback() {
                    messageDiv.innerHTML = 'There was an error
        looking up your position';
            }
        </script>
    </head>

    <body onload="initLocation()">
        <div id="message">Looking Up Location</div>
    </body>
    </html>
```

This code is a good test of the HTML5 geolocation API. Here's how the code works: `navigator.geolocation.getCurrentPosition` requests a position, which polls the hardware device's GPS feature or a computer's router for location information. If successful, the `successCallback` function displays the latitude and longitude coordinates onscreen. If the information is not available, the `There was an error looking up your position` message appears.

2. Open **L10-geolocation.html** in a Web browser. If the browser supports geolocation, you should be asked for your permission for the browser to track your physical location, as shown in Figure 10-3. Click **Allow once** or a similar command, depending on the browser you're using.

Figure 10-3

The browser prompting for permission to track your physical location

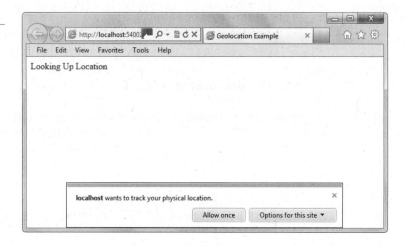

3. Your coordinates display, similar to that shown in Figure 10-4.

Figure 10-4

The display of coordinates using the geolocation application

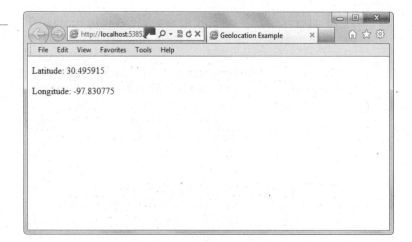

4. Close the file and Web browser but leave the editing tool open if you plan to complete the next exercise during this session.

+ MORE INFORMATION

The Microsoft "Geolocation" Web page at http://bit.ly/IZ7Lut offers links to creating a location-aware Web page and Internet Explorer tutorials. You should also check out the "12 Cool HTML5 Geolocation Ideas" article in *MSDN Magazine* at http://msdn.microsoft.com/en-us/magazine/hh563893.aspx.

Understanding Web Workers

Web Workers are scripts that run in the background, performing calculations or other actions that allow for a more responsive user interface.

CERTIFICATION READY
Which types of applications use Web Workers?
4.6

Web Workers are APIs that allow scripts to run in the background as parallel threads. These background threads can connect to multiple Web pages, fetch real-time data like stock updates, make network requests, or access local storage while the main HTML document responds to the user input like tapping, scrolling, and typing. Web Workers help keep your user interface responsive for users.

Web Workers objects run in isolated threads—they do not act directly on the main HTML document or the DOM. That means you don't use document or `getElementById` in your script. (You can use `setTimeout`, `setInterval`, and `XMLHttpRequest`.) Instead, Web Workers pass information through messages, executing code from a JavaScript file separate from the main HTML document.

To use a Web Worker, you first need to create a Worker object in your main HTML document, as follows:

```
var worker = new Worker('worker.js');
```

When the browser interprets this line, it creates a new worker thread, and then starts it with the following method:

```
worker.postMessage();
```

The `postMessage()` method accepts a string or JSON object as its argument. All browsers support passing a string message, but only the latest versions of the major browsers support JSON object passing.

As a simple example of message passing with a Web Worker, the following is a script in the main HTML document:

```
var worker = new Worker("doWork.js");
// Watch for messages from the worker
worker.onmessage = function(e){
  // The message from the worker
  e.data
};
worker.postMessage("start");
```

The following code might appear in the doWork.js file:

```
onmessage = function(e){
  if ( e.data === "start" ) {
    // Perform an action or computation
    done()
  }
};
function done(){
  // Send results to main document
  postMessage("Hello, I am done");
}
```

Instead of using the `onmessage` event handler, you could use `addEventListener()` in the main HTML document, like this:

```
worker.addEventListener('message', function(e) {
```

CREATE AND RUN A WEB WORKER

GET READY. To create and run a Web Worker, perform the following steps:

1. In an editing or app development tool, create a file named **L10-worker.html** with the following content:

```
<!doctype html>
<html lang="en">
<head>
<script>
var worker = new Worker('doWork.js');

// Send a message to start the worker and pass a
variable to it
var info = 'Web Workers';
worker.postMessage(info);

// Receive a message from the worker
worker.onmessage = function (event) {
  // Do something
  alert(event.data);
};
</script>
<title>Web Workers Example</title>
</head>
<body>
</body>
</html>
```

2. Create a JavaScript file named **doWork.js** in the same folder as worker.html, with the following content:

```
onmessage = function(event) {
  var info = event.data;
  var result = 'Hello ' + info + ' everywhere';
  postMessage(result);
};
```

3. Open **L10-worker.html** in a Web browser. The alert box should display, as shown in Figure 10-5.

Figure 10-5

The result of running a Web Worker

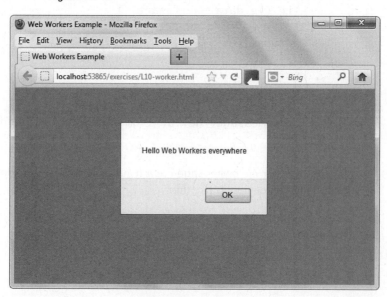

4. Click **OK** to accept the settings and close the alert box.

5. Close the files and Web browser but leave the editing tool open if you plan to complete the next exercise during this session.

Understanding WebSockets

> The WebSocket API enables you to open a persistent connection between a client and a Web server, and exchange text and binary files. WebSockets reduce the amount of overhead required for real-time communications.

WebSocket is an API that offers full-duplex communication, which is simultaneous two-way communication, through a single socket over the Internet. Developers use WebSockets mainly for real-time Web applications like chat, multiplayer online gaming, and stock quotes.

To understand the power of WebSockets, you need a little background on what came before. Originally, when a user entered a URL in a Web browser or clicked a link on a Web page, the browser contacted the appropriate Web server for the page. Whenever the user wanted to update or refresh something on the page, the browser would fetch a whole new page from the Web server. You might still see this when clicking through a photo gallery. Each time you click to a new photo, the page refreshes and you sometimes have to scroll back to the gallery.

Technologies such as AJAX made it possible to refresh only a portion of a Web page. Comet and similar "push" technologies introduced *polling*, in which a browser would contact the Web server periodically (sometimes constantly) to see if new information was available to present to the user. The problem with polling is that many requests are made to the server to check for new data, which can cause performance problems.

WebSocket technology creates a persistent connection between a client and a Web server, so that either one can send data to the other at any time. The persistent connection greatly reduces the amount of overhead required for the communication channel.

CERTIFICATION READY
How do WebSockets reduce performance problems associated with real-time applications?
4.6

To establish a WebSocket connection, the client and server change from the HTTP protocol to the WebSocket (WS) protocol during their initial handshake. After a connection is established, the client and server can exchange both text and binary files in full-duplex mode.

There are three primary events associated with WebSocket communications:

- onopen: When a socket opens
- onmessage: When a message has been received from the Web server
- onclose: When a socket closes

You'll see each of these events in the code snippets in this section. First, let's look at the JavaScript that opens a WebSocket connection:

```
var host = 'ws://example.com';
```

Notice the use of ws rather than http in the URL. You can also use wss for secure WebSocket connections, just like you use https for secure HTTP connections.

After initializing a Web connection, you should test it to make sure it was successful. You can test by using the onopen event handler to know when the connection is opened. Here's one example that opens an alert box when the socket opens:

```
socket.onopen = function(){
    alert("Socket open");
}
```

Here's another onopen example that displays a message:

```
socket.onopen = function (openEvent) {
document.getElementById("serverStatus").innerHTML =
          'Socket open';
};
```

Now you're ready to send and receive data. To send text-based messages to the server, use the send ('*message*') method on the connection object. The code for sending a text-based message is:

```
socket.send('message');
```

A simple way to send binary data is to use a binary large object (Blob). A ***Blob*** is simply a data type that can store binary data, like images or multimedia files. To send a file as a Blob, you can use this code:

```
var file =
document.querySelector('input[type="file"]').files[0];
socket.send(file);
```

Then, to receive messages from the server, you can use the onmessage callback:

```
socket.onmessage = function(msg){
    alert(msg); //Received!
}
```

Finally, to close a connection, use the onclose event handler, like this:

```
socket.onclose = function() {
    alert("Connection closed.");
};
```

The WebSockets API specification is still in draft format as of this writing, and WebSockets is not supported by all Web browsers. To get a feel for using WebSockets, complete the following exercise.

➔ CREATE A WEBSOCKET TO TEST BROWSER COMPATIBILITY

GET READY. To create a WebSocket that tests whether your browser supports WebSockets, perform the following steps:

1. In an editing or app development tool, create a file named **L10-WebSocket.html** with the following content:

```
<!doctype html>
<html>
<head>
<script type="text/javascript">
    function WebSocketTest() {
        if ("WebSocket" in window) {
            alert("Your browser supports
WebSockets.");
            // Open a WebSocket
            var socket = new
WebSocket("ws://localhost:9998/echo");
            socket.onopen = function () {
                // Connected, send data
                socket.send("Connected");
                alert("Connected.");
            };
```

```
                    socket.onmessage = function (e) {
                        var received_msg = e.data;
                        alert("Message received.");
                };
                    socket.onclose = function () {
                        // WebSocket closed
                        alert("Connection closed.");
                };
                }
                else {
                    // Browser doesn't support WebSockets
                    alert("Your browser does not support
            WebSockets.");
                }
        }
    </script>
    </head>
    <body>
    <div>
        <a href="javascript:WebSocketTest()">Click to run
        WebSocket demo</a>
    </div>
    </body>
    </html>
```

2. Open **L10-WebSocket.html** in a Web browser.

3. Follow the prompts displayed by the program. If your browser supports WebSockets, the first alert box that appears is shown in Figure 10-6.

Figure 10-6

An alert box confirms that your browser runs WebSockets

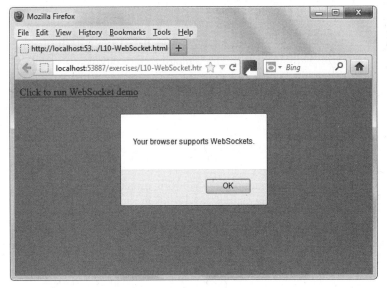

4. Click **OK** to accept the settings and close the box.

5. A second alert box should appear, stating that the connection is closed, as shown in Figure 10-7. Click **OK**.

Figure 10-7

An alert box confirms that the connection is closed

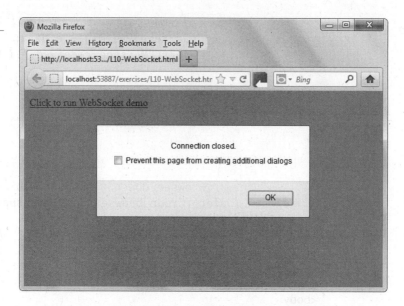

6. Close the file and Web browser but leave the editing tool open if you plan to complete the next exercise during this session.

➕ **MORE INFORMATION**

To learn more about WebSockets, visit the Microsoft "WebSockets" Web page at http://bit.ly/JXDAYN.

Using File API for File Uploads

You can use the File API to upload individual or multiple files from a local disk or a device's local storage to a remote server. You can also display uploaded image files in a Web application.

The *File API* allows a browser or application to upload files from local storage to a remote server without the need for a plug-in. For example, using File API, you can make an Open dialog box appear and allow the user to select an image file. When the user clicks OK, a thumbnail of the image file displays in the Web application. Developers use File API in games and applications that work with media files, in offline mail clients, photo editors, and video players.

The File API uses several interfaces for accessing files from local storage. Some of the interfaces are:

- `File`: Includes read-only informational attributes about an individual file, such as its name and media type, and reads in the file as a URL
- `FileList`: An array-like sequence of File objects; includes dragging a folder of files from local storage
- `Blob`: Provides access to raw binary data
- `FileReader`: Provides methods to read and display a file

CERTIFICATION READY
Which element do you use to load a file using the File API?
4.6

An easy way to load a file is to use the input `type="file"` element. Using the input `type="file"` element returns the list of selected File objects as a `FileList`. The code might look like this:

```
<input type="file" id="input"
onchange="handleFiles(this.files)">
```

To enable the user to load multiple files at once, add "multiple" before onchange, as follows:

```
<input type="file" id="input" multiple
onchange="handleFiles(this.files)">
```

 CHECK BROWSERS FOR FILE API COMPATIBILITY

GET READY. To check the major browsers for File API compatibility, perform the following steps:

1. In an editing or app development tool, create an HTML file with the following content:

```
<!doctype html>
<html>
<head>
    <meta charset="utf-8" />
    <title>File API Browser Support Check</title>
<script>
if (window.File && window.FileReader && window.FileList &&
window.Blob) {
    alert('Hurray! This browser supports File APIs.');
} else {
  alert('This browser does not fully support File APIs.');
}
</script>
</head>

<body>
</body>
</html>
```

The if statement checks for support of the File, FileReader, FileList, and Blob APIs. If the APIs are supported, the "Hurray" message appears. Otherwise the second message appears.

2. Save the files as **L10-FileAPI-checkBrowser.html** and open it in each of the major Web browsers. The display shown in Figure 10-8 appears when File APIs are not supported.

Figure 10-8

Message showing File APIs are not supported

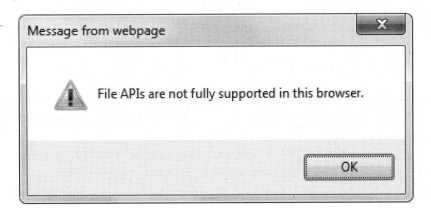

Message from webpage

File APIs are not fully supported in this browser.

OK

3. Close the file and Web browsers but leave the editing tool open if you plan to complete the next exercise during this session.

■ Accessing Device and Operating System Resources

↓ THE BOTTOM LINE The Windows Runtime environment enables developers to access in-memory resources as well as hardware using APIs.

CERTIFICATION READY
What operating system environment is responsible for access to devices, local storage, and more?
4.7

As you learned in Lesson 1, the Windows Runtime (WinRT) is the operating system environment responsible for access to devices, media, networking, local and remote storage, and other items. This is the environment in which developers test their applications and where users run the apps. A developer can use APIs and the runtime environment to request access to user devices and memory within an application.

The following sections walk you through in-memory resource access, and device and operating system access, which are functions of the WinRT.

✚ MORE INFORMATION
A list of Windows Runtime and Windows Library for JavaScript APIs is at http://msdn.microsoft.com/en-us/library/windows/apps/br211377.aspx.

Accessing In-Memory Resources

The Web Storage API includes local storage (for persistent data) and session storage (for temporary data).

The Web Storage API provides a client-side method for saving session information locally within the browser or device memory. The `localStorage` method allows users to save larger amounts of data from session to session (persistent data), whereas the `sessionStorage` method keeps data only for one session (until the browser is closed). The data is stored in key/value pairs for both types of Web storage.

Local storage is persistent data and is useful for things like online to-do lists, contact lists, calendars, and saved shopping cart data. You want this information to be available to the user after the browser closes and the user reopens it at some point. The information is held in persistent memory of Web applications and mobile devices. *Session storage* is temporary data that's kept for only one session, until the browser is closed. All of the data in a session is saved in session storage and then erased from session storage when you close the browser tab or window. An example of the proper use of session storage is a ZIP code lookup program.

In JavaScript, you use the `localStorage` and `sessionStorage` objects with the following methods to manage key/value pairs:

- `setItem(key,value)`: Adds a key/value pair to the storage object
- `getItem(key)`: Retrieves the value for a specific key
- `removeItem(key)`: Removes a key/value pair from the storage object
- `clear()`:Removes all key/value pairs from the storage object

This is the generic code for adding a key/value pair to a `sessionStorage` object:

```
sessionStorage.setItem('key', 'value');
var myVar = sessionStorage.getItem('key');
```

CERTIFICATION READY
Which JavaScript method do you use to add a key/value pair to a sessionStorage or localStorage object?
4.7

This is the generic code for local storage:

```
localStorage.setItem('key', 'value');
var myVar = localStorage.getItem('key');
```

The getItem() and removeItem() methods use the same syntax. Using sessionStorage.clear() removes everything from the list.

 USE THE LOCALSTORAGE OBJECT

GET READY. To save a value to local storage, perform the following steps:

1. In an editing or app development tool, create a file named **L10-localStorage.html** with the following content:

```
<!doctype>
<html>
<head>
<title>localStorage Example</title>
    <script type="text/javascript">
      function load() {
        var value = localStorage.getItem("myKey");

          if (!value) {
            alert("Item not found, adding to
localStorage");
            localStorage.setItem("myKey", "myValue");
            }
          else {
            alert(value + " found!");
            }
        }
</script>
</head>
<body onload="load()">
</body>
</html>
```

2. Open **L10-localStorage.html** in a Web browser. Because the value "myValue" has just been passed and the session is current, you should receive an alert box similar to Figure 10-9. Click **OK** to accept the settings and close the alert box.

Figure 10-9

The first alert box indicates the value is being added to localStorage

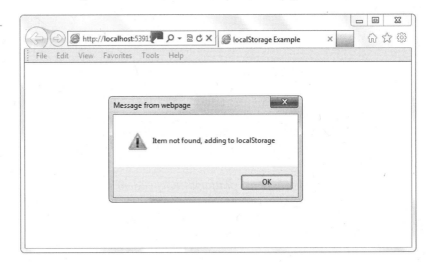

3. Close the Web browser, and then reopen **L10-localStorage.html**. Now you should see the alert box shown in Figure 10-10. The value was saved in local storage and persisted between browser sessions.

Figure 10-10

The second alert box confirms that the value was saved

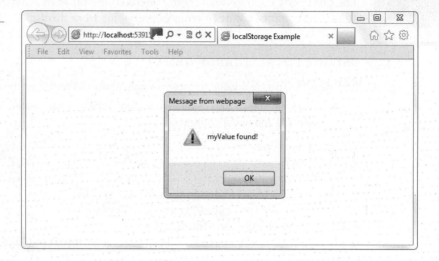

4. Close the Web browser.

5. In the HTML document, change each instance of localStorage to **sessionStorage**.

6. Save the file as **L10-sessionStorage.html** and open it in a Web browser. Notice what displays in the alert box.

7. Close the Web browser, and then reopen **L10-sessionStorage.html**.

8. The alert box message should be the same—that the value was not found. This is because you closed the Web browser, which cleared the value from session memory.

9. Press **Ctrl+R** or click your browser's refresh button. An alert box appears, confirming that the value is found.

10. Close the file and Web browser but leave the editing tool open if you plan to complete the next exercise during this session.

➕ MORE INFORMATION

The Microsoft "HTML5 Web Storage" Web page at http://bit.ly/JeXIJU provides the API for persistent storage of key-value pair data.

Accessing Hardware Capabilities

Platform-independent applications run on a variety of desktop and mobile operating systems, and device-independent applications are device agnostic. You use JavaScript to access the Windows Runtime APIs for hardware devices.

HTML5 is considered *platform-independent*. That means you can use the HTML5 family of technologies to create Web pages and apps that run on different desktop and mobile device operating systems, such as Microsoft Windows, Internet Explorer, and Windows Phone. You can also run them in Mac OS X, Android, iOS, and Blackberry OS. Because HTML5 is built on an open standard, users of HTML5 apps do not have to download a plug-in or use devices that have plug-in support. Instead, you can use any Web browser, whether on your PC or mobile device, and get the same rich Web experience.

CERTIFICATION READY
What does device-independent mean?
4.7

A program or interface that runs software that produces similar results on a wide variety of hardware is also called *device-independent*. With HTML5, along with CSS and JavaScript, you can easily create device-independent applications. Some of hardware capabilities you can access with device-independent applications are GPS, Accelerometer, and camera.

In a nutshell, you use JavaScript to access the Windows Runtime APIs for hardware devices.

UNDERSTANDING GLOBAL POSITIONING SYSTEM (GPS)

Global positioning system (GPS) hardware, which is usually a chip or circuit board, is a receiver that communicates with satellites to provide a device's precise location in longitude and latitude coordinates. Most modern phones are now equipped with GPS functionality, as are laptops with WiFi and/or cellular broadband.

The Geolocation API you learned about earlier in the lesson works with the GPS chip to gather raw geolocation data.

UNDERSTANDING ACCELEROMETER

Many mobile devices include orientation and motion sensors, which detect the orientation and motion of the device and use that information as input. For example, as a user holds the device and swings his arm back and above his head, and then swings the arm forward as if executing a tennis stroke, the device recognizes and records the motion.

An *accelerometer* is a device that measures acceleration, which is a change in speed or direction over a period of time. The Accelerometer sensor detects forces applied to the device, such as movement (up, down, sideways) and gravity. In Windows-related systems, specific APIs retrieve raw motion data from Accelerometer sensors, and then the Motion API combines the data from those sensors and crunches the numbers that result in easy-to-use values.

The `devicemotion` event provides the acceleration of the device, in Cartesian coordinates, and the rotation rate. A snippet of JavaScript that receives `devicemotion` events is as follows:

```
window.addEventListener("devicemotion",
function(event) {
        // Process event.acceleration,
event.accelerationIncludingGravity,
        // event.rotationRate and event.interval
    }, true);
```

TAKE NOTE*

Two related sensors are Compass and Gyroscope. The Compass sensor determines a device's orientation relative to the Earth's magnetic north pole. You can use the Compass sensor along with the appropriate APIs to create apps for geocaching and navigation, for example. The Gyroscope sensor uses motion (rotational forces) to detect the rotational velocity of the device along its three primary axes.

ACCESSING A CAMERA

The W3C HTML Media Capture specification uses a capture attribute with the input element to capture data from cameras, camcorders, webcams, microphones, and so on. For example, the following generic code uploads an image from a device's camera:

```
<input type="file" accept="image/*" capture="camera">
```

However, this construct has limited support, working only with select mobile browsers. There is movement toward the `getUserMedia()` method along with the navigator object as an alternative, which accesses a device's local camera and microphone stream. `getUserMedia` plays well with the new HTML5 audio and video elements. Here's a code snippet that provides access to a device's hardware:

```
navigator.GetUserMedia('audio, video',
function(localMediaStream) {
  var video = document.querySelector('video');
  video.src =
window.createObjectURL(localMediaStream);
}, onFailSoHard);
```

The specification is in flux, so you should expect changes over time as the specification is modified and browser vendors adopt the technology.

→ **EXPLORE HARDWARE CAPABILITIES**

GET READY. To explore hardware capabilities, perform the following steps:

1. Visit the "Quickstart: detecting location using HTML5" MSDN Web page at **http://bit.ly/LerKIW**.
2. Copy and paste the JavaScript sample code into an editing or app development tool, and save it as **L10-geo-ms.html**.
3. Open **L10-geo-ms.html** in a Web browser and test the application.
4. Compare the longitude and latitude coordinates with L10-geolocation.html, which you created in an earlier lesson.
5. Visit the Microsoft "Quickstart: Responding to user movement with the accelerometer" MSDN Web page at **http://bit.ly/J70A58**.
6. Read through the JavaScript sample code and the HTML sample markup.
7. Answer the following questions, researching parts of the code and markup if necessary:
   a. Which function establishes a connection with the default accelerometer?
   b. Which function captures new accelerometer data?
   c. Which elements write new values to the screen?
8. Close all open files and programs.

➕ **MORE INFORMATION**

Learn more about camera-related APIs at this MSDN Web page: http://bit.ly/K2Lf5E. To explore Windows Runtime components, go to this MSDN Web page: http://bit.ly/HWTZJL.

SKILL SUMMARY

IN THIS LESSON YOU LEARNED:

- A touch-enabled device interprets finger movements on a touch screen, called gestures, and converts them to instructions for an application. Many gestures have mouse equivalents.
- The primary touch events are `touchstart`, `touchmove`, `touchend`, and `touchcancel`. The primary gesture events are `gesturestart`, `gesturechange`, and `gestureend`.

- The Web Hypertext Application Technology Working Group (WHATWG) maintains a living HTML specification that includes APIs that were not originally part of the HTML5 specification. These include Geolocation, Web Workers, WebSockets, and File API.
- The Geolocation API gets a user's geographical coordinates (latitude and longitude). The API can also show a map with a marker showing the user's location based on the coordinates.
- Web Workers are scripts that run in the background, performing calculations or other actions that allow for a more responsive user interface.
- The WebSocket API enables you to open a persistent connection between a client and a Web server, and exchange text and binary files. WebSockets reduce the amount of overhead required for real-time communications.
- You can use the File API to upload individual or multiple files from a local disk or a device's local storage to a remote server. You can also display uploaded image files in a Web application.
- The Windows Runtime environment enables developers to access in-memory resources as well as hardware using APIs.
- HTML5 Web storage includes local storage (for persistent data) and session storage (for temporary data).
- Platform-independent applications run on a variety of desktop and mobile operating systems, and device-independent applications are device agnostic. You use JavaScript to access the Windows Runtime APIs for hardware devices.

■ Knowledge Assessment

Fill in the Blank

Complete the following sentences by writing the correct word or words in the blanks provided.

1. The action an application takes in response to a gesture is called a _____ event.

2. _____ data provides raw location data, such as longitude and latitude, or meters.

3. _____ are APIs that allow scripts to run in the background as parallel threads.

4. The _____ API offers full-duplex, two-way communication through a single socket over the Internet.

5. The _____ API allows a browser or application to upload files from local storage to a remote server without the need for a plug-in.

6. A program or interface that runs software that produces similar results on a wide variety of hardware is also called _____.

7. An _____ is a device that measures acceleration, which is a change in speed over a period of time.

8. A _____ touch screen is made up of several layers, the topmost of which flexes when pressed and pushes into the layer underneath. Sensors detect the pressure, which is how the system knows which part of the screen has been pressed.

9. A _____ is a data type that can store binary data, like images or multimedia files.

10. Comet and similar "push" technologies introduced _____, in which a browser would contact the Web server periodically (sometimes constantly) to see if new information was available to present to the user.

Multiple Choice

Circle the letter that corresponds to the best answer.

1. Which type of touch screen requires conductive properties?
   a. Capacitive
   b. Resistive
   c. Electronic
   d. none of the above

2. In JavaScript, which of the following contains a reference to all points of contact with a touch screen?
   a. Touch object
   b. Identifier
   c. Touchlist
   d. Manifest

3. Which API defines an interface that provides a device's location, usually using latitude and longitude coordinates?
   a. WebSocket
   b. Geolocation
   c. Web Workers
   d. File

4. Web Workers do *not* use which of the following?
   a. setTimeout
   b. setInterval
   c. XMLHttpRequest
   d. getElementById

5. Which of the following are good examples of Web applications that benefit from WebSockets? (Choose all that apply.)
   a. Chat
   b. Address book
   c. Multiplayer online gaming
   d. Stock quotes

6. Which API enables you to upload images and immediately display thumbnails in HTML documents?
   a. WebSocket
   b. Geolocation
   c. Web Workers
   d. File

7. Which API uses ws rather than http when referencing URLs?
   a. WebSocket
   b. Geolocation
   c. Web Workers
   d. File

8. Which method allows users to save relatively large amounts of data that persists from browser session to browser session?
   a. localStorage
   b. sessionStorage
   c. postMessage
   d. addEventListener

9. Which method accesses a device's local camera and microphone stream?
   a. `getUserMedia`
   b. `sessionStorage`
   c. `addEventListener`
   d. `getCameraSound`

10. Which mobile device sensor detects the force of gravity along with any forces resulting from the movement of the device?
    a. GPS
    b. Compass
    c. Accelerometer
    d. Gyroscope

True / False

Circle T if the statement is true or F if the statement is false.

T | F 1. The W3C was formed by Apple, the Mozilla Foundation, and Opera Software to define and document the HTML5 specification.

T | F 2. In JavaScript, the touch object detects input from touch-enabled devices.

T | F 3. Civic data is location data that's more easily understood by humans, such as a map or an address like 637 Park Street.

T | F 4. Developers test their applications and users run the apps in the WinRT environment.

T | F 5. The press and tap gesture is an equivalent to a left-mouse click.

■ Competency Assessment

Scenario 10-1: Understanding Gestures

Jerome is a co-worker and budding developer who is experimenting with a touch-enabled application. He wants to know which gesture mimics a mouse click. What do you tell him?

Scenario 10-2: Gathering Customer Location Data

Austin Energy and Light wants customers to log in to their Web site and use an application that pinpoints their exact location. The application must be very responsive to the user experience, and allow users to continue filling in form data. The location data will be sent to handheld devices that technicians use in the field to quickly locate customer homes and businesses. Which technologies do you suggest the company explore?

■ Proficiency Assessment

Scenario 10-3: Understanding Device Motion

Vong is a programmer for a major smartphone manufacturer. She was recently assigned to work on a device motion project with a development team. She wants to quickly understand the difference between the Accelerometer, Compass, and Gyroscope sensors. What do you tell her?

Scenario 10-4: Exploring Web Storage

Vong has returned with a new question about Web storage. She believes Web storage refers to saving files to a cloud service over the Web, but that doesn't make sense in relation to her smartphone project. How do you clarify Web Storage for her?

Appendix A
Exam 98-375 HTML5 Application Development Fundamentals

Exam Objective	Skill Number	Lesson Number
Manage the Application Life Cycle		
Understand the platform fundamentals.	1.1	1
Manage the state of an application.	1.2	1
Debug and test an HTML5-based touch-enabled application.	1.3	1
Publish an application to a store.	1.4	1
Build the User Interface by Using HTML5		
Choose and configure HTML5tags to display text content.	2.1	2
Choose and configure HTML5 tags to display graphics.	2.2	2
Choose and configure HTML5 tags to play media.	2.3	2
Choose and configure HTML5 tags to organize content and forms.	2.4	3
Choose and configure HTML5 tags for input and validation.	2.5	3
Format the User Interface by Using CSS		
Understand the core CSS concepts.	3.1	4
Arrange user interface (UI) content by using CSS.	3.2	5
Manage the flow of text content by using CSS.	3.3	6
Manage the graphical interface by using CSS.	3.4	7
Code by Using JavaScript		
Manage and maintain JavaScript.	4.1	8
Update the UI by using JavaScript.	4.2	8
Code animations by using JavaScript.	4.3	9
Access data access by using JavaScript.	4.4	9
Respond to the touch interface.	4.5	10
Code additional HTML5 APIs.	4.6	10
Access device and operating system resources.	4.7	10

A

Absolute positioning, 100–102
 with multi-columns, 101
Accelerometer, 263
Access data, 225–227
Adding elements, 209–211
 to display, 210
Animated boxes creation using canvas, 222–224
Animations, 173–179, *See also* Canvas
 coding using JavaScript, 216–219
 creating, 216–219
  interactive animation, 218–219
  simple animation, 216–219
 using CSS, 178–179
 3D, 173–179
Application Cache (AppCache), 231–232
 for offline files, 11–12
Application container, 8
Application life cycle, managing, 1–20, *See also* HTML5
 AppCache for offline files, 11–12
 application states, understanding and managing, 10–12
  application state, 11
  localStorage, 10
  persistent state information, 11
  session state, 11
  sessionStorage, 10
  storing state data using local and session storage, 11–12
 platform fundamentals, 2–10
  app samples, exploring, 8–10
  application container, 8
  application package, 8
  application programming interface (API), 7
  credentials, 10
  host process, 7–8
  identity permissions, 10
  metro style user interface (UI), 3
  packaging, exploring, 7–10
  permission sets, 10
  runtime environment, exploring, 7–10
  Windows Runtime (WinRT), 7
 publishing an application to store, 16–17
 touch interfaces and gestures, 12–13
 Windows Store marketplace, 16–17
Application package, 8
Application programming interface (API), 4, 7
Application samples, exploring, 8–10
Application state, 11
Article element, 61
Aside element, 61–64
 adding to HTML document, 63–64

Attributes, 23–24, 33, *See also* Input attributes
 global attributes, 24
Audio element, 47
Audio tags, 4, 47–49
 audio element, 47
  working with, 48–49
Autofocus attribute, 79
Automatic hyphenation, 152
Automatic validation, 82

B

Background gradients, 164–166
Basic markup, HTML, 22–29
Blob, 256
Block content flow, 96–98
Block-level element, 113
Border, 112
Border-radius property, 160
Bounding box, 102
Browser compatibility, WebSocket to test, 256–258

C

Cache, 231, *See also* Application Cache (AppCache)
 cache manifest, 11
Callback, 204
Camera, 263–264
Canvas
 canvas object, enhancing, 184–185
 graphics creation with, 38–42
  canvas basics, 39–40
  outline of a shape, 40–41
  shape creation, 39–40
 instead of SVG, 44
 manipulation with JavaScript, 220–224
  animated boxes creation, 222–224
  canvas element, 220
  clockface creation, 220–222
Capacitive touch screens, 244
Cascading style sheets (CSS), 2, 32, 87–109, 137–158, *See also* CSS
  essentials; Graphical interface management
 appropriate tools, 88–89
 basic Web page creation, 90–91
 content and style, separating, 91–92
 content flow, 87–109
  managing, 96–98
 CSS3, 88
 declarations, 92–94
 fonts and font families, 94–96

Cascading style sheets (*continued*)
  HTML and, link between, 89–91
    simple use of CSS with HTML, 89–90
  positioning, 87–109
    absolute positioning, applying, 100–102
    float positioning, applying, 99–100
    positioning individual elements, 99–102
  scrolling overflow, 102–104
  selectors, 92–94
  styling, 87–109
  text flow management using, 137–158
    between multiple sections, using regions in, 139–155
    CSS Regions, Microsoft's implementation of, 142–145
    flow around a floating object, CSS exclusions in, 152–155
    overflowing text, 142
    readability of text ptimization, columns and hyphenation in, 145–152, *See also* Columns; Hyphenation
    through containers dynamically, 140–145
Child items direction in a flexbox, changing, 122–126
Civic data, 250
Class, 93
Client-side validation, 82
Clockface with moving hands, creating, 220–222
Codec, 45–46
Coding essentials, 189–214
Columns
  creating, 146–150
    column-count, 146
    column-gap, 146
    column-rule, 146
    multi-column layout, 146, 149
    three columns, 148
  to optimize text readability, 145–152
<Command> element in HTML5, 31
Complex objects, transmitting, 227–229
Compression, 46
Computer program, 190
Containers, flowing content through, 140–145
Content, 112
  containers, 140
  of elements, 208–209
    content visible on screen, 208–209
    updating, 208–209
  flow, managing, 96–98
    block flow, 96
    content overflow, managing, 102–105
    hidden overflow, 104–105
    inline flow, 96
    visible overflow, 104–105
  HTML5 tags to organize, 54–72
  overflow, managing, 102–105
  source, 140
  and style, separating, 91–92
Cookies, 11, 235–237
Credentials, 10
CSS essentials, 110–136
  content, ordering and arranging, 126–128
  user interface (UI) content arrangement, 111–114
    block-level element, 113

    border, 112
    content, 112
    Flexbox Box model, 113, *See also individual entry*
    Flexbox for simple layouts, 112–114
    grid for complex layouts, 112–114
    Grid Layout model, 114, *See also* Grid layouts
    inline elements, 113
    margin, 112
    padding, 112
    parent/child relationship, 113
    vendor prefix, 111
CSS Regions, *See* Regions, CSS

D

2D rotation, 171–172
3D rotation, 171–172
2D scaling, 169–170
2D skewing, 172–175
3D skewing, 172–173
2D transformation, 167–169
3D transformation, 167–169
Data, 224–229
  accessing, 215–242
  complex objects, transmitting, 227–229
  parsing, transmitting, 227–229
  sending and receiving, 224–229
  types, 233
Datalist element, 79
Debugging, 13–16
Declarations, 92–94
Definition list, 71
Deprecation, HTML5 elements, 32–33
  <acronym>, 33
  <applet>, 33
  <basefont>, 33
  <big>, 33
  <center>, 33
  <dir>, 33
  effects of deprecated elements, 34
  <font>, 33
  <frame>, 33
  <frameset>, 33
  <noframes>, 33
  <strike>, 33
  <tt>, 33
Device and operating system resources, JavaScript coding for, 243–267
Device-independent hardware capability, 263
Device resources, accessing, 260–264
Devicemotion event, 263
Display
  add an element to, 210
  hiding parts of, based on user action, 206–208
Doctype, 25–26
Document Object Model (DOM), 7, 141
Drop shadow, 161
Dynamic application, 190

E

Elements, 23, *See also* Content: of elements
  accessing, 201–203
  adding elements, 209–211
  audio, 47
  hiding, 206–208
  locating, 201–203
  showing, 206–208
  updating the content of, 208–209
  video, 45
Email attribute, 78
Empty tags, 22
Encapsulation, 226
Entities, 24–25
Event handler, 204
Events, listening and responding to, 203–206
Extensible Markup Language (XML), 42

F

Figcaption elements, 35–38
Figure elements, 35–38
File API compatibility, 259
File API for file uploads, 258–259
  interfaces for accessing, 258
Files, 229–233
  loading and saving, 229–233
  local file, accessing, 229–231
Flexbox/Flexbox Box model, 113
  child items direction in a flexbox, changing, 122–126
  for content alignment, direction, and orientation, 114–128
  flexbox items, 114, 116–128
    with flex function, creating, 120–122
  flexbox with flexbox items, creating, 119
  flex-order property, 127
  order of flexbox, reversing, 124–126
  proportional scaling within, 116–122
  for simple layouts, 112–114
  working with, 116–128
Flex-order property, 127–128
Float positioning, 99–100
  with multi-columns, 99–100
Floating object, creating text flow around, CSS in, 152–155
  CSS exclusions, 152–154
  positioned float, 152
Fonts and font families, 94–96
  monospace font family, 94–95
  sans serif font family, 95
Footer element, HTML document creation with, 6
Form creation, 77–81
  simple Web form, 79–81
Form input, 73
Forms, 73–81
  HTML5 tags to organize, 54–72
  form input, 73
Functions, 193
  creating and using, 193–196
  JavaScript function, 194–195

G

Gaussian blur filter, 180–182
Geodetic data, 250
Geolocation, coding to capture, 249–252
  geolocation API, 250
Gestures, 12–13, 245
  capturing, 246–249
  responding to, 246–249
Getelementbyid() method for user input, 202–203
Global attributes, 24, 54
Global positioning system (GPS), 263
Gradients, 164–166
  background gradients, 164–166
    applying to a box, 165–166
  linear gradient, 164
  radial gradient, 165
Graphical interface management using CSS, 159–188
  canvas to enhance GUI, 182–185
  2D rotation, 171–172
  3D rotation, 171–172
  2D scaling, 169–170
  2D skewing, 172–173
  3D skewing, 172–173
  2D transformation, 167–169
  3D transformation, 167–169
  2D translation, 168–172
  gradients, 164–166
  graphics effects, creating, 160–166
    shadows, 161–163
  rounded corners, creating, 160–161
    border-radius property, 160
  SVG filter effects, applying, 179–182
    Gaussian blur filter, 180
Graphical use interface (GUI)
  canvas to enhance, 182–185
Graphics, 34–44, *See also* Media: HTML5 tags to play
  canvas, graphics creation with, 38–42
  HTML5 tags to display, choosing and configuring, 34–44
    alternate image for older browsers, 41–42
    figcaption elements, 35–38
    figure elements, 35–38
    raster image, 35
    vector image, 35
    web page, image display in, 37
  SVG, creating graphics with, 42–44
  working with, 215–242
Grid for complex layouts, 112–114
Grid layouts, 114, 128–133
  for content alignment, direction, and orientation, 128–133
    grid cells, 129
    grid items, 129
    grid lines, 129
    grid tracks, 129
  creating, using CSS properties for rows and columns, 130–132
    simple grid layout, 130–131
  grid templates, 132–133
Grid templates, 132–133

H

Hardware capabilities, 264
  accessing, 262–264
    device-independent, 263
    platform-independent, 262
Header element, HTML document creation with, 56
Hidden overflow, 104–105
Host process, 7–8
HTML5, 2–10
  APIs, coding, 249–259
    to capture geolocation, 249–252
  apps, 5–7
    app manifest, updating, 5
    building app, 6
    debugging, 6, 13–16
    deploy, 6
    developer resources, 4, 6–7
    packaging, 6
    project planning, 5
    testing, 6, 13–16
    UI designing, 5
    validation, 6
    writing code, 6
  HTML5 standard, exploring, 4
  user interface building by, 21–52, *See also* Media:
      HTML5 tags to play
    simple Web page, markup of, 26–29
    tags to display graphics, 34–44, *See also under* Graphics
    tags to display text content, 29–34, *See also under* Text
    valid, 26
  new features, 4
    application programming interfaces (APIs), 4
    audio and video tags, 4
    canvas, 4
    geolocation, 4
    media queries, 4
    modernizr, 4
  new in, 3–5
  platform-independent, 3
  slate/tablet applications, skills and content for, 13
  validating a package, 14–16
  validating HTML5 code, 14
Hypertext Markup Language (HTML), 2, 22, *See also* HTML5
  attributes, 23–24
  basic markup, 22–29
  doctype, 25–26
  element, 23
  empty tags, 22
  entities, 24–25
  essentials of, 22–29
  nesting elements, 24
  page structure, 22–29
  renders, 22
  tags, 22–23
Hypertext Transport Protocol (HTTP), 11
Hyphenation, 150–152
  automatic hyphenation, 152
  to optimize text readability, 145–152
    ms-hyphenate-limit-chars, 150

ms-hyphenate-limit-lines, 151
ms-hyphenate-limit-zone, 150

I

Identifiers, 195
Identity permissions, 10
Iframes, 142
Images, 219–224
In-browser calculator using JavaScript, 199–201
Individual elements, positioning, 99–102
Inline content flow, 96–98
Inline elements, 113
In-memory resources, accessing, 260–262
Input attributes, 77–81
  autofocus attribute, 79
  email attribute, 78
  pattern attribute, 78
  placeholder text, 78
  required attribute, 78
Input, HTML5 tags for, 72–83
Integrated Development Environment (IDE), 88, 190
Interactive animation, 218–219
Interactivity, 190

J

JavaScript, 189–214, 216–219
  animations coding using, 216–219
  canvas manipulation with, 220–224, *See also under* Canvas
  coding, 243–267, *See also under* Touch interfaces
    accelerometer, 263
    camera, 263–264
    civic data, 250
    geodetic data, 250
    global positioning system (GPS), 263
    in-memory resources, accessing, 260–262
    polling, 255
  jQuery, 197–199
  managing a form with, 233–235
  multi-statement JavaScript program, 192–193
  simple JavaScript program, creating, 190–192
  UI updation by using, 199–211, *See also under*
      User interface (UI)
  use in user form input validation, 233–235
  variable use in, 196
JavaScript Object Notation (JSON), 228
jQuery, 197–199

K

Keyframes, 177

L

Launcher icon, 5
Library, 197–199
Linear gradient, 164

Lists
    creating lists, 69–72
      tags in, 64–72
    datalist element, 79
    definition list, 71
    ordered list, 69–70
    unordered list, 69–70
Local file, accessing, 229–231
Local storage, 10, 237–239, 260–262
    save to, 238
    storing state data using, 11–12

M

Margin, 112
<Mark> element in HTML5, 31
Markup language, 2
Markup validation service, W3C, 15
Media, 21–52
    HTML5 tags to play, 45–49, *See also* Audio tags; Video tags
    queries, 4, 127
Menu element, 72
Methods, 189–214
Metro-style user interface (UI), 3
Microsoft's implementation of CSS Regions, 142–145
Monospace, 94–95
Multi-column in CSS3, 146–147
Multi-column layout, 146
Multi-statement JavaScript program, 192–193

N

Named flow, 140
Namespace, 8
Nav element, 59–61
    adding to HTML document, 60–61
Nesting elements, 24
.NET framework, 10
Non-contiguous content flow between regions, 139

O

Onload event handler, 204–206
Opacity, 163–164
Operating system resources, 260–264
Ordered list, 69–70
    creating, 72
Overflowing text, 142

P

Padding, 112
Page structure, HTML, 22–29
Parent/child relationship, 113
Parsing, 227–229
Pattern attribute, 78
Permission sets, 10
    identity permissions, 10

Persistent state information, 11
Perspective, 173–179
    3D, 173–179
Placeholder text, 78
Platform-independent, 3, 262
Polling, 255
Positioned float, 152
Process, 8
Proportional scaling within flexbox, 116–122

R

Radial gradient, 165
Raster image, 35
Recursion, 216
Regions, CSS, 139
    creating, 143–145
    Microsoft's implementation of, 142–145
Renders, 22
Required attribute, 78
Resistive touch screen, 244
Reversing order of flexbox, 124–126
Rotation, 171–172
    2D rotation, 171–172
    3D rotation, 171–172
Rounded corners, creating, 160–161
    box with, creating, 162–163
Rules, 89
Runtime environment (RTE), 7

S

Sans serif font family, 94–95
Scalable vector graphics (SVG), 34, 42
    canvas use instead of SVG, 44
    creating graphics with, 42–44
      SVG vector graphic, 43–44
    filter effects, applying, 179–182
      Gaussian blur, 181–182
      offset, 181–182
Scripting language, 2
Scrolling overflow, 102–104
Section element, HTML document creation with, 57–59
Selectors, 92–94
Semantic HTML, 54–55
Semantic markup, 54
Separation of content and style, 91–92
Server-side validation, 82
Session state, 11
Session storage, 10, 260
    storing state data using, 11–12
Shadows, creating, 161–163
    box with, creating, 162–163
    drop shadow, 161
    h-shadow, 162
    v-shadow, 162
Shape creation, using canvas, 39–40
    outline of a shape, 40–41
Shapes, 219–224

Simple grid layout, 130
Simple Web form, creating, 79–81
    using <p> tags, 81
Simple Web page, 26–29
    creating, 26–29
    markup of, 26–29
Skewing, 172–173
    2D, 172–175
    3D, 172–173
Slate/tablet applications, HTML5 skills and content for, 13
Software Development Kit (SDK), 14
Storing state data using local and session storage,
        11–12
Subroutines, 197

T

Tables
    creating tables, 64–69
        tags in, 64–72
Tags, 22
    use to add structure to HTML document, 55–64
Testing HTML5 apps, 13–16
Text, 21–52
    HTML5 tags to display, choosing and configuring,
            29–34
        alternate text for older browsers, 41–42
        <b>, 30
        <em>, 30
        HTML 4 text-related elements with new meaning or
                functionality, 29–31
        <i>, 30
        <small>, 30
        <strong>, 30
        text-related tags in web page, modifying, 30–31
    flow management using CSS, 137–158, See also under
            Cascading style sheets (CSS)
    new text elements in HTML5, 31–32
        <command>, 31
        <mark>, 31
        mark element use, 32
        <time>, 31
    text elements not used in HTML5, 32–34, See also
            Deprecation, HTML5 elements
<Time> element in HTML5, 31
Touch event, 245–249
Touch interfaces, 12–13
    capacitive touch screens, 244
    JavaScript coding for, 243–267
    resistive touch screen, 244
    responding to, 244–249
        gesture events, 245
        primary JavaScript touch events, 246
        touch object, 246
        touchlist, 246
    touch screen capability detection, 247–249
    touch-screen simulator or emulator, 13
Touch object, 245–246
Touchlist, 245–246

Transformations, 167–169
    2D, 167–169
    3D, 167–169
Transitions, 173–179
    creating using CSS, 176–178
    3D, 173–179
Translation, 168–172
    2D, 168–169
Transparency, 163–164
Typography, 166–167

U

Uniform resource locator (URL), 47
Unordered list, 69–70
User form input validation, JavaScript use in, 233–235
User interface (UI), 3
    building, by using HTML5, 53–86, See also Forms; Validation
        article element, 61
        aside element, 61–64
        content, 54–72
        footer element, 6
        form creation, 77–81
        forms, 54–72
        header element, 56
        input, 53–86
        input attributes, 77–81
        lists, using tags to create, 64–72
        menu element, 72
        nav element, 59–61
        organization, 53–86
        section element, 57–59
        semantic HTML, 54–55
        simple Web form, creating, 79–81
        tables, using tags to create, 64–72
        using tags, 55–64
        validation, 53–86
        values, 77–81
    content arrangement by using CSS, 111–114,
            See also under CSS essentials
    updating by using JavaScript, 199–211
        content of elements, 208–209
        display parts hiding based on user action, 206–208
        elements, locating and accessing, 201–203
        elements, showing and hiding, 206–208
        events, listening and responding to, 203–206
        getelementbyid() method for user input, 202–203
        in-browser calculator, 199–201
        onload event handler, 204–206

V

Valid Web page, 26
Validating a package, 14–16
Validating HTML5 code, 14
Validation, 81–83, 203
    automatic validation, 82
    client-side validation, 82
    fields addition to Web form, 83

HTML5 tags for, 72–83
    server-side validation, 82
Values, 77–81
Variable, 195
    in JavaScript program, 196
Vector image, 35
Vendor prefix, 111
Video compression, 46
Video element, 45
Video tags, 4, 45–47
    attributes available, 45
    compression, 46
    video compression, 46
    video element, working with, 46–47
Visible overflow, 104–105

W

Web form, 72
    creating, 79–81
        using <p> tags, 81
        validation fields addition to, 83

Web Hypertext Application Technology Working Group
        (WHATWG), 249
Web Open Font Format (WOFF), 166–167
Web page, image display in, 37
Web safe, 166
WebSockets API, 255–258
    in browser compatibility test, 256–258
    polling, 255
    primary events associated with, 255
Web worker API, 252–255
    creating, 254–255
    running, 254–255
Windows Runtime (WinRT), 7, 260
Windows Store marketplace, 16–17
World Wide Web Consortium (W3C), 2
    CSS validation service, 15–16
    markup validation service, 15
WWAHost.exe, 8

X

XMLHttpRequest API, 225